CREATIVITY AND INNOVATION

REINHOLD MANAGEMENT REFERENCE SERIES
Carl Heyel, *Editor*

In Preparation

Contract Research, *by Archie M. Palmer and Murray Berdick*

Guide to the Use of Management Consulting Services, *by Philip W. Shay*

Handbook of Corporate Public Relations, *by Paul Burton*

Published

Dynamic Work Simplification, *by W. Clements Zinck*

Management Games, *by Joel M. Kibbee, Clifford J. Craft, and Burt Nanus*

CREATIVITY
AND
INNOVATION

JOHN W. HAEFELE

Research Chemist, Procter and Gamble Company

New York

REINHOLD PUBLISHING CORPORATION

Chapman & Hall, Ltd., London

To My Mother and Father

FOREWORD

John Dewey has remarked that in all ages, man has made discoveries, but that it has been reserved for this age to *discover the process of discovery*. Recently Walter Mitchell, Jr., Executive Director of the Society for Advancement of Management, in inaugurating the Society's Advanced Management Course, stated that "tomorrow's top manager must be almost instinctively keyed to innovation. More specifically, he must appreciate the need of innovation, its proper timing, and its multiplier effect, and be able to manage innovation, encourage it, inspire it, and, where possible, author it."

We need only place these two comments—one by a leading figure in education, the other an official pronouncement of the leading professional society devoted to scientific mangement—in the perspective of the current research and development "explosion," to have ample justification for the inclusion of Dr. Haefele's study of creativity and innovation in the Reinhold Management Reference Series.

Reinhold's recently published "Handbook of Industrial Research Management" is an example of the authoritative information now available on the organization, staffing, direction, and accounting control of this vital function. However, there is need for an orderly examination into, and prescription for, the very essence of research and innovation—*the creative process itself*. Is creativity something that "just happens"—or is it something that can be stimulated, strengthened, and guided?

This book brings to management and to the creative worker the fruits of research that has been done *on* research, and on creative work in general: what the creative process is and how it works . . . practical information on individual and group aids to creativity, with case experience in applying "brainstorming" and other widely used techniques . . . early identification of creativity in an individual . . . establishment of the most productive creative climate.

Like all the books in this series, this volume has been organized to provide a broad view of the field for those with a general interest, followed by detailed supporting chapters of interest to those with specialized responsibility. For the generalist, Part I, "The Anatomy

v

of Creativity," sets the stage, and Part II, "Putting Creativity to Work," provides immediate practical application ideas. For the specialist in research, and for all whose inclinations and opportunities invite a more detailed pursuit of the subject, Part III provides further comments in depth, and the Appendices give documentation and additional insights.

While the "applied" aspects of the book dwell on creativity and innovation in business and industry and in the natural sciences, the author takes the position that creativity and the creative process are the same in all fields of endeavor. "The physicist studying the nature of gravity in the university laboratory, and the industrial chemist formulating a new floor polish, may both create new combinations of social worth, and in so doing, use the same creative methods, from the same basic motivation . . . The painter's picture, the inventor's machine, the novelist's book, and the engineer's bridge, are the men's responses to problems which they faced and solved." Examples are freely drawn from the fields of music, literature, and art to supplement those from the fields of business and the natural sciences. Spreading the subject before us from such a variegated palette on such a broad canvas is in keeping with the Society for Advancement of Management's concept of true management development, which "calls for pushing through to a depth of knowledge and *conceptual understanding* which will provide [the manager] with a *systematic and effective way of thinking*—about his environment, his work, his responsibilities, and himself."

With the foregoing as a statement of intent, we invite to this type of conceptual understanding the following classes of readers:

Top management people, who will wish to explore the opportunities for greater creativity and innovation in their organizations.

Directors of Research, who are faced with the problem of securing maximum return from the high-priced professional talent at their disposal.

Executives in other areas of management—advertising, merchandising, etc.— where creativity is at a premium.

People with *top functional responsibility in training and executive development,* who, in addition to the broader view, will be interested in the more detailed discussion and examples.

Educators interested in ways to develop creativity.

Scientists and others in the creative areas of their companies who will make use of their guidance for self-improvement.

CARL HEYEL, *Editor,*
Reinhold Management Reference Series

PREFACE

In an age when not only commercial life, but the very life of our nation depends upon keeping a lead in scientific development, the values to be gained from a greater understanding of creativity need hardly be dwelt upon. Yet the study of creativity has suffered comparative neglect even to the most recent times, and it is this neglect to which this book is directed.

The nature of creativity and the theories about it are here discussed with continuous attempts to relate this knowledge to the importance of creativity in *business,* especially in the expanding field of industrial research and development. Here the need to consider "frontier thinking" is especially apropos, since despite the spectacular exponential rise in research and development, the fact remains that only a small fraction of total funds expended in this activity is on fundamental research.

The need for a good climate for creativity must be understood by the "practical businessman," and he must appreciate the reasons why an organization must make certain concessions to the creative man. The research manager and scientist will in addition be interested in enhancing their understanding of creativity, as will, indeed, many general readers whose principal outlet for creativity may be outside the boundaries of their bread-winning activities.

This book is intended to accomplish three specific things:

(1) Provide a fairly complete review of the literature, with special effort to show the *development* of principles rather than to give a mere statement of them. With this in mind, considerable specific material in the form of tables and diagrams has been included—although much of this supporting documentation has been developed as an Appendix, in order not to impede continuity in the coverage of the subject as a whole. This material is drawn or condensed from the original sources, to show the type of work that has

been done and to emphasize the gaps in our knowledge of this important and fascinating subject which are still to be closed.

The literature of creativity is important. The creator should be as conversant with this literature as he is with that of his special subject. How inefficient it is to spend years in mastering a specialty, and then to work at its frontiers with an undeveloped creative potential!

(2) Present new material which the author has developed during a study extending over more than ten years. Among the new ideas offered, the most important are: the CNB method; the resurgence of creativity at great age; the importance of verb responses to the Kent-Rosanoff type tests; possibilities in creativity rankings of tests in conjunction with "inverse factor analysis"; and the relation of Spearman's fundaments and relations to creativity and to the basic nature of creative aids.

(3) Pinpoint the ways in which managements of business enterprises can enhance creativity, and discuss the various group and individual aids to creativity which have thus far been developed, and which may be applied more effectively in the light of the general discussion provided here. These include "brainstorming," the so-called Gordon method, and programs developed by leading corporations to enhance creative thinking.

A scientist declared that in his education, including graduate work, he received no instruction in creative method beyond a few desultory talks with one professor. These matters apparently were considered outside the important part of his educational program. It is highly probable that almost none of the research staff employees who are expected to do the foundation work of creative thinking for a large industrial laboratory have had any instruction in creative method. As a result, in each man creativity develops haphazardly, and his best creative years may be gone before he begins to understand how his own mind functions for discovery.

The material to be covered in reviewing the subject of creativity and its branchings is derived from a variety of sources. There are, first, the anecdotes by creators of how they accomplished their works. These are reports by the great minds which created all civilization, and we should be willing to trust and learn from them. It is irrelevant whether some of the material comes from science, some from music, and some from art: they are all talking about the same thing. For example, Lehman has studied creative workers' production in relation to age without regard to field of work, and has made important deductions about creativity by correlating the quantitative results so obtained. Then there are the thoughtful analyses of creativity in diverse fields by many writers such as Wallas and Beveridge.

Experimental investigations of creativity are strikingly few, and divide into these methods: First, analysis is made of questionnaires filled out by members of a particular discipline, including music (Bahle), mathematics (Hadamard), invention (Rossman), and science (Platt and Baker). Second, creators in a particular discipline report their thoughts while in the process of producing an example of their art (Patrick, Vinacke). Third, creativity tests are administered to samples from the general population, and deductions made (Guilford). Fourth, such psychological methods as the Rorschach and Thematic Apperception tests are applied to outstanding persons in various disciplines to break out the common underlying characteristics of psychological significance (Roe).

Additionally, there are many related fields which yield material of important consequence for creativity. Among these are the psychological literature on concept formation and problem solving, as well as writings on intelligence testing, intuition, imagination, and (as will be seen) word association. Some of the experimental work will be presented in tabular form for consideration and analysis.

But how sparse is the literature of creativity in comparison with the importance of the subject! Of 121,000 titles listed in *Psychological Abstracts* in 23 years, only 186 were given as definitely concerned with creativity. This amounts to less than two-tenths of one per cent of abstracts over a quarter of a century. In chemistry, the creative process was last examined on a major basis by Platt and Baker, as published in the *Journal of Chemical Education* in 1931. This article is not even indexed in *Chemical Abstracts* under the authors' names, nor under "creative thinking," "imagination," nor even under the catchall "science."

The purpose of the following list (which makes no pretense of being complete) is to mark certain milestones, and especially to show the increasing tempo of recent work. Important material much earlier than 1881, but in slim quantity, could be quoted, which might include even Bacon and Plato.

1881	Souriou	Theorie de l'invention
1896	Helmholtz	Vortrage und Reden
1900	Ribot	Creative Imagination
1908	Poincare	Mathematical Creation
1910	Ruger	Puzzle Solving
1924	Heidbreder	Experimental Study of Thinking
1926	Wallas	Art of Thought
1928	Bancroft	Methods of Research
1929	Laycock	Adaptability to New Situations
1931	Rossman	Psychology of the Inventor
1931	Spearman	Creative Mind
1932	Platt, Baker	Relation of Scientific Hunch to Research
1932	Bulbrook	Experimental Inquiry into Insight
1933	Claparede	La Genese de l'hypothese
1935	Duncker	Zur Psychologie des Productiven Denkens
1935	Patrick	Creative Thought in Poets
1937	Patrick	Creative Thought in Artists
1938	Patrick	Scientific Thought
1945	Hadamard	Psychology of Invention in the Mathematical Field
1946	Wiegand	Motivation in Research
1949	Hutchinson	How to Think Creatively
1950	Beveridge	Art of Scientific Investigation
1951	Flesch	Art of Clear Thinking
1951	Roe	Psychological Studies of Physical/Biological Scientists
1951	Guilford	Factor Analysis of Creativity
1952	Eindhoven, Vinacke	Creative Processes in Painting
1954	Rogers	Toward a Theory of Creativity

A lively interest has more recently been in evidence, in numerous articles and in such books as Patrick's "What Is Creative Thinking?", W. I. B. Beveridge's masterful "The Art of Scientific Investigation," and Flesch's popular, but thoughtful, "The Art of Clear Thinking." The attack is gaining momentum. Several symposia on creativity have been held in recent years, at which valuable papers were presented. The need to develop young scientists in increasing numbers has been an important factor. Some universities have opened courses in creativity and some business enterprises have instituted deliberate attempts to stimulate creativeness, as have the armed forces.

From 1930 to 1939 the *Industrial Arts Index* listed no papers on creative ability. From 1940 to 1949 it listed nine; from 1950 to 1954, eight; from 1955 through 1956, twenty-three; and from 1957 through 1958, twenty-one. Yet no recent, broad review exists on this most important subject, with so active a current interest.

Let me deal here with certain philosophic aspects of the subject, since in the text I refer to them only indirectly. Creativity is defined in this book as *the ability to make new combinations of social worth.* Roland Glie has written that "in technology, the search for truth *per se* has no place." The question then arises, should a special viewpoint be adopted in writing about creativity for an audience that will include a significant proportion of people with management responsibilities, particularly *industrial* management, where creativity in technology is a desideratum? The answer, I submit, is no, and the reason is that the search for truth (leaving out of consideration the impossibility of defining this word) is only a part of the subject of creativity. Again, the stand taken is the same as that of many other writers, namely that creativity and the creative process are the same in all fields of endeavor. The physicist studying the nature of gravity in the university laboratory, and the industrial chemist formulating a new floor polish, may both create new combinations of social worth, and in so doing use the same creative methods, from the same basic motivation. The relative social value of their work-products is a philosophic concept.

Recently, the University of California's Institute of Personality Assessment and Research (IPAR) postulated three categories of creativity: *

(1) The creation is an expression of the inner state of the creator.
(2) The creation is a response to meet externally defined needs and goals.
(3) The creation is both of these.

I see these distinctions as ones of convenience for discussion, and not of basic importance. The creative workers in all of these categories are seeking to solve the problem of creating new combinations of social value within the particular disciplinary skills they happen

---

* Carnegie Corp. of N. Y., *Quarterly*, Vol. 9, No. 3, July 1961.

to possess. Whether they add little or much of themselves does not seem a particularly important criterion. The painter's picture, the inventor's machine, the novelist's book, and the engineer's bridge, are the men's responses to problems which they faced and solved.

It has been needful to refer occasionally to personal experience, which is the only creative mental activity a man can ever *know* for himself. Therefore, where necessary to the argument, personal instances have been used to illustrate certain points.

Credits for material extensively reprinted from the literature have been given elsewhere. For permission to use these quotations my thanks are due to the copyright holders.

A special acknowledgement is made to Mr. Maurice Nelles for use of the "smog" example from his article, "Deliberate Creativeness in Science and Engineering," *The Chemical Bulletin,* February 1953. This example was particularly apt for use in Chapter 5.

Thanks are also due to Dr. J. F. Lawrence of Richardson, Bellows, Henry, and Company, for preparing Chapter 9 on "Creative Personality," and to Dr. H. A. Edgerton of the same firm for consultation in and heavy contribution to Chapter 12, "Creativity Testing." Finally, an acknowledgment is due from the writers to the general editor of this series, Carl Heyel, for his assistance in the organization of the material and in its final presentation.

Needless to say, the full responsibility for what he has written rests upon each writer; and in particular, the opinions expressed by me are personal, and not officially those of the Procter and Gamble Company.

JOHN W. HAEFELE, Ph.D.

Cincinnati, Ohio
May 25, 1962

CONTENTS

APPENDICES

PART I

THE ANATOMY OF CREATIVITY

1. THE CREATIVE PROCESS

In London one spring evening in the 1850's, late riders on the open air bus must have watched with some amusement the behavior of a young man who was seated well forward. He was a young foreigner, a student, and there may have been suspicion of indulgence in liquid cheer. His head was thrown back, and he looked toward the bright sky with his face alight. Now and again his hands lifted to gesture, or seemingly sketch something in the air. Presently he sat bolt upright, and then gradually settled again into his seat with a pleased sigh. The onlookers would undoubtedly have said, "Now, this lad is certainly going home from a call on a young lady and he unconsciously sketches her face from memory." They could not know that the face of *his* fair one was an association of atoms—and quite polygamous.

Let the young student, Friedrich Kekulé, tell his side of the story. He was returning from a visit to a friend who lived a considerable distance away. They had been talking chemistry, as usual. On the bus, his thoughts continued:

"I fell into a reverie, and lo, the atoms were gamboling before my eyes! Whenever, hitherto, these diminutive beings had appeared to me, they had always been in motion; but up to that time I had never been able to discern the nature of their motion. Now, however, I saw how, frequently, two smaller atoms united to form a pair; how a larger one embraced two smaller ones; how still larger ones kept hold of three or even four of the smaller; whilst the whole kept whirling in a giddy dance. I saw how the larger ones formed a chain, dragging the smaller ones after them, but only at the ends of the chains. . . . The cry of the conductor 'Clapham Road' awakened me from my dreaming. But I spent a part of the night in putting on paper at least

3

sketches of these dream forms. This was the origin of the *Structurtheorie.*" (Japp, Kekulé Memorial Lecture.)

Now the *Structurtheorie* was a concept of tremendous import, at that time urgently needed to coordinate the accumulating facts of organic chemistry. But our present interest is in the psychology. For Kekulé shows us three things, surprising to many: the creative thinking took place as the free manipulation of symbols, nonverbal, and fast; the big insight came at a relaxed time, like playing; it came in a flash. Kekulé's preceding work, and prior mulling over the problem, are implicit. Lest anyone think it was too easy, let it be said that Kekulé was an indefatigable worker, known to his friends as a "walking encyclopaedia," of chemical information. He drove himself hard in his work, to the detriment of his health in later life.

How can such a tenuous thing as creativity be seized and analyzed, with a view of appropriating to oneself the creative method, and enlarging one's talent for bringing into being new combinations of value—the essence of creativity? Only, as always, by searching out what has been learned in the past, and adding to it what one can. Such experiences as Kekulé's have been widely reported from the arts. One or two other anecdotes may be cited—not to imply that all of us can achieve in the way indicated, but to highlight certain underlying principles. Thus Henri Poincaré wrote:

"For fifteen days I strove to prove that there could not be any functions like those I have since called Fuchsian functions. I was then very ignorant; every day I seated myself at my work table, stayed an hour or two, tried a great number of combinations and reached no results. One evening, contrary to my custom, I drank black coffee and could not sleep. Ideas rose in crowds; I felt them collide until pairs interlocked, so to speak, making a stable combination. By the next morning I had established the existence of a class of Fuchsian functions, those which come from the hypergeometric series; I had only to write out the results, which took but a few hours.

"Just at this time I left Caen, where I was then living, to go on a geologic excursion under the auspices of the school of mines. The changes of travel made me forget my mathematical work. Having reached Coutances, we entered an omnibus to go some place or other. At the moment when I put my foot on the step the idea came to me, without anything in my former thoughts seeming to have paved the way for it, that the transformations I had used to define the Fuchsian functions were identical with those of non-Euclidean geometry. I did not verify the idea; I should not have had time, as, upon taking my seat in the omnibus, I went on with a conversation already commenced, but I felt a perfect certainty. On my return to Caen, for conscience's sake I verified the result at my leisure."

Again, this time in mathematical creation, a pattern can be seen: creative thinking by *free manipulation of symbols*, nonverbal and fast; *insight* at a relaxed time, in a flash. It does appear that, in order to create, the first thing to do is to board a bus!

This, then, is the creative process: a *new combination* formed from pieces already in the mind by symbolic manipulation during dissociated thought. It is the same in the arts as in science, as numerous musicians, artists, and poets separately attest. With them, too, the ideas came at a relaxed time, were relatively effortless, and developed fast. The *work* had gone before. This can be verified by reference to Ghiselin's Symposium, where the comments of men of many disciplines are recorded. The point is important, because it means that an appropriate citation from a musician or poet as to his method of work is fully applicable to creativity in science. To illustrate this, the present writer has used a minority of literary and artistic references, along with a majority of instances drawn from scientific fields, to develop creative principles.

The purpose of this book is to consider the nature of creativity from as many points of view as possible, including the historical, the experimental, and the psychological, with attention also to related aspects of thinking. Creativity is defined as the ability to formulate new combinations from two or more concepts already in the mind. This definition covers the arts as well as the sciences, a symphony or a novel as well as a chemical investigation. For every creation is a new combination, of numbers, colors, notes, chemicals, mechanical elements, or words. It may be a political solution, a mathematical proof, a lyric subject, a scientific discovery, a character to be delineated in a novel, or an idea for a painting—in each case a particular person has a goal he wants to attain. The method is the creative process. It is initiated by a felt need, a "thorn in the flesh," an envisioned and desired result. It is achieved by formulating a new combination of two or more concepts that were already in the mind. The concern here is with creative effort at the level of solid new achievement of recognized social worth. Creativity should be concerned with the significant. This does not mean that small creative acts should not be studied to learn about the process by which the big ones were accomplished. But the idea of creativity to produce something of serious social value is implicit. One of the most important aspects of creativity will for our purpose therefore be the study of the mode of creation of solutions to difficult problems—a major concern of industrial management.

In brief, creativity is the *ability* to make new combinations. The creative process is the *means* to make them. The new combination is termed an innovation. High creativity is the ability to make innovations of especially great social worth.

In many cases, more especially in the fields of science and technology, creative effort becomes a problem situation, particularly when work is begun toward a tangible result. In technical work, as well as in business, to "define the problem" has become a practical cliché and a sacred cow. But it is also good advice. Let it be imagined that Leonardo da Vinci, in pursuing the creative bent supported by his patron, has just now finished a picture. The patron has seen and praised, and implied that he would like another, different and even better. Leonardo then has the problem of painting another picture. After he so decides, he has the problem of finding a suitable subject. The solution to this problem is the girl Mona Lisa. Having found her, the problems of posing her, understanding her character, and giving the portrait the da Vinci touch, arise in order. This artistic endeavor is in no way different from the attitude of the chemist who has completed an investigation, and now asks himself," What shall I tackle next?" In each case, there is, first, the problem of casting about and searching for the next creative object; then there is the problem of carrying the position by creative attack which bears the individual impress of the creator.

The motivation of such work is twofold. In the first place, a man gains his living and satisfies his basic food, sex, and social drives by the practice of his discipline. In the second place, the activity during the execution of the creative work is pure joy.

The growing interest of industrial management in creativity, especially of technical employees, is recognized. There is evident throughout management literature a strong desire to foster creative ability and creative climate—the subject of a later chapter. The most important reason for this is the significance which new products have assumed in today's business. To provide these has demanded the creation of a multi-billion-dollar research and development activity, A company must participate in this activity if it is to have a chance to compete in the market. Management has seen this, and now faces the dilemma that creativity needs freedom in order to function, but also needs direction in order to generate profits. Consequently, management must have an understanding of the principles of creativity to ensure wise decisions in this area.

Beyond this, the potential rewards, individual and social, in a larger understanding of creativity are obvious. Suppose we could identify creative persons at an early age, bring them to maximum capacity earlier, keep them active through a lifetime, and not risk the loss of potential geniuses! We might have several men of the highest creative ability where now there is one, and fifty of talent, where now there are only a few.

More than this, everyone must create solutions to problems, and each could learn to do it better. The creative techniques would be largely applied to catalyze the development of the social sciences as well as of physical science, which now dangerously outstrips them. From the development of a more complete knowledge of man can stem a balanced world society.

Finally, creative activity at the highest level is among the greatest of all human ecstasies, and often brings moments of high personal drama.

This book purposes a review of the extant knowledge of creativity and a reworking of this material in the following directions:

Aids to individual creativity.
Aids to group creativity.
Creativity tests.
Aspects of creativity in the world today.

The principles of creativity have not even begun to be applied as far as they may. In thinking about creativity, one must be prepared to deal with intangibles. But to minimize this, let the facts that *have* been established and the best judgments that have been projected from them be set forth. The approach here will be to use available evidence in as much detail as necessary to set forth the principles of creativity. Then the way to use the principles will be considered, to show how deductions from them reveal individual and group aids and guides to creative climate.

The principles derive from the knowledge of creative personality, and the several stages of the creative process. By logical deduction from, or extension of, the principles, the reasons appear for such individual aids as how to study your own creative method, or how to prime the pump to set your creative activity in motion. Or, the "why" develops for such widely discussed group aids as "brainstorming," Gordon and G. E. procedures, or for some of the improvements in group methods and suggestion systems which will be discussed. The principles show the biggest step toward improving creative climate; and they show how to interview for, test for, and study creativity.

Moreover, in management, a man *must* take account of the principles deriving from the creative personality and creative stages, not alone for his own progress, but for the proper development of those who report to him. This knowledge shows the way to establish climate suitable for growth—and in the special case of research, the way for it to be fruitful and creative.

Some preliminary examples of how this understanding works can be given for the very well known procedure of brainstorming (described more fully in Chapter 10). In brainstorming, a group of people gather, are given a problem, and respond verbally. All ideas are recorded. All contributions are welcome, and all criticism is barred. "Hitch-hikes" on others' ideas are welcomed, and indeed, are given the right of way. This was the procedure as originally defined.

The principles of creativity, as will later be developed, permit two immediate deductions:

(1) If the problem is simply "sprung" on the group, there is no time for the creative stages of gathering material and mental scanning. Therefore, it is better to reveal the subject for discussion to the participants in advance. Thus opportunity is gained for some preparation, and as a bonus, some incubation, or mulling over, before the brainstorming session.

(2) As the session proceeds, many new avenues of approach and association stimuli are brought to the attention of each participant under "hot" conditions of interest and drive. Later, incubation on these is bound to occur, whence further ideas arise. Therefore, it should be fruitful to provide a mechanism for collecting these aftermath ideas and add them to the list assembled during the session.

Both of these deductions, showing how to use the knowledge of creativity, were made by the present author in this theoretical way prior to their publication; both of them were later published,* and are now routine parts of the brainstorming method.

Another deduction may be made about brainstorming from the basic principles of creativity: a man creates from pleasure in creation itself, from pride in his achievement, and from desire to better his life position in the areas of all the basic drives of food, sex, and social status. All these imply *recognition*. The brainstorming technique does not attach ideas to their originators. The principles say that this must be done to get the best ideas. It is as easy to take originators as it is to take ideas from a tape recording. Why bother? Because you will get better ideas that way! If the man who produced the *winning* idea in the session is recognized for it, he will be stimulated by his success and its recognition to produce an even better idea the next time. In creation perhaps more than anywhere, nothing succeeds like success.

The principal function of a brainstorming session is to feed new, pertinent, perhaps remote associations to the one or two high-creatives in the group under prime conditions of motivation, interest, permissiveness, and opportunity for achievement. As for the other

---

* *Machine Design,* April 2, 1956; *Printer's Ink,* April 27, 1956.

participants, "they also serve...." The principles also give the following on brainstorming: Quantity is wanted, in the hope that in much quantity there may be some quality. The question should therefore be so structured that it will have many answers, usually rather specific. Examples are a name for, a slogan for, ways to use, or to do, something. For instance, it is required to name a new face cream, provide a slogan for a safety campaign, invent different ways to use Scotch tape or aluminum foil, imagine opportunities to use an extension phone, or think of how to interest new groups of consumers in a given product. For questions of this type, brainstorming is relatively more effective than are other methods.

To understand and make use of the principles of creativity, it will be necessary to know the traits and quirks of the *creative personality* and the component parts, the intermeshing gears, of the *creative stages.* If they are to be used freely and confidently, these principles, like those of any other subject used a great deal, must rest on a solid foundation of intimate acquaintance with the historical development of the subject and the basic literature from which the knowledge is derived. This will be covered in the first part of the book.

The kinds of deductions that can be made and the manner of their derivation will then be discussed in the latter part, which will thus serve for training each person to use the principles for himself. For example: Give insight, i.e., ideas, a chance to occur by taking time out for dissociated thought; when insight comes, record it; allow opportunity for *full* realization of coordinate and supplementary thoughts, as well as the clear perception of the next hurdle. To "know thyself" in the creative sense is to know your creative faculty as you know your golf skill.

As a matter of personal interest, the present author made a point of recording, over a considerable period, the time, place, and circumstances of any new ideas that occurred to him in the fields of this book and of his chemical research. By keeping this catalog, insights were caught that otherwise would have been missed. We must give insights into problems a chance to emerge. Beyond that, we can have more creative ideas right away, simply by taking note of the ones that are now escaping.

Every person as he goes through life must be creative to some degree, because he must continuously create solutions to presented problems. These new combinations are for the most part new simply to the individual, and while useful to him, have no larger, social worth. The toddler, examining the bric-à-brac of the living room faster than his harried mother can retrieve them from his grasp, is posing his own problems and solving them creatively. In school, learning in some cases may partake of the creative process. A composition written, or a social situation adjusted to, may be creative behavior. Solving an algebra problem is discovery and invention, and carries its attendant satisfaction. The answers to questions in psychological tests for creativity are new combinations for the individual.

In business, in courtship, in marriage, in family relationships, we all create solutions to problems every day. But solutions to *difficult* problems are founded on years of effort, of training, and of learned creative rapport, even though their expression may quite commonly mature in a sudden burst of insight. It is striking to detect the symbolism, the speed, the effortlessness, of such insight, but one must think also of the vast conglomeration of material whence the unconscious has crystallized a coordinated unit by a sudden compression of much work in a small compass of time and space.

To summarize: Everyone is to some degree creative; all of us create answers to problems as we live. The theme of this book is new creation of social value; but the study of creativity at lower levels is admissible, in order to learn about it. Creation, especially in the realm of technology, is in large measure problem solving. It is the same in all fields of endeavor, is backed by the same motivation, and indeed will be shown to develop by the same process.

2. THE CREATIVE STAGES

The elements that go into the creation of solutions to difficult problems have been divided into from three to seven separate categories or stages by workers in different fields. They all developed very similar analyses. This suggests the important point that the process is the same whatever the area of its exercise. Thus, knowledge gained regarding the process will have broad applicability.

Following are the stages in creative thought postulated by serious investigators, in historical order:

By Helmholtz:

(1) Preparation.
(2) Incubation.
(3) Illumination.

By Graham Wallas, following Helmholtz, adding one:

(1) Preparation.
(2) Incubation.
(3) Illumination.
(4) Verification.

By James Webb Young:

(1) Assembly of material.
(2) Assimilation of material in our mind.
(3) Incubation.
(4) Birth of the idea.
(5) Development to practical usefulness.

By Joseph Rossman:

(1) Observation of a need or difficulty.
(2) Analysis of the need.

(3) Survey of the available information.

(4) Formulation of objective solutions.

(5) Critical analysis of the proposed solutions for advantages and disadvantages.

(6) Birth of the new idea, the invention.

(7) Experimentation to test out the most promising solution; perfection of the final embodiment by repeating some or all of the previous steps.

By Alex Osborn:

(1) Orientation: pointing up the problem.

(2) Preparation: gathering pertinent data.

(3) Analysis: breaking down the relevant material.

(4) Hypothesis: piling up alternatives by way of ideas.

(5) Incubation: letting up, to invite illumination.

(6) Synthesis: putting the pieces together.

(7) Verification: judging the resultant ideas.

It will be clear that all have given essentially the same process as Wallas, though Osborn gives synthesis in place of the usual illumination. Verification is the word commonly used to mean elaborating or developing ideas. What the expanded lists have really done is to amplify the preparative stage. Rossman points out the importance of appreciating that there *is* a problem. This is significant, because explicit statement of the problem is often the real creation, the answer then being more or less obvious. A good example of this is Henry A. Wise Wood's story. He noticed "that in machines for smoothing the interior of printing plates, the resulting chips would continue to lie in the machine and injure the following plate unless carefully removed by hand." The solution: turn the machine upside down. The real invention: realization of the problem.

Rossman is also quick to point out that, given a major illumination, the process of creation may be repeated on a minor scale in the subsequent development toward verification.

No rigid insistence on the order of the steps of the process of origination is intended, since they interweave, and the entire process may occur in building a segment of a larger creation. The present writer will use the following convenient list:

(1) Preparation.
(2) Incubation.
(3) Insight.
(4) Verification.

In each of these stages there is an emotional complement to consider.

No question should arise regarding the need for preparative work to acquire the necessary knowledge, or for a desire to solve the problem, or for doing something about developing the idea that finally comes. The possible moot points are incubation and insight. These mean, simply, a wait after preparation, and the more or less sudden birth of the good solution-idea—what Gerard has aptly called "the arrival of the fittest."

The value of a wait after preparation, and the sudden birth of ideas, are common knowledge. It is in the explanation of these phenomena that psychologists and thinkers in general have differed. Incubation is unconscious cerebration to some; to others it is fading of the irrelevant. Insight is sudden birth to some; to others, what is left after the fading of the irrelevant. These conflicting points of view will be discussed again in a later chapter. Here we subscribe to the viewpoints of unconscious cerebration and sudden birth, largely because this is what the creators themselves have believed and reported, as will now be shown.

Joseph Rossman, a U. S. patent examiner, in his book, "Psychology of the Inventor," analyzed the replies of 710 inventors to a questionnaire sent out by him. The author has tabulated the quotations in Rossman's Chapter VI from 28 of these respondents, on the mental processes of inventors, with respect to these particulars: Did the ideas come suddenly? In a period of relaxation or after rest? Was the mental visualization of the idea relatively complete before committing it to paper? Did they feel that subconscious processes were involved? Such comments were counted only if overt and explicit. The results:

Of the 28 inventors—

Eight made no comment in any category.
Six attributed their ideas to unconscious development.
Six visualized the invention complete with moving parts

and in detail before making any drawing.

Twelve declared that the ideas came in periods of rest and relaxation.

Ten declared that ideas habitually came to them out of the blue.

Remembering that these comments are voluntary and spontaneous, one sees in them striking support to incubation and insight as stages of creative thought. The number of unprompted references to the unconscious is surprising.

Flesch has neatly summarized the variety of occasions reported for the occurrence of ideas to chemists:

Sunday in church as the preacher was announcing the text.

At three o'clock in the morning.

In the evening when alone in the study room.

In the morning when shaving.

In the early morning while in bed.

Just before and just after an attack of gout.

Late at night after working intensively for some hours.

Invariably at night after retiring for sleep.

In the plant one Sunday morning about 9 A.M., when no one was around.

In the morning while taking *two* baths.

While riding in an early train.

While resting and loafing on the beach.

Flesch also added in interesting detail some other cases of bright ideas, which came on a picnic, on a trip to Labrador, in the middle of the night, and riding through town in a car at 6 A.M., after a night making the rounds.

In the summary of the replies to their questionnaire relating to the "scientific hunch," Platt and Baker reported that 41 per cent declared their hunch came from subconscious or unconscious thought. The notion of "unconscious cerebration" as the principal means of solution of difficult problems is tremendously popular among creative workers. Kipling and Stevenson have written whimsical accounts of its operation in their work. Kipling declared that a demon seized his pen when his good work was being done, and he did little more than watch its motions and read the words it set down. In the case of the Mowgli stories, his demon failed to lend his aid on two. These, which he had written, as it were, alone, he destroyed, "and was better pleased with the remainder."

Stevenson speaks of "... the little people ... my Brownies ... who do one-half my work for me while I am fast asleep, and in all human likelihood do the rest for me as well, when I am wide awake and fondly suppose I do it for myself." Handel to the end of his life believed that his work was given him from outside, and many other creators, especially in the arts, but many in science too, have believed the same.

Lowes showed that every item in "The Ancient Mariner" had been dropped into "the deep well" by Coleridge, often long before the composition of the poem. It does seem that every element in a creation must have been in the prior knowledge of the originator. What comes out of the blue is a new combination. But if one analyzes back, the component parts are seen to have been in the mind all the time, just as Lowes indicated. That is why it was to Darwin that the evolutionary concept occurred, but Handel composed "The Messiah."

It is proposed in this book that unusual creative ability is largely compounded of two things:

(1) Unusually skillful rapport with the unconscious.
(2) Unusual symbolization of a nonverbal character.

Elaboration of these will appear in the chapters to follow, as they deal successively with the creative stages of preparation, motivation, incubation, insight, and verification. First, however, we wish to allude to the important *experimental* results on the stages obtained by three workers in this field: Catherine Patrick, W. E. Vinacke, and J. Eindhoven. (The interested reader is referred to Appendices A and B for details.) Working with poets and artists, with respective control groups of nonpoets and non-artists, Patrick differentiated experimentally the four stages of creative thought as specified by Wallas, and made clear the importance of early ideas, and how often they appear in the final product. Patrick was the first to show the interweaving of the stages: revision work started early; insights to embellish occurred even when the creative work was nearly completed.

Eindhoven and Vinacke also observed painters in action. The stages of creative thought were again identified. The interplay of the stages was further clarified: the stages are continuing, the process is dynamic. The stages of creativity are not stages at all, but processes which occur during creation. "They blend together and go along concurrently."

Both Patrick and Vinacke compared work in a creative field by persons skilled in the particular art as against unskilled. It appeared that the creative *method* was the same in the two groups, the difference in performance being attributable to greater technical skill. Both groups took about the same time, did the work in essentially the same way, and returned for later sessions in about the same proportion. They both made preliminary sketches, produced early ideas, incubated them, and revived and modified them. The work described employs the heuristic method, to study a factor at two different levels.

Although the experiments show that the stages of creativity interweave, that creativity itself is dynamic, and that its processes do not necessarily go through the stages in the order given, the stages will serve as convenient headings for the discussion in the next five chapters.

3. EMOTIONAL FACTORS IN CREATIVITY

The entire creative process is charged with emotion.

It goes without saying that any chance of solving a problem presupposes interest in it, and more, an intense desire to solve it. "With men, as with horses, it is only when something is tugging at the heartstrings that there is real straining" at the load.

Since the stages of creativity interweave, this chapter will consider the role of emotion in the whole creative process. The creative stages, and their affective complements, in brief, are:

Preparation = Organization of material: desire to solve.
Incubation = Wait after preparation: frustration.
Insight = Birth of the clarifying idea: thrill of solution, and anxiety of separation.
Verification = Development and proof: satisfaction **of** reaping, and removing separation.

Most important, and needing the most discussion, is the initiating drive, because without it nothing happens. But it shows feedback from the other stages.

Motivation in the Preparative Stage

The motives which together furnish the drive to conclude a major creative effort comprise a highly complex system. True, all may be referable ultimately to Weinland's three F's of food, family and fame. But beyond this concept, many specific spurs to action can be isolated. They lead one to ultra-meticulous preparation. They lead him to feed pertinent associations into the creating mind under activating conditions which maximize the likelihood of favorable collisions. Different aspects of this motivation are:

The practical—the three F's.
Satisfaction—in creating, in the resultant achievement, in service.
Anticipation—of the joy of insight.
Freedom—from frustration.
Challenge.
Basic psychology—sublimation.

Three closely related motivations are: the spur of keen competition, *esprit de corps* within the framework of that competition, and loyalty to an inspiring leader. These are powerful mainsprings of action which are summed up in the military mind as morale. Lord Kelvin established a fortunate interplay of these motives in his brilliant group of students who helped lay the foundations of modern physics, and who included Wilson—of cloud chamber fame—and Sir Ernest Rutherford. Eyring has described the marvelous creative give and take of G. N. Lewis' group at Berkeley, which produced three Nobel Prize winners in physical chemistry.

Such interplay has been the rule throughout history with the famous schools of philosophy, of art, and of science. When these motives of competition, group pride, and admired leaders exist in a given group of personalities, all are stimulated. If a great creator has that communicable fire, his students become disciples, and achieve by emulation. The contact first sparks creativeness, and then performance.

Teeple * shows how this works, and incidentally, how climate and freedom and recognition and competition catch men up in the joy of achievement:

> ".... the time and patient money being available, you start picking men here and there who like work and responsibility ... The only bait needed is the picture of a big pioneer work to be done, the promise that a man can have all the work, responsibility, and freedom from bossing and interference that he is capable of taking, and the assurance that the work will be completed. Then you watch them grow ... One day it becomes an organization, a living, growing, cooperating entity, working toward a definite end,

* *Industrial and Engineering Chemistry*, **22**, 575, June 1930. Copyright 1930 by American Chemical Society and reprinted by permission of the copyright owner.

disregarding personal discomfort, 115 degrees in the shade, or twenty-four hours a day. It is no longer a place for the weak, the petty, or the deadwood, the man who is not contributing his best feels lost and fades away. When this peak has been reached, you go fishing and let them alone while they finish the job. You see it is really very simple. There are men in plenty who will work their heads off intelligently and accomplish really marvelous things if you will but realize, and make them realize, the dignity and importance of their work . . . Above all they must be freed from petty nagging, freed from gloom spreaders, and freed from a voice at their elbow constantly dictating just how and when and where each move should be made."

A vision of contributing to the good of mankind is often a strong incentive, as in the field of social service, and in the willing sacrifices frequently made in medical research.

Confidence in the issue of the creative task is mentioned, especially, by Le Chatelier. He observes that "great men have concerned themselves with great problems," and recommends confidence that a problem is important, that the answer will be new and useful, and that *you* can get it.

A creative worker does not develop much drive without such confidence, and this confidence feeds upon the expressed faith by others that he will succeed. The most tangible expression of such faith is the actual commission to undertake a specific act of creation. He then has the powerful motivation of knowing that success will be rewarded, and that the product will be used. The story of countless masterpieces has been, first the commission, then the inspiration. It was on commission that Mozart wrote the great opera "Don Giovanni," and Verdi "Aida." On commission, paintings are painted, literature written, and discoveries made. Always implicit in the mind as work proceeds is the hoped-for recognition for good work, the commissioned reward, and the use or enjoyment of the product by mankind.

Once interest is aroused, there is the simple joy of exercising a well-understood creative skill, just as a good golfer or bowler enjoys his game. Easton suggests, as a method of getting started in a creative activity, that one begin on a puzzling phase of the work. Soon attention is engaged, interest aroused, and creative imagination lends its aid. Problems challenge. Finally comes the joy of solution, the triumph, the "insight thrill." This may be the pleasure of a partial solution of one phase of the work, or it may be a giant step of understanding, or it may even be merely a resolution of the next progressive step to take, the next experiment to perform.

A final motive comes in preparation, when the effort has not evoked solution of the problem. It is the wish to have the mind freed of the frustration, to be rid of the not knowing. A parallel is the insistent nagging in the brain, much like a barely perceptible physical discomfort, until an urgently desired or needed memory is recovered. Related to this is the feeling of a reader who "can't put down" a good book. His frustration, or suspense, is momentarily to be relieved by exposure of the author's insights.

All forms of creative imagination imply elements of feeling, and all emotional dispositions influence the creative imagination. There are "the fertile artifices generated by envy, jealousy, enmity, vengeance." Love creates an imaginary being, of more or less close resemblance to actuality. Sorrow has been worked out in music and poetry and other creative tasks, as have sublimations of the powerful unconscious drives. It is possible that the obscure motive of the need to sublimate is the most fundamental of the creative drives, with all the rest stemming from it.

Rossman's questionnaire to 710 inventors enabled him to give the following list of frequency of mention of their motives:

Love of inventing	193
Desire to improve	189
Financial gain	167
Necessity or need	118
Desire to achieve	73
Part of regular job	59
Prestige	27
Altruistic reasons	22
Laziness	6

The desire to improve existing devices is nearly identical with love of inventing, and together the two add up to a large proportion of the total. Rossman points out work that confirms his tabulation. Studies at Bryn Mawr showed that 66 of 171 inventors recorded their joy in manipulating materials, in experimentation, and in exploration. Anne Roe, reporting on personality studies of eminent physical and biological scientists, concluded: "All had in common a driving absorption in their work. They work all day, every day, with few vacations, because they would rather be doing their work than anything else."

The motives of love of invention and love of work, as stated above, are based on recognition and use of the product. These motives are especially noticed and mentioned because they are in the forefront in the actual doing.

Besides anticipation of insight, there is in the motivation of the preparation stage another feedback, namely, anticipation of esthetic satisfaction in the product of insight—in the verification. As the sculptor chips, or the painter paints, or the writer writes, even at the beginning of the work the general feel and total impression of the finished unit is available to him.

As a special aspect of emotion in the preparative work, some associations necessarily gain favor and preference over others in the creator's mind, and, for help or hindrance, receiving an affective tag. These words, phrases, symbols, and hypotheses have, indeed, great value for one alone.

Thus motivation draws a profile of the creative personality, for the later portrait (Chapter 9): desire to solve, desire to serve and be recognized for it, confidence in creative skills, ability to bear and utilize incubative frustration, joy in the beauty of the solution, in its reward, and in the use of the achievement. What a tremendous experience must it be, in the case of genius, to *know*—to know calmly with cold certainty—what you can do, and see before you the problem, as a meal spread for the gourmet palate, and have the commission to solve it! *Then* is born "The Mona Lisa," or "Don Giovanni," or the great coordinating theory of relativity. Yes, there is stumbling along the way. There are hesitations. But far ahead is glimpsed, as Mozart wrote, "the feast."

Emotion—Other Stages

In the solution of difficult problems, the complex spectrum of drives in the preparative phase must spend itself without solution or even much apparent progress. With a feeling of discouragement and of tiredness, the prepared material is committed to unconscious incubation. If the preparation has been well done, the process of incubation takes place, and may lead to insight. But without motivation, the unconscious will not usually be bothered, and there will be no incubation.

A fertile field for the analysis of creativity might be found in the analogy between the unconscious of discovery and the unconscious of psychiatry. In the unconscious of psychiatry, the repression of unacknowledgeable material leads to symbolic dreams. In the unconscious of discovery, frustration and preparative material lead to creation. To speculate along this line: when a problem is undertaken, interest is awakened. It is kindled as information is assembled, arranged and rearranged. With failure to solve come fatigue and frustration. In those moments when the preparative effort slackens and stops, and incubation begins, there is a let-down, discouraged feeling. The conscious turns to other things. As with an unresolved psychic conflict, the organized body of preparative material, plus frustration, are pushed into the unconscious. Thus the means and energy to continue action are available. The means of alleviating the frustration are at hand by finding the correct answer to the problem. But as a supplement to this view, the man skilled in the art of creative thinking learns to transmit the task to the unconscious with great confidence—a kind of slow expectancy.

After the tension of the incubation comes the elation of insight, which has aptly been named a "eureka." There should be some psychic energy relation between the desire in preparation and the tension in incubation or the elation in insight. There is a licking of the mental chops in satisfaction over the coup that has been brought off. Then follows a flood of associated material and conclusions, methods of verification, and development. There ensues feverish activity, to set all these in order, and strong conscious effort to realize their full potentialities.

The parallel shown in the following is of interest:

Frustration	Psychic pressure built up by repression
↓	↓
Insight	Decision to talk out
↓	↓
Elation	Burst of expression

This series has been suggested: interest ⟶ frustration ⟶ anxiety ⟶ elation ⟶ feverish activity. In the end, only desire can drive the preparative work to be well done; only desire can result in frustration—men are not frustrated when they do not care. Only intense desire can arouse anxiety; only fruition of intense desire can evoke elation, and spur the feverish activity of verification.

The desire is transmitted to the unconscious as anxiety-tension. Can the unconscious be otherwise stimulated? The ice is thin, but these comments are offered for expansion in the next chapter. The unconscious loves symbols, not words. Use preferred symbols, and words which have especial value for you.

The sci-artist finds deep satisfaction—and deep ego involvement —in the esthetic beauty of his creation or discovery. At the same time, he feels strange in the new territory, apart from his fellows. This emotion has been named by Rogers the anxiety of separation. In an atmosphere of permissiveness the worker achieved the breakthrough. But he keenly feels the need of verification and communication to draw his fellows to himself in the new area, to "gain acceptance of the general mind."

Thus, there is the *necessity* to communicate in order to remove the separation and cash the reward. As Wiegand observes:

> "... the kudos of accomplishment are not subject to surtax or attrition by tradesmen. A prime motivation for research personnel is the identification of their accomplishments with their own names.... The widespread assurance that the work of each individual is going to be tagged with that individual's name all the way up the line to the top is a *sine qua non* of research motivation."

Furthermore, Wiegand declares, the scientist is as attached to his discovery as any artist to his painting or author to his book. The reason is that discovery is itself an art: it is only verification of the discovery that is science. Indeed, it is for the most part in verification that the classical scientific method as taught in university courses is applied. Discovery is made with the creative imagination. By comparison, verification, though necessary, is hackwork, except to the extent that the creative imagination must function again and again to invent the means of verification, the devices of proof.

Once a problem takes the attention, it seems to catch and hold interest by some kind of psychic law. You cannot let go. It is reported that Queen Victoria, given ELTABYRA, spent the entire night seeking the anagram! Everyone enjoys riddles, puzzles, and contests needing skill, because they represent insight and creation keyed to a minor level of effort. When one is reading for pleasure, he readily gives the task fully energized attention, because he is repeatedly held in the suspense of incubation, followed by reliving the insights of the author. A most pertinent observation on the joy of reading, or seeing a play, opera, or movie, is that in a short space of time one repeats the insight thrills the creator experienced over months, all the while expending his own energy, to his great satisfaction.

In games such as bridge, poker, and chess, there is insight to enjoy. Sometimes the play of a difficult hand, or the planning of a complex series of moves, needs the expenditure of full, if momentarily exercised, creative power.

The popularity of the detective story is an interesting case. The reader repeats the insights of the writer. He also repeats the insights of the detective. Then he further strives to achieve his own solution of the crime, or insight, in competition with the detective—hence the reader's disgust should the detective pounce upon and closely inspect a small, unidentified object, and not let him in on it.

Most cultural pleasure is vicarious insight. Even in spectator sports, by identification with the hero, there is insight into the muscular skills he exerts for his achievements.

Enjoyment is thus second-order creation.

A problem in the area of industrial research that has been skirted is the following: with the present emphasis on large research teams tackling phases of a problem, whence is to come the joy in a man's own artistic creation? In an assignment to a small segment of a problem, whence is to come the joy of working on something big? Even the team may have only a little problem. If the team succeeds, it is a *team* creation. There is loss of individual motivation. (A method to be described later will set a man loose part time on something big, in competition with others. Thus his contribution to the ultimate result will be clearly defined by his own hand.)

Management's concern with the motivation of all employees is the subject of many books. With regard to creative technical employees, motivation is a most important part of creative climate (see Chapter 13), and the following usual but very fundamental factors apply:

> A clear commission.
> Confidence in the man.
> A clear reward.

The difficult task is to identify the reward, or reward-system, which different men or groups of men value. Some of the reward must be paid in advance, in the form of a loosening of organizational control as far as possible in granting freedom to work. This freedom extends in many directions, and the required degree is sometimes organizationally difficult.

A facet of the reward problem is to consider the creative scientist's inner visualization of himself as a Discover. This ideal is limited for the industrial scientist by his industrial situation, his employee situation, and his secondary social status vis-à-vis management. Rewards are concerned with mitigating or removing these blocks by pay, bonuses, status symbols, and freedom. The principles of creativity teach the best reward of the creative researcher: not administrative responsibility, but recognition of his creative capacity; then a new and larger commission, and free opportunity to fulfill it. That means status and freedom of the kind that management itself enjoys, but with an entirely different responsibility—the responsibility to *create*. An awareness of how important this is comes with the realization that what the R&D men do now will be half the business in a decade. Creative scientists will not consistently seek to join management ranks if the alternate path of staying on the line of direct creation is made equally attractive. One of the important things management can do is to provide the means to make this alternate path available.

When the research man has attacked his problem with desire and solved it, the thrill of insight is another, and large, part of his reward. Then management can help with a sympathetic hearing, to mitigate the "anxiety of separation" from his fellows the creator feels when the moment comes that he must communicate his discovery. The man may begin to feel some concern about the newness of his proposal. He can minimize this anxiety of separation by intelligent orientation of his presented material. Management can help with a sympathetic ear. Serious consideration must be given even if ideas seem wild or ridiculous. If sound judgment then rejects them, the rebuff—for so it will be regarded—should be softened with appropriate explanations.

In summary, the three F values of food, family, and fame to be obtained through the conception and communication of a significant new discovery are the basis of creative drive. Operating as a supplement along the way is joy in the work as it seeks to give definite and esthetic form to the nebulous; as it distills the essence of a new association; as it boldly denies that there is nothing new under the sun, by formulating the absolutely new from the old.

4. PREPARATION

Creative effort becomes a problem situation as soon as effort begins to realize a tangible result. Let it be assumed that an individual has a problem and has the motivation to seek its solution. The problem can be in any discipline, but the specific discussion to follow will be largely in terms of physical science. The worker, then, starts with a basic training, which has prepared him to handle himself in the area where he wishes to work, and with some information which bears more or less directly on the problem.

In its first presentation, the problem will be somewhat nonspecific, as when an industrial researcher is assigned the problem of curing smog, or evaluating the silicones in the product line, or developing a synthetic shampoo. In general terms, the necessary work then becomes:

(1) To restate the problem in more effective terms.
(2) To decide directions in which material must be developed.
(3) To activate the results of this mental analysis toward solution achievement by manipulation of the material.

A little thought will show that these steps would serve as well to implement the creation of a new symphony as of a new product. The steps have many aspects which require discussion. But first, it will be helpful to understand just what creativity is in its simplest terms. It is useful to consider the brief equation,

$$A + B \rightarrow C$$

where A and B represent two concepts established in the mind, which come together and in some way engage to produce the new thing, C. The arrow in the equation has the meaning of "yields" or "produces." The purpose of the preparative work is to put A and B into the mind and activate them; of incubation, to get them together; of insight, to perceive C, with or without A and B, which may no longer be needed; of verification, to *realize* C. The purpose of this chapter is to discuss the nature and activation of A and B.

The symbols A and B can be conceived as very simple or very complex. Examples of their meaning will be given, which will show that C is a new combination of them, often self-evident, once the correct A and B are set side by side.

Example 1 (Adapted from Nelles)

A: The gases of car exhausts contribute to smog, which is dangerous to health and dangerous in other ways.

+

        +

B: Gases can be passed through chambers which absorb and modify them.

↓

        ↓

C: Put a suitable reactor in the car exhaust train.

Example 2

A: Matches often burn down too far and sear the fingers; they also continue to burn after being tossed away, and ignite fires.

+

        +

B: Paper and fabrics are easily rendered nonflammable by soaking in solutions of certain salts.

↓

        ↓

C: Soak the finger end of the match to render it nonflammable. Fire will go out before the fingers are reached, and the treatment will mitigate, though not solve, the problem of starting fires, since the match will go out sooner.

Example 3

A: In Osborn appeared the story of an idea contributed by a laborer in a factory suggestion system, which proposed windows in the doors leading from the locker rooms, without which "it makes collision." The polite reply pointed out the loss of privacy.

+

        +

B: In the newspaper, a story appeared telling how windows, designed to be opaque from the outside looking in, had been put in place in a girls' dormitory—the wrong way!

↓

        ↓

C: Use one-way windows on locker-room doors—set, of course, the right way.

The author actually obtained C by the A-B combination indicated. The unaccompanied idea C popped in the middle of the week, along with a couple of expletives, after "it makes collision" happened to him. That week-end in the public library he happened to come across the story of A again, and realized in a flash and for the first time the A and B content of C and their sources.

Example 4 (Adapted from Flesch)

A: In 1940, England desperately needed material help, but there was no political possibility of the United States granting a sizable
\+ monetary loan.

\+

B: In community life, a neighbor will often borrow one's garden hose,
↓ and in return lend the use of his lawn mower.

↓

C: Destroyers for bases, lend-lease.

Example 5

A: Thin films react exceptionally fast. A thin film of rubber can be dried down from an aqueous dispersion, and then made much thinner still by two-way stretching over the top of a shallow dish,
\+ which it will grip at the edges, and so remain in position.

\+

B: A reagent in the dish prior to hooking on the film could be caused
↓ to react rapidly with the thin film either as liquid or vapor.

↓

C: New rubber products, formed in the stretched condition, by reaction with, for example, iodine, stannic chloride, etc.

In doing such work by prior introduction of sulfur into the film, for example, hard rubber was cured in the stretched condition.

For a classic example, the story of Newton's concept of gravitation can be cast in this form:

Example 6

A: There was the knowledge of the rate that the moon deviated from
\+ the straight line which it would follow were it not for the earth.

\+

B: There was the knowledge of the rate of fall on an object—let it be
↓ an apple for sentiment's sake—toward the earth.

↓

C_1: There is a relation between A and B. . . . The relation was deter-
↓ mined and the rates were found to be equal. Then,

↓

C_2: The same force acts on both!

These illustrations bring out two things of interest: (1) A, besides its factual content, usually states or implies the difficulty or need; (2) when the right B is present with it, the solution becomes suddenly obvious. After dozens to thousands of B's have been matched to A in the conscious or unconscious mind, it is no wonder that the right one excites the "eureka" feeling.

Actually, the situation is more complex than matching many B's to one A. Many B's must be matched to *each* A, and there may occur a large number of A's. The problem is known, and it is in every A, overtly or implicitly. But the particular, complete form of each A depends on the terms in which it is expressed. There will be many ways, some much more fruitful than others.

In the Newton example, the elements are quite complex, A involving directly the first law of motion, as well as careful astronomical observations transformed into suitable mathematical form. A and B can even be two large branches of knowledge which, in a powerful insight, are brought into relation by a coordinating theory. In the case of Darwin's evolutionary concept:

Example 7

A: There is the knowledge of comparative biology and the broad families of organisms diverging into numberless species.

\+

\+

B: There is the knowledge of competition for the food supply and general economic welfare in human society.

↓

↓

C: By natural selection resulting from competition, favorable mutations are kept and unfavorable ones weeded out, to produce new species.

The idea of survival of the fittest came independently to A. R. Wallace during an illness. He read Malthus' *Principles of Population*, describing the checks to human population, and how these eliminate the least fit. Wallace says:

> "Vaguely thinking over the enormous and constant destruction this implied, it occurred to me to ask the question, 'Why do some die and some live?' and the answer was clearly that on the whole the best fitted live. . . . Then it suddenly flashed upon me that this self-acting process would improve the race . . . the fittest would survive. Then at once I seemed to see the whole effect of this."

It occasionally happens that a pattern, A, has been poised and waiting for B for years. When B is presented, they rush together to give C at once. Victor G. Bloede worked for several years on the problem of sun-fast colors for window shades. He relates:

"I had finally given it up as a practical proposition.... One day I was examining some samples of raw cotton, among them being several of a dark, ecru color instead of white. These samples the party said were called 'sanded' cotton, colored by nature through falling upon red soil, the color being beaten in by the rain, and not removable by any method of bleaching known to the arts. Instantly the hunch flashed in and said this is the way to produce what you have spent long months of work on. And so it proved to be ... and gave rise to a very profitable industry still flourishing."

Diagrammatically (Figure 4-1), suppose that in an important conference a pattern had been building during the discussion, so that a, b, c, d, have been forged and interrelated. The thought B then is introduced, and someone is inspired to state the completed complex C. This is insight, and the seeing of things as wholes in the Gestalt psychology.

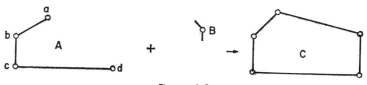

Figure 4–1

In the foregoing example, the arrangement of A and B has been such as to make C quite clear; however, this is not always the case. Even with the correct A and B, the solution C may require further effort. Commonly, only A is in the mind in various forms and arrangements. One has then to toss in a lot of things and hope that one of them is B and that A and B will get together. The source and arrangement of different B items are the principal object of the preparative *search*, once the problem A has been explicated.

Where do B items come from? They come by analysis of the problem and decision to devote thought and effort in a certain direction. Or B may already be in the mind, and its fusion to A may be a rapid process or a slow one.

The preparation stage, then, is restructuring of the problem, asking the question in as many ways as possible, and following along the direction each structuring suggests. How is the material assembled and how are the pieces fitted? To answer this, the work of five men in different directions will be described, and then these pieces of information will be dovetailed to unify the preparative activity. In several cases, the work described for one man is representative of the field, and others might have been named.

Poincaré

Poincaré has given several personal experiences of the work-incubate-solution process and has pointed out that hard, preparative labor, resting on a firm foundation of solid mathematical training, was necessary to produce useful results. The work consisted of manipulative trial of the thought-up material, and much of it was not even used in the finale. Such apparently fruitless labor must be done, said Poincaré, to produce the necessary ideas, activate them, and afford opportunity for relationships among them to develop. Then one night, ideas rose in crowds, and interlocked with one another to form patterns. The esthetically pleasing patterns were the more useful ones. Insight came.

Armstrong

One of the most interesting commentaries on the operation of the creative mind is the study of Shakespeare's idea clusters by E. A. Armstrong. An idea cluster is the group of words and ideas that are associated in one person's mind with a given word. The Association and Gestalt schools of psychology can deal with these in their theoretical developments, but the clusters themselves are facts. Armstrong shows how, in the plays, time and again, groups of words and ideas tend to occur together. Such a group is seen as an idea cluster. One word or association arouses another, so that in a passage of any length where one or two words of a cluster are used, many of the others will have been fitted in as well. There was a definite group of associations surrounding the concepts of *kite,* and *beetle,* and *crow.* Armstrong shows that for Shakespeare "crows rather than seagulls fly over the white cliffs of Dover."

The present author has used Armstrong's idea to verify that the three-ply association of "the lunatic, the lover, and the poet" occurs in the plays no less than six times. The duo of lunatic and poet occurs four other times; and the duo of lover and poet, twenty-one other times. The association of lover, poet, and heart occurs eleven times; of lover, poet, and moon/sun/planet, seven times.

An image cluster will reappear after an absence, wax or wane, gain or lose elements, and so blossom again with new components. Shakespeare's characteristic style derives much from the tendency of his mind to fulfill a large portion of a cluster in a passage once it was started by revival of the other associated images. In his later period, they lacked room, and indeed seemed to "gate-crash his verse." This observation may be a comment on the creative mind—that the older, more practised mentality is not now so much changing and expanding a cluster as economically trying to use in a short space all the compact unit to which maturity has reduced the associated group.

The infallible cluster reproduction shows how the mind works to create. When a stimulus recalls any remote or central unit of a cluster, the whole will be activated. Shakespeare's work shows how, when one idea was started, then others, both words and images, alike in sound or in meaning, or even opposites, all were activated and reproduced. The process continued for some time and might be strung out over many lines before the strings initially sounded ceased to produce their overtones. Each cluster has some commonly and some more seldom used components. The composition of the cluster is the limitation that the mind has in that area. A new idea derives from elements in two clusters—perhaps from the more seldom used elements.

The different modes and types of association of Shakespeare are tabulated below. These examples are included here to illustrate some of the ways of thought continuation and thought completion that Shakespeare used, but which are common to all men (cf. also page 250).

Coordination: peacock-turkey—i.e., one bird, another bird.

Predication: perfumes-sweeten—i.e., a noun, then a verb appropriate to context.

Coexistence: prunes-stewed (frequent, common use together).

Identity: unlessoned-unschooled—i.e., synonyms.

Motor speech forms, associated in proverbs or daily speech: cat-mouse.

Word completion: ever-everlasting.

Clang: Kate-cat.

Rhyme: nit-wit.

Naturally, these are all examples in some way of the basic of contiguity. Some important special processes are specified by Armstrong. Image clusters appearing somewhat separated in an earlier work may occur closer together in a later work. If the mood or atmosphere of a passage is similar to an earlier context, the same images may appear. An image, having occurred close to another image, tends to be accompanied by it or a similar image on another occasion. An image frequently calls forth its opposite. Frequently it is the sound of the word rather than its meaning which is significant for Shakespeare's associative activities. (Similar memory processes, especially memories from reading, have been analyzed by Lowes for Coleridge's "Ancient Mariner.") Incidentally, clusters represent absolute proof of whether Shakespeare wrote a certain passage or not. The clusters are fingerprints of the mind.

Why is all this important? First, because the mechanism of creativity (in poetry) stands revealed. Second, because a word or image can activate a cluster. It is the *clusters* which, in Poincaré's phraseology, have hooks, rise in crowds, are activated, some more, some less, interlock, and form patterns, until an especially fruitful combination gains ascendancy.

Flesch

In "The Art of Clear Thinking," Rudolf Flesch defines thinking in this beautifully simple way: "Thinking is the manipulation of memories." This definition fits even creative thinking, and the $A + B \rightarrow C$ equation, where the memories A and B coalesce in the new idea C. In other parallel lines of *searching* thought, the memory wanted may be a forgotten name, address, or fact. Or the memory may be a recalled personal experience. Such recall is accompanied by a strong rush of emotion, of sadness, gladness, or anger, just as the new idea is conceived with joy. The creative thought differs in that the product is new.

Flesch discusses the action of the mind in seeking a forgotten memory or a solution to a problem as analogous to an electronic scanner. Insight is experienced when a recalled pattern "matches the pattern of the situation before you." The mental scanner needs, first, to know when it has the right combination, and second, to have an open channel to communicate. Scanning takes place during incubation and reflective thought and times of quiet. The first item is achieved by correct asking of the question, which amounts to economical specification for the scanner to sort ejects and rejects. The second item, the open channel, is achieved by allowing time for reflection and insight, and by forming the habit of recording insights which flash skittishly across the conscious and are gone. This has been mentioned on page 10, and it will be considered again under individual aids, as one of the most important things anyone can do to stimulate his own creativity.

This picture develops:

> Preparation specifies the problem.
> Preparation selects and activates clusters.
> To the specifications, the mental scanner manipulates the clusters.

Duncker

In using a scanner, the punched-in specifications are all-important. Karl Duncker's important paper "On Problem Solving" has discussed the establishment of the best specification of the problem, the economical way to ask the question. Duncker's chief contribution to creativity is his detailed analysis of what the preparative work is: restructuring of the problem, asking the question in as many ways as possible, and following the direction that each structuring suggests; seeking and supplying information needed so that each structure can have the concrete material to *be* a structure, not a skeleton; searching in all ways to acquire marginal knowledge about the subject; and deliberate application of heuristic methods of reasoning to the restructurings and the accumulated specific material belonging to each.

According to Duncker, when an individual has discerned and accepted a problem, an interplay occurs in attempting solution. "From above," by thought, a model of search is formulated. "From below," the environment—materials and their arrangement—signals the operator and shapes the model of each in its plastic form(s). A model of search is a general framework of complexity suited to the problem, to which particular pieces can be fitted at will and judgments made about the result. The framework covers the whole problem. Its vague and general character is rendered just specific enough to fix it in useful form. The properties of this important concept will be discussed further.

Duncker is concerned with:

Recognition of the problem.
The model of search, how it is forged.
The kinds of events which aid a closure or solution.
The kinds of events which hinder a closure.

He studied these questions by posing problems of considerable difficulty, and analyzing subjects' verbal comments as they strove to solve them.

Duncker states that explication of a problem in different directions takes place until the optimum statement results, and one perceives a way to the answer, or at least a good experiment to perform, or an important missing piece of information to seek. These way-stations Hadamard calls "relay results."

One famous example Duncker uses is the ray problem: "Given a human being with an inoperable stomach tumor, and rays which destroy organic tissue at sufficient intensity, by what procedure can one free him of the tumor by these rays and at the same time avoid destroying the healthy tissue which surrounds it?" To this, one subject produced the following:

Send rays down the esophagus.
Desensitize the healthy tissues by a chemical injection.

Expose the tissue by operating.

Decrease the *intensity* of the rays while on their way.

Swallow something opaque to the rays to protect the stomach walls.

Alter the location of the tumor. How?

Introduce a drainage tube.

Move the tissue toward the exterior.

Vary the *intensity* of the rays.

Adapt the healthy tissues by previous *weak* use of the *rays*.

Somehow use diffuse rays . . . dispersed rays . . . stop. . . .

Send broad and weak bundle of rays through a *lens* adjusted so that the tumor lies at the focal point.

Send *weak rays* from *different directions* to *converge* on the tumor.

The italics are the present author's, and show the progress of the thought.

In one of Duncker's geometry problems, restructuring took the form of a good diagram. The real task was to construct, to the given, a mirror image.

When the mind is actively considering a problem, and making progress toward solution (Duncker's closure), how does it utilize certain material to favor the tendency toward solution? Duncker offers the following observations on this question: The easiest solution of a problem turns out to be, simply, if *a,* then *b.* Effort successfully directed to reduce the problem to these terms will favor the tendency to closure. Such reduction of the problem may come when *b* can be read from *a* because *a* has been suitably restructured in a proper model of search. Let objects be sought which have the property *b,* and let three classes exist which have the properties *bc, bd,* and *be.* If, to a general model in the mind one adds *c* characteristics, he is going toward *bc,* but away from *bd* or *be*—which will be unfortunate if one of them is the answer. In creative work, one must always be ready to shift his ground to overcome this.

The "thirteen problem" of Duncker asked, "Why are such numbers as 246,246, 181,181, and 903,903 all divisible by 13?" According to his analysis, the mind, directed to the problem, might ask "What kinds of theorems that I know would apply here? . . . Is it something

to do with the sum or other property of the repeating integers? ...
Or is it that the numbers have a common divisor divisible by 13?
... Yes, that divisor is 1001."

From this problem three interesting heuristic methods arise. The
first is to ask, "What kind of a theorem applies here" or "Shouldn't
theorems about this be looked up?" The second is the technique of
writing the simplest example, 100,100, which immediately produces
1001. So also does the third method, the technique of examining
neighbors: the difference between two consecutive numbers, say
234,234 minus 233,233, is 1001.

The thirteen problem was given to seven groups, each receiving
different help:

a. All the numbers are divisible by 1001.

b. The number 1001 is divisible by 13.

c. If a common divisor of numbers is divisible by 13, all are divisible
by 13.

d. If a divisor of a number is divisible by p, the number itself is
divisible by p.

e. Different numbers can have in common a divisor which is in
turn divisible.

f. Look for a more fundamental common character from which the
divisibility by 13 becomes evident.

w.a. Without aid.

The results:

Group	No. of Subjects	% Who Solved
a	22	59
b	10	50
c	13	15
d	22	14
e	10	0
f	13	15
w.a.	26	8

Evidently, the kinds of events which the tendency to a closure
can use to accomplish the closure are signals which are well-suited
because specific. Only the direct and specific aids improve performance significantly in the table above. As will appear several times
later, to get only 50-60 per cent success the experimenter practi-

cally reveals the answer. Without aid, only 8 per cent solved the problem, and this, when the question had already been structured for them. The creator must himself see the problem, ask the correct question, and select the pertinent from a tremendous mass of material before him. That is why high creative talent is rare.

In one of Duncker's displacement of function problems, three candles were to be mounted on a wooden door. A number of objects to use were spread on a table. From the materials on the table, the solution was to select thumb tacks and match boxes to provide the supports. Match boxes filled with matches are unit articles and possess a fixation of container, requiring forcible rearrangement of association paths to displace to another use. Now in one experiment, part of the instructions were, "The solution object is green, look for something green." Subjects went right to the green match boxes and used them. Banal? Perhaps. But see the advantage of a proper model of search which suits the solution-object well!

It is clear that the chance of solving a problem is much increased if one can select the right, specific clue from the mass of data before one. Such selection needs the creative taste that is developed by studying the methods and products of the great creators.

It has been said that it is more difficult to ask a question than to answer it. Duncker is concerned to ask the question the best way. Often the difficulty is to know what qualifications to strip from the statement in order to simplify, but not oversimplify, the problem. Actually, the very best way to ask the question will not be known until the answer is known. The restructuring accomplishes the seeking, and arrangements and rearrangements, of the preparative material, the activation of clusters, and the specification of the mental scanning. This specification includes both the question and the setting up of the models in which the cluster-substitutions can be made.

More will be discussed later about the tremendous aid a model or hint may be in obtaining solution. Now, let it suffice to recall the great creative strides that have been made in cultural history by certain schools of painting, poetry, philosophy, or psychology. The very things a school provides are: first, a model established by the founder of the school, on which creative changes may be rung by his followers; and second, a clear-cut question to be answered.

A good example is the group of impressionist painters—Monet, Manet, Sisley, and Pissarro. The scope of the creative work of their school derives from these propositions:

Example 8

A: Light is the real subject of pictorial art; anything is worth painting
+ to show a special effect of light upon nature.
+

B: In painting, use on the palette only the pure colors of the spectrum, and get modifications by small (point) applications of
↓ the pure colors side by side.
↓

C: An impressionistic work of art.

Here is a framework and a method within which men of training and talent can turn out a deluge. The model of search (find an unusual light effect) and the method (point dabbing) invite creation. The selection of a subject will depend on the interactions of a man's light-beauty-nature clusters with his other clusters, operating within the framework of A.

As a chemical illustration, to complement Example 8, in carrying out the work described in a paper by the present writer on mercaptan synthesis, two chemical models of search were explicated:

$$HSCH_2CON\text{———}X \qquad HSC_2H_4N\text{———}Y$$

To these models were synthesized a wide variety of mercapto-amides and N-mercaptoethyl compounds. There were minor insights on methods, on reactions, and on unusual compounds, such as the first heterocyclic quaternary mercaptans. The important thing here is to note the similarity of these specific chemical models to the one the impressionistic painters set up. It is a kind of algebra, where one sets up x and then solves for it. For the best chance to reach the goal, give to x a prägnant signal.

As an end result of preparation, the question may well be cast in the form A of the equation $A + B \rightarrow C$.

Hadamard

The analogy of creative thinking to electronic scanning is only partial, because on the machine the specifications can usually be punched only in a set form. But for mental scanning the specifications can assume a wide variety of forms—words, images, symbols, and drawings—corresponding to different ways in which the question is asked.

In "The Psychology of Invention in the Mathematical Field," Jacques Hadamard has devoted an entire chapter to the use of symbols in thinking. The subject of the symbolization of thought in problem solving will be discussed in detail below; the purpose now is to emphasize the fact that part of preparative labor is symbolization. This enhances the specification of the problem, may provide the clearest restructuring, and will activate new clusters for consideration. The symbolization may take several forms: such as a graph, not too carefully specified, suggesting the goal; or diagrams; or some attractive, vague patterns, embracing as much as possible of the total content of the question; or a blue-sky visualization in terms of maximum hopes, to help build motivation. For example, in the smog problem (p. 29), the statement of the problem can be a graph of oxidative rates, or a diagram, or a picture of two cars illustrating before and after conditions of effluent gas, or even clear and murky views of a landscape or skyline.

Thought may also be supported by nonsense words, and even by rhythms. Hadamard says:

> "Signs are a necessary support of thought. For socialized thought (stage of communication) and for the thought which is being socialized (stage of formulation), the most usual system of signs is language properly called; but internal thought, especially when creative, willingly uses other systems of signs which are more flexible, less standardized than language and leave more liberty, more dynamism to creative thought."

The mind generates images, and the unconscious loves symbols, not words. Therefore,
  (1) Many ways besides words should be used in the preparative work, and in formulating the problem.
  (2) Some of these ways should appeal to emotion.
  (3) Some of these ways should use senses other than sight.

Discussion

The preparative work is to:

See the problem.

Analyze directions of study.

Assemble material.

Work it over in order to

    (a) Activate clusters and make available their unconscious, contiguous members.

    (b) Reformulate the specifications of the problem.

    (c) Establish symbolization.

If solution is not then attained, the motivation and the active stirring of this polypreparative labor provide energy to keep the work going during incubation. The deliberate commitment to the unconscious may itself be an overt act of importance.

The work of these five men has been interpreted by the present writer to amplify the process of preparation. Thus:

Poincaré: Hooked items of thought interlock.

Armstrong: The items are members of clusters.

Flesch: The clusters undergo a scanning.

Duncker: Specifications for the scanning derive from the model of search.

Hadamard: Symbolization is diverse, to broaden and sharpen specifications.

For the manipulation of the material, conscious or unconscious, a kind of open framework (A) is provided as a model on which substitutions (B) can be made in the *search* for C.

The paradox is that in order to avoid following the wrong road, as many elements as possible of the model of search are kept vague and fluid, while the specific clues are fitted and matched in turn. On the subject of keeping elements of the model of search vague and fluid, there is much affirmative testimony, for example by Hadamard above, and by Ghiselin, Van Gogh, McKellar and Ribot.

Van Gogh, in preparing to paint, said he would "strive in the early stages to keep vague."

Ghiselin said of constructing poetry: "Half the trick then lies in keeping the object spotted in the central furnace-light of the aroused excitement while the construction of the poem goes on in relative shadow, as if it were a thing of slight importance. For under these circumstances the structure may be played with freely ... and freedom ... is preserved to the last moment of creative labor."

McKellar notes that in the Mona Lisa, the eyes and the corners of the mouth are left indistinct. The painting *is* great because it enforces audience participation. "Leonardo blurs precisely the features in which expression resides, thus compelling us to complete the act of creation."

Ribot shows how images may be of different clarity: first, a loved one's face; then, some object, as a book; and finally, a schematic image. Ribot says, "This image is little more than a shadow. It is subject to rapid manipulation, examination of results of additions and subtractions, etc."

The present author has slightly modified the following examples from Duncker to show how vague images might be manipulated in the manner of Ribot. Above the line, things are vague; below, a clear object emerges.

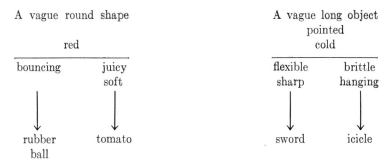

By rapid substitution of particular traits, numerous images may be successively and rapidly reviewed. Instead of one item, every item of a roused or activated cluster may be substituted. It is in this way that an item may appear in the solution to a problem without ever having been handled directly in the preparative labor. One element of a cluster is so handled. Later this triggers solution because another element of the cluster is the thing (B) actually needed.

Vagueness does these things: It helps avoid fixation and mental blocks, and it allows facile and diverse substitution.

The way in which preparation is begun has been emphasized by several writers. About initiating a creative task, Schiller said, "Intellect has withdrawn the watchers at the gates; ideas rush in pell-mell; only then does it review and inspect the multitude." There is search to establish valuable directions of exploration, and develop specific material within each area, according to judgment as to its relative worth. Schiller's thought is parallel to the instructions in brainstorming: Give all ideas, the wilder the better, and defer judgment. Deferring judgment is withdrawing the watchers at the gate.

5. SPECIAL ASPECTS OF PREPARATION

The stage of preparation has been visualized as comprising the selection and activation of idea-clusters for scanning within an established loose framework or model, e.g., a scientific hypothesis or established art form (sonnet, fugue, portrait). It is now desired to consider in detail certain aspects of polypreparation, including the following:

> Restructuring
> Symbolization
> Analogy
> Heuristics
> Check Lists

Restructuring

This discussion is in addition to the description already given of Duncker's ray problem (p. 36). Maurice Nelles relates how one of the consultants of his company, riding in a cab on a visit to Los Angeles, was caught in smog. This led him to consider the influence of car exhaust upon it, and produced the creation flash: make something to put on a car to prevent it from putting out noxious gases. By restructuring, the suggestion was made to oxidize the noxious gases catalytically, and the problem was finally cast in the form: What is that material over which the gases can be passed which will with adequate efficiency convert them to innocuous substances?

The development of this was, briefly:

> Q_1: *Smog*
> *Exploration:* Car exhaust is cause
> Absorb or modify
> Oxidize
> Q_2: *Restructure*—Oxidation-chamber in exhaust train

In general terms, the restructuring is the search, the hunting, for pertinent clues and for areas to explore,

Q_1	Exploration	$Q_2, Q_3, \ldots \ldots Q_n$
General		Specific
Problem	$\longrightarrow$	Question or
Area	Restructuring	Questions

$Q_2 \ldots Q_n$ are relay results, insights into useful things to do to help solve the problem. At the same time a model of search, a framework to be fitted, a hypothesis, is drawn. In the above example, the hypothesis is oxidation, and the things fitted are material $+$ catalyst charges for the canister.

For another instance, let it be supposed that the problem is to make a longer-wearing tire. It is known, or learned, that synthetic rubber polymerized at low temperature ("cold rubber") shows sharp improvement in abrasion resistance. The problem solution is to make the tire tread from rubber polymerized at a temperature many degrees lower than now used. But in so lowering the temperature it is found that an antifreeze must be added to the mix. Then, in the cold, the rate of conversion becomes impractically slow. Eventually, the problem of a longer-wearing tire reduces to this: Find a catalyst system to polymerize rubber in a non-freezing mix at the present rate of conversion but at a significantly lower temperature.

By such restructuring are elicited concrete things on which to go to work. Then begins the process of spot-check experiments, consultations, discussions, reading, and attending conventions where the latest information on polymerization and catalysts is discussed. These methods of search are directed not only to the problem but also to surrounding or halo material, such as:

> How much slow-down in rate occurs when the temperature of present mixes is lowered?
> High speed formulas used at present.
> How have others modified their formulas in coming down from hot mixes in the past to lowest present temperatures of polymerization?
> General methods of speeding up reactions.
> General theory of polymerization.

General theory of kinetics.

Fastest known present polymerizations.

Thus, given a problem, there is the task of restructuring, and supplying material that appears pertinent to each structure. Now, each structure is an A. For one of them a B is sought, and it is not known if it will come from something that seems directly pertinent or from halo material. All that can be done is to multiply the number of possibly pertinent associations in the brain. There, outside of consciousness, they combine and recombine with knowledge already present—and the unconscious may never forget any experience—until a useful pair appears. Restructuring establishes new directions of search. Material is developed by deliberate effort to expand these new directions, and create a framework-hypothesis to work to. New statements of the problem follow, which are verbal, and geometric, and miscellaneous *new symbolizations*.

Symbolization

Since the concern is with major creative projects, it is assumed that no pains need be spared in the preparative work. There is general agreement on the advice to state the problem clearly in words, and properly organize all the material. To this should now be added the advice to make liberal use of nonverbal symbolization. The unconscious is to act in incubation. It loves symbols, not words. And there is no loss of effort, for drawings and symbols are a powerful aid to conscious thought as well. Naturally, their use is not here suggested as something new in creative work. It is not. But many employ them far less than they should. Then, too, there are types not so commonly resorted to.

Symbols are familiar, to illustrate and greatly clarify syllogisms (Figure 5-1).

Some interesting points on symbols and problem solving appeared in Karl Duncker's ray problem. The required solution was to use a lens to converge rays on the tumor. The subjects were assumed to be unaware that the rays in question are not deflected by ordinary lenses, but "this fact is of no consequence from the viewpoint of the psychology of thinking," in Duncker's view. The problem was presented to the subjects with one of three schematic symbolizations, shown as a, b, and c in Figure 5-2.

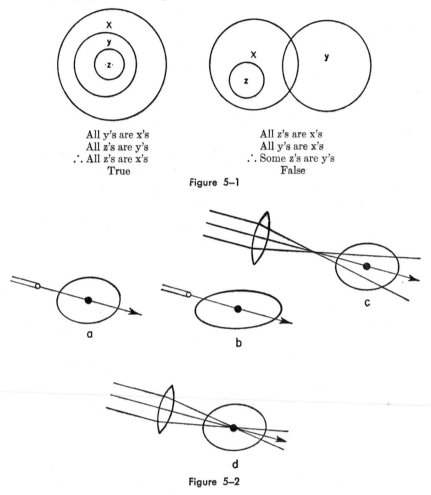

All y's are x's
All z's are y's
∴. All z's are x's
True

All z's are x's
All y's are x's
∴. Some z's are y's
False

Figure 5–1

a

b

c

d

Figure 5–2

With the narrower ellipse, b, subjects fell into the error of commenting on the shorter path, with less tissue in the way, saying, in effect, "If you must burn tissue, at least take the shortest path." This is a correct statement, but not a correct answer. It shows how a variation in diagram can influence thought. With a there were three successful solutions out of 75; with c there were three out of five. It was easy to displace the lens, as shown in d. (It has been repeatedly demonstrated that with the answer virtually given away, only half the subjects achieve a solution.)

All organic chemistry grew by manipulating symbols, first in two dimensions, then in three. Today, the greatest chemists play with models in which the units represent atoms cut to a relative scale of size, and with correct angles of attachment to one another.

It has been remarked that all chemists could profit from a required course in art, because the artist deals in symbols, and some of the most important advances in modern chemistry are in reality advances in the ideas which symbols convey. The ability to get ideas from symbols, and the scope of the ideas which such symbols convey, are some of the responsibilities of chemical education.

In particular, artists manipulate symbols by processes of exaggeration, distortion, and abstraction. The chemist does the same with *his* symbols. Kekulé's benzene chain seized its tail in its mouth, a fruitful distortion indeed. Pauling considered dynamic, resonating symbols, and distortion of bonds to accomplish reactions. As with distortion, so with exaggeration and abstraction, as in van't Hoff's tetrahedral abstraction of carbon valences, or the exaggeration of extending simple reactions to the polymerization of giant molecules.

Duncker shows a geometry problem where solution is elementary when a mirror image of the given figure is drawn to it. There is much psychological sense in this. According to William James, a new perspective may be gained by viewing a landscape (or a problem diagram?) from the side, or upside down. An inverted painting gives a fresh sense of tint and shading, and a new judgment of balance. The illusion of the moon's great size near the horizon disappears if you bend over and observe it from between your legs. To lie on the floor and look up at someone talking is to find the seldom-noticed animation of the lower lip most remarkable. To reverse a graph, to enlarge parts of a diagram at the expense of others, even to consider it upside down, may help insight.

Platt and Baker advise looking "for a central assumption, commonly supposed to be beyond question, but false."

Flesch recommends, "Look for a seemingly irrelevant key factor in the situation, or a seemingly unsuitable pattern in the mind."

Let the tremendous meaning of powerful symbols be considered. Advertising men seek to attach to their copy such symbols as these:

the dove of peace, the valentine heart, the spring lamb, the flowers for the beloved, the alma mater, the national anthem, the flag, the church ritual.

One of the interesting things in connection with symbolization is the various ways in which writers have symbolized creativity itself. Pacifico plays tic-tac-toe to show mechanisms of thinking and methods of improving it. True graphs the ups and downs of preparative effort and fatigue and the complex interactions of the unconscious work. These diagrams can be found in the appropriate references. Two have been reproduced here (Figures 5-3 and 5-4). Von Fange

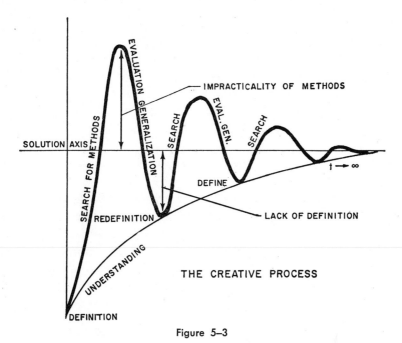

Figure 5–3

(E. Von Fange, from *General Electric Review,* July 1955, by permission.)

shows the creative process as a wave form diminishing along the axis. Hutchinson depicts a creative flow chart.

Models are symbols. So are concepts. A dog is many dogs. A geometric design is many figures. Working to a model on which to ring changes is a sure way to creation. Thus a school of painters or writers follows the master. The preliminary sketches of painters, to which they later create the finished art, are often relatively small. These models serve especially well to show the relationships of the parts, which are then incorporated with more detail in the larger work. The condensed and annotated sketch, to one artist, was worth far more than a photograph, which, indeed, he called "worthless."

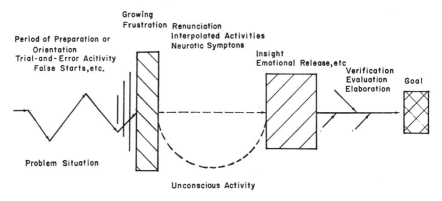

Figure 5–4. Flow chart of the Creative Process.

(From E. D. Hutchinson, "How to Think Creatively," p. 41, copyright 1949 by Pierce & Smith. By permission of Abingdon Press)

Turner watched clouds until an effect took his fancy, then recorded it in miniature on a sheet the size of a letter page. Millet drew a picture in his notebook 2½ x 3, later expanded it. Another worker would use a picture the size of a postage stamp in his planning. This tendency was noted as a common practice of the professional artists by Eindhoven in his artist experiment.

The above has prepared the way for the elaboration of symbolization in three directions:

(1) As representation.
(2) As the creation itself.
(3) As response to promotive conditions.

As Representation

Symbolization is a representation of the problem. For the smog problem, the real visualization is an *image* of air clear-to-see-through coming out of an exhaust pipe. This reduces to the *state-*

ment in words already derived above. The statement can also be an *arrangement in space*. The chief point here is the use not only of verbal symbols, but also of diagrams, and of representations involving all the senses, not just sight. The statesman may visualize his problem as a dove of peace (symbol) sitting on the Kremlin (symbol) and cooing (auditory) to another dove of peace sitting on the Capitol (symbol).

As the Creation Itself

It may even be that the symbolization *is* the creation. Sibelius, walking by the seashore, became suddenly aware of a disgusting smell from some decomposing fibrous material. Later he started humming, and wrote a grotesque capriccio. The musical composition symbolized the olfactory experience. Weber made the Freischütz laughing chorus from the false intoning of the responses of an old woman in church. He designed the march in Oberon to match heaps of tables and chairs in a closed café. The music symbolized the size, variable height, and arrangement of the visual percept.

Promotive Conditions

There are promotive conditions which enhance the progress of symbolization and thence of creation. A part of this is the provision of a model or framework. From the above discussion, the framework is a desirably vague symbol of the finished and unified whole which will be realized as piece by piece is created in the mind and inserted in its proper place in the framework. Numerous examples are available from recognized creators.

Browning, planning "The Ring and the Book," said: "I went for a walk, gathered 12 pebbles from the road, and put them at equal distances on the parapet that bordered it. These represented the twelve chapters into which the poem is divided." Thus, Browning set up a symbolic framework.

Poets have widely reported getting sounds before the meaningful words. These sounds undoubtedly provide a model or framework for the final creation. This is readily recognized in Wordsworth's "booing" and Yeats's "buzzing," the noises they made aloud as they composed. For Yeats, again, a poem appeared "as a persistent musical phrase, a set of rhythms and sounds demanding words." Wilbur thought of the incubation of a poem as first a retreat from language to a preverbal condition, with such fundamental images (for framework) as "lightness, darkness, rising, falling." Another poet rattled a stick against fence palings to help establish a desired rhythm. Tartini composed to phrases from Petrarch, which he wrote in cypher at the top of his manuscript.

One may speculate that the idiosyncrasies for which many creative workers are famous are related to the arrangement of framework. "Ibsen used to keep a number of little images on his writing desk; they helped him in his work of composition, he said, but declined to say how, adding, 'That is my secret.' " Possibly he assigned his characters' names and traits to the figures, and moved them around on his desk to help visualize the scenes and action of his plays. "Kant used a certain tower, visible from his study window, as a sort of mental focus for thinking out his categories." Stevenson liked bare and white-washed walls—on which to project mental images?

In the above discussion, framework is viewed as somewhat more general, and model, as more specific.

Especially in the technique of the theater are symbols important. There is identification with one or more characters, and moment by moment re-creation of the playwright's insights. In order to gain these pleasures, the onlooker co-operates with the playwright to yield the common basic assumptions of the theater, such as location in time and space, three-walled room, passage of time, English speech of foreigners, etc. But the skilled writer goes beyond this and in subtle ways persuades the onlooker into easy granting of the necessary concessions. He uses devices to lower personal thresholds in the direction of a hypnoidal or suggestible state. This is done by the poet, the novelist, and the musician as well as the playwright. Examples are: screams heard off-stage before or in the early action of a mystery play; Big Ben striking to suggest London; austere settings for tragedy; the drums in "The Emperor Jones"; and the endless beating of the rain in "Rain." Thus, music, setting, early sound and action induce a mood to accept and actively identify in what follows, however far removed from usual experience.

Can one develop techniques to use this symbolism—this great and subtle power of suggestion—to induce creative mood and promote creative thought? The executive office is very carefully arranged to provide an atmosphere which makes it easy for the occupant to do his job. Would it not be worth the effort for a creative worker to arrange the conditions in his workroom in such a way as to weaken barriers to creativity and persuade the mind and psyche into easy granting of the concessions (abeyance of judgment, relaxation of censorship, spirit of play) that are necessary for creativity to flourish?

Supertags

For each individual, some symbols or concepts are "supertagged." Melville Cane liked to write about snow, and a disproportionate number of his poems were about it. A writer in Ghiselin's Symposium comments that many authors have favorite words that appear again and again. As with words, so with shapes. There are shapes that one likes to use in drawing diagrams. There are certain relationships that one prefers to graph. As one works on a problem and develops several hypotheses, some have more appeal than others. One hypothesis may soon become like the home team: you root for it and want to see it win.

It is a matter of observation that symbols, ideas, and hypotheses soon acquire an emotional accompaniment. Symbols in many cases have great emotional impact, as in personal religious and love symbols. Many plays and movies gradually build up values for certain symbols until their strategic use has tremendous power. "The Four Feathers," A. E. W. Mason's famous novel, later made into a movie, is one example among many. Here is a man who is accused by four of his associates as a coward, and receives from each of them a symbolic white feather. Later, in each case after an act of great heroism, each is asked to take back the feather he gave. Another example is the impact a song may acquire. In the movie, "Since You Went Away," a wife receives a music box as a Christmas gift from her husband in military service, who sent the present before he was reported missing and presumed dead. The music box plays the tune, "Together," which was their special courtship song. It evokes a

whole lifetime of associations for the wife, and suggests and tele-
scopes them for the audience. In respect to emotional content, the
symbols used in thinking both (a) exemplify the discussion of Chapter 3 on emotion and creativity, and (b) aid the progress of creation
by supplying psychic energy, inasmuch as the emotional content of
the symbol means motivation.

It therefore seems reasonable advice to use favored symbols deliberately in formulating problems. There is usually an unconscious
basis for this preference. Therefore, the unconscious work may be
aided.

Abstract and Concrete

Symbolization should be directed to move from the abstract toward sense experience, and to appeal to other senses than sight.
This has been touched upon above. Sibelius transmuted odor to
sound. Weber changed sight to sound. Poets change nonspecific
sound to words. Heidbreder's work on concepts will be discussed in
detail later. Here it is noted that one important finding was an experimental confirmation of common knowledge, namely, the fact
that concrete form is more quickly comprehended than abstract
form, and that the latter is more quickly comprehended than even
such a simple, pure abstraction as number. A face was recognized
before a geometric figure, and both before the numbers 5 or 6. So,
in the smog problem, "oxidation chamber in exhaust train" is less
meaningful than an imaginative flow-chart diagram.

Duncker's thirteen problem showed abstract aids to be of no help
at all, and possibly a hindrance; and statements of a problem in
glittering generalities or broad abstractions are useless except as
take-off points. Take "smog is bad." The work of preparation is to
develop from this a specific model of search with components just
vague enough to avoid fixation and facilitate substitution. Correspondingly, an abstract hint is bad because the hint itself has to
be restructured and related to the problem while *it* still remains
abstract.

Symbolization should strive for concreteness. Poetry itself is so
meaningful because it establishes relations between the abstract

and the concrete. Poetry equates abstractions and ideals to simple acts and percepts. It requires the "almost seeing and feeling" of concrete things first. Then comes the extension to spiritual values. A rose is described, and then abstracted to mean love.

Other Senses

Poets also, more than the ordinary man, achieve analogies between the senses:

>   ".. fine honey of song notes—*Swinburne;*
>   ".. light like lulled music sleeping"—*Shelley.*

Symbols, especially nonverbal ones, serve to establish relationships between one sense and another. This is undoubtedly important. Gerard makes the point that many words describing thought refer to sight, for example, insight; vision, evidence (Latin, *video*); contemplate (*contemplor,* I view); consider (*considero,* I look closely at). Such dominance of sight may be a limitation on creativeness. Another limit is that with age, thinking tends to become more and more verbal, and less creative. The American psychologist, Titchener, strove to keep his thinking youthful by deliberate use of other-than-verbal imagery.

It might be possible to aid creativity by attempting to construct auditory, taste, odor, and tactile symbolizations of the problem. For example, in Duncker's ray problem, one might think of a ray machine, humming away at a certain intensity, strong enough to damage normal tissue. When turned down, this hum will not damage either the normal or diseased tissue. But the reduced hum can be heard just as well as before with a little focusing.

A symbolization to one sense can have meaning to others. Willman showed that a composer could match music to horizontal, slanted, and zig-zag lines. Weber matched music to a random pattern of furniture placement.

Woodworth, in his "Psychology," shows that to the *word* stimulus "red," subjects were prone to reply with "blue." But to the presentation of the *color* red as a stimulus, responses were diffuse.

These results emphasize the interrelation of the senses. To the extent that one can learn to use all his senses on a problem, he can increase his creativity. There is no way of knowing which sensory combination will serve best for any given problem. Considering the mind as a scanning system, to bring more senses into play is to increase the span of material to be scanned, yet increase selectivity. Selectivity is enhanced because more, and different, specifications have been added for the combination sought. There tends to be too much dependence on the visual and the verbal. How to involve several senses in a problem is a subject for study and development of methods.

Factors of Mental Ability

The modern knowledge of factor analysis affords strong reason for structuring a problem into symbols as well as prose. Two well-established factors are the verbal and the spatial. Both of these are not necessarily found in a highly developed state in the same individual. A person may be most facile in conceiving figures in space, yet relatively inarticulate. This was shown by Sharp in 1899. She gave a group of seven subjects a series of tests of memory, images, imagination, attention, and observation. Some shone in verbal tests, some in spatial, a clear indication of the varying quality of different factors in the subjects. Recently, Anne Roe studied small groups of eminent physicists and biologists, to delineate the personality-intelligence profile of creative scientific workers. Her ratings comparing verbal and spatial tests showed numerous instances where better-than-average skill with words accompanied less-than-average ability to visualize in space. Examples of the reverse were also found, as well as instances of superior skill in both directions. Average, here, refers to the mean for the group of scientists concerned. Clearly, the best creative thinking requires that material be supplied to match not only one's optimum factors, but the others as well. Cooperation of all the factors is the desired end.

It has been developed that, as thinking progresses, the problem is cast into new symbolizations, which in turn involve new clusters, new senses, and new mental factors.

Restructuring $\longrightarrow$ Material to work up $\longrightarrow$ Symbolization $\longrightarrow$ New relationships.

The symbolization might take several forms: a graph, a diagram, a pattern, a picture to promote motivation. The deliberate broadening of the symbolization is preparative work. The development of new relationships is preparation too.

Analogy

This topic might well have been discussed under symbolization. The direct basis of much creative activity is analogy: "a relation of likeness between two things, or of one thing to or with another, consisting in the resemblance not of the things themselves, but of two or more attributes, circumstances, or effects." The foregoing is Webster. A leading psychologist of the turn of the century, Charles Spearman, gave this definition: "First a pair of ideas is given, between which a relation has to be cognized; and then this relation has to be applied to a third idea, so as to generate a fourth one called the correlate."

The best correlation in an early study of tests of originality was with analogy. Aristotle declared, "Metaphor is the special mark of genius, for the power of making a good metaphor is the power of recognizing likeness." Ribot goes so far as to say, "The essential, fundamental element of the creative imagination is the capacity of thinking by analogy .... that is, by partial and often accidental resemblance." Knowlson makes a point of the value of a rich feel for analogies, and asserts that this can be developed to a pitch that at first seems improbable. It should not be overlooked that one of the best kinds of training in creativity is to look for analogies constantly.

An analogy is a kind of mirror image—not in a plane mirror, but in a more or less distorting one. Examples are very common. The child at play endows everything with life, by personification. Resemblances by the hundreds are the clichés of everyday speech, for instance, red-blooded man, brave as a lion, quiet as a mouse, cold as ice, etc.

William James states that high creativity comes with an "ability for 'similarity association' to an extreme degree"—that is, the ability to think in analogies. One is not to heed the old bugbear that it is risky to reason by analogy—a pat phrase. If the purpose is creation, the greater danger is *not* to reason by analogy. After all, any creative act is a risk. James gives examples of how powerful, comprehensive, and inclusive in content an analogy can be:

> Light blue is a feminine color.
> A blotting-paper voice.
> A mind like Roquefort cheese.

These suggest how much material a good analogy can crystallize and unify.

The important thing is that analogies and other poetic devices are relations: and insight is seeing relations. The $A + B \rightarrow C$ equation is a new relationship. A creative method is to establish two poles, i.e. words or concepts, and develop relations between them. The question, "List uses of a brick," often used as a creativity test, is answered by relating the brick in various ways to other physical items: a door to stop, an enemy to hit, or a weight to support.

Heuristic Methods

Heuristics are theorems that may apply. They aid in the detection of useful preparative material and its handling. Often, the insight obtained as a relay result is a remembered rule to apply to a certain segment of the material. Heuristic methods have been especially well summarized by Polya:

> Have you seen the problem before in slightly different form?
> Do you know a useful theorem?
> Have you seen a problem with a similar unknown?
> Here is a solution to a similar problem. Can you use its
>   results?
>   method?
> Can you restate the problem?
> Can you solve a part of the problem?
> Try a related problem, which may be
>   more general,
>   more specific,
>   analogous.

The application of sound reasoning and logic to the material worked with is the most effective way to detect avenues of search and consciously exploit the resultant material. Scanning of the field, and logical judgments of the material produced are evident in the progression of thoughts developed on the ray problem, page 36. But conscious manipulation and reasoning are only parts of the preparation for the discovery, or answer to the difficult problem, which is more susceptible to insight than to logic. Discoveries and solutions, as new combinations, are less likely to result from logic than from imagination, precisely because the needed new results are *less* logical than other, more mundane ones. Where reasoning comes into its own again is in the work of verification, for selecting, arranging, and judging among the means of realization and communication.

Beveridge emphasizes that discovery is an *art*. His chapters on imagination, intuition, and reason are part of a step-by-step consideration of the ways, means, and methods of exploratory science. Logic and reason are declared to be more concerned in verification than elsewhere. Often, when they are used to develop a hypothesis, the hypothesis may be entirely wrong, but valuable discoveries ensue just the same. Ideas mature in the unconscious. Opportunity must be afforded for that, and for emergence.

On the role of reason, Beveridge says, "Research must often be guided by personal judgment based on scientific taste. . . . After the initial, empirical experience opening up the field, rational experimentation has led to a series of relatively small but important improvements. . . . The role of reason in research is not so much in exploring the frontiers of knowledge as in developing the findings of the explorers." Others have made comments of similar nature.

This section cannot be left without mentioning the fallacy of the scientific method. This is one of the most widely accepted fallacies in productive thinking, and whole college courses are taught upon it. The scientific method is simply an accepted or required way of reporting results. After the result is obtained by fumbling and struggling toward insight, reason develops the answer and arranges the material so as to arrive at the solution prettily. But the work wasn't *done* that way. Some highly skilled men who developed a complex computer said, "First we juggle the circuits until it gives the right answers, and then we work out the mathematics." Later, in the university, the professor presents the math first, then the circuits. On this point, F. C. S. Schiller declared: "The analysis of scientific procedure . . . . has not tried to describe the methods by which the sciences have actually advanced . . . . but has freely rearranged the actual procedure. . . . For the order of discovery there has been substituted an order of proof."

Check Lists

Check lists are aids applied to carry forward solution of the problem, either directly, or by detecting new areas to work over. They are employed as a means of forcing the mind at least to consider specific categories. Various types have been given by Flesch, Osborn, Reiss, von Fange, and Whiting. Check lists as aids to individual creativity are discussed in Chapter 11. For the present, a few examples of the genre will be given, from Osborn:

> To what other uses can this be put?
> Something similar I could copy?
> Make it bigger? Smaller?
> What if it is reversed?
> What can it be combined with?
> What about using half of it? Part of it?

These are simply stimulative questions. A more remote type the present author uses is, "If I had something with this unusual property, what could I do with it?" If a good idea results, then ask, "Well, what actually comes as close to this 'something' as possible?"

Management

What should management's viewpoint be?

The keyword is *tolerance*—of apparent inaction. In his industrial research experience, a worker may feel he never has enough time to prepare properly for a new problem. Management should strongly curb a natural desire to pressure the man to write up a project sheet and begin work too soon. It takes a long time to store up the lightning of insight, but only one second to discharge it. The early preparation on a scale worthy of a difficult problem takes time—time to learn and time to reflect.

Even on theoretical grounds, the loss in curtailed preparation is too great to countenance. A creative man is paid to do one thing—to achieve insight. If he is rushed, and fails to achieve insight, the money is wasted. If he is rushed, and his insight is incomplete, the loss is much greater than an extra week's salary for preparation or even cogitation. The man has got to stare out of the window, even if in doing so, he violates the Protestant ethic (work; don't shirk!). Richness of insight, as well as greater certainty of it, justifies the idea of the Creative Lodge (Chapter 13) for maturing the early preparation.

The Stage of Preparation—Summary

It will be seen from all the above that not everything which takes place in the creative *stage* of preparation is strictly preparative work. In this first stage, besides pure preparation, there are insights which are relay results and which refine and further refine the statement of the problem until either the issue—what should be done—is clear, or the solution is evident. If the case is one of much complexity, refinement of the problem-statement occurs in several fields, requiring investigation to gain information in those directions. These several statements are polypreparative in that they are symbolizations of different types (verbal, diagrammatic, analogic) and even designed to appeal to different senses.

In this chapter, several different ways of symbolizing creativity, from the especial viewpoint of preparative work, have been discussed:

(1) Diagrams of Pacifico, True, Hutchinson, and von Fange.

(2) The equation, $A + B \rightarrow C$.
   A problem, two pieces of information, and the new combination.

(3) $Q_1 \longrightarrow$ Restructure $\longrightarrow Q_2 \ldots Q_n$
   Refinement of the original question.

(4) Problem $\longrightarrow$ Material $\longrightarrow$ Restructuring $\longrightarrow$ Symbolization $\longrightarrow$ Relationships $\longrightarrow$ Insight

In the solution of difficult problems, these processes require time. There are periods of thinking, and periods of seeking needed material, and periods of rest. The periods of rest are not idle. Development goes on during them, though psychologists do not agree as to what this developmental process is.

The work of preparation is:

(1) Multiple restructuring.
(2) Spatial symbolization
     By graphs
     By diagrams
     By some vague, inclusive organization or framework
     By some motivating visualization.
(3) Other-than-visual definitions of the problem.
(4) Accumulation of the necessary supporting material.
(5) Development of analogies.
(6) Application of heuristic methods.
(7) Application of stimulative questions.
(8) Use of supertags.
(9) Consideration of remote viewpoints.

In guiding the preparative work, a thorough, professional knowledge of the principles of creativity is useful. This knowledge will have guided each worker to an understanding of the operation of his own creative bent. It will have guided him, during the attentive study of master creations and their way of coming into being, to develop a creative taste for application to his own work. On this matter of taste it is as difficult to be specific as on taste in dress or décor. If a man is himself creative, and studies creations of the past, he will begin to understand why certain details are right in a Mozart opera, a Turner landscape, a Shakespearean drama, or a scientific investigation. It is in these details—where no word or brush stroke or note or weighing is too small to receive lavish care—that the masterpiece differs from the mediocre. There is pleasure in such understanding, and a duty for each creative worker to adapt as he can to his own work.

Symbols that are developed in the preparative work should be selected to have these properties:

       To be simple.
       To be concrete.
       To be liked.
       To utilize the individual's strongest factors.
       To promote interrelation of the senses.

Why all this?

It has been assumed the creative objective is worth the effort, and the question is, *what* effort. All this extensive preparation is worthwhile because:

(1) It makes insight more likely.
(2) It makes insight more complete.

To the extent that the spadework has been unstinted, the insight-harvest is richer, broader, and more fruitful. Because of the extra areas of knowledge filled in, with which and among which relationships were established in the preparative labor, extra results and remote consequences ensue. The insight to the problem may lead to discoveries aside from the original purpose.

If the experimental fittings to the model of search do not suit, and solution of the problem is not achieved, even with willingness to strive beyond fatigue, then work is stopped. One does something else. The problem is committed to the unconscious. This should be an overt act. If the preparation has been well done, the process of incubation—the subject of the next chapter—takes place there, and may lead to insight.

6. INCUBATION

In the old Egyptian wisdom it was said, "The archer hitteth the mark, partly by pulling, partly by letting go."

Incubation as an interval between preparation and insight is a fact of experience, without regard to the theories promulgated about it. When a problem weighs on the mind, it keeps recurring, even when one is otherwise engaged. Everyone has had a personal experience of this kind: He may have collected information on a certain subject at random, and over an extended period. Later he sits down to write up his material in organized form, and behold, it emerges from the subconscious, neatly arranged and docketed. The age-old device for a knotty problem is to "sleep on it" and enlist the aid of incubation. Very simply, this is a time of waiting—when the preparative work has been brought to an end without solution of the problem. The end of incubation is the attainment of insight. This may come with dramatic suddenness, in a moment when the problem is not being worked on at all. In the more prosaic case, however, insight follows quickly upon resumption of the work. What went on in the interim is by far the least understood facet of the creative process.

The period of incubation is everywhere acknowledged. As Ghiselin says of creation, there is "universal need for a gestation period ... long or short, it must be endured." This implies that during incubation something goes on besides waiting. There is a large body of evidence for making this inference, including the definite reports of creative workers, and some careful psychological analyses.

The chief evidence of incubation is the appearance of insight. Suddenly, where a myriad of facts were all in confusion, order now prevails, and the essential point is perceived with clarity. Something must have occurred to achieve this organization.

Their own reports show that creative workers use incubation deliberately as their method of achievement. Amy Lowell speaks of "the idea dropped into the subconscious, like a letter into a mail box." Walter B. Cannon asserted:

"As a matter of routine, I have long trusted unconscious processes to serve me—for example when I have had to prepare a public address. I would gather points for the address and write them down in rough outline. Within the next few nights I would have sudden spells of awakening, with an onrush of illustrative instances, pertinent phrases, and fresh ideas related to those already listed. Paper and pencil at hand permitted the capture of these fleeting thoughts before they faded into oblivion."

The experimental evidence about incubation of Patrick was presented in Chapter 2. But on this point there is even more powerful proof. John Livingston Lowes, in "The Road to Xanadu," analyzed the content of Coleridge's poems, *The Ancient Mariner* and *Kubla Khan,* idea by idea, and sometimes word by word. For his analysis he checked the source material of the voluminous reading Coleridge had done, and the planning notes he had made. The ideas and imagery in the poems were individually traced, with some suggestion of how particular pieces had come together or were modified. Lowes shows that these definite items of Coleridge's experience were joined or fused (they are here interpreted as A + B → C examples):

Glossy fish in ocean	+	Coiled water snakes	→	Coiling, glowing water snakes
A (source 1)		B (source 2)		C
Rosy light	+	Electric morn	→	Morn of rosy light
A (source a)		B (source b)		C

The slow development of the planted seed is described by Lowes in admirable detail. It is of great interest to learn how the material resulting in the *Ancient Mariner* was activated by discussions during the long walks with Wordsworth and his sister. The original material and poetic result of this activation strongly support the hooked atoms of Poincaré. The A and B are fed into the mind and in time yield the product C, an image, a stanza, or just a needed bit of business about seamanship.

Such an analysis of material and results has been done about Lewis Carroll by A. L. Taylor in "The White King." The clusters of Shakespeare represent related material. The anticipated, expected, and attained development of material dropped in "the deep well" of the unconscious is mentioned by many others, as James, Ghiselin, Tate, Hart, and Spencer.

Most counsel on improving and increasing creative production has centered in this: Do a good preparative job, then give incubation a chance. This is the theme, for example, of J. K. Williams' book, "The Knack of Using your Subconscious Mind." Rudolf Flesch says, "Give the unconscious a chance." If one has a difficult problem to solve, W. H. Easton's advice is to work up to an impasse, then relax. All this, in effect, is simply that a two-day method of problem solving is more *efficient* than a one-day method. As Stevenson said, his Brownies did at least half his work while he slept. He hit the mark by letting go.

There seems to be a good chance that if preparation has been adequate, and the motivation is there, and opportunity is allowed, then insight will emerge. The preceding discussion has presumed a difficult problem, one requiring long, varied, and meticulous preparation. This kind of detailed preparation has been advocated in readiness to commit to the unconscious for incubation. Much about preparation is known: restructure, study, motivate, symbolize. Something is also known about insight and how to evoke it: a quiet time, and readiness to note it. But creators have not been successful in explaining incubation. They talk about inspiration; they adopt special methods to evoke creative mood. But they have not been able to tell what they have learned empirically, the technique of how to take out a problem and look at it to see how far it has advanced, how to reenergize the incubation, how to prime it with some new, pertinent material.

Shakespeare and many others must have known the techniques of creation, and how to control their own minds and bodies so that the creative process could take place, and the goals which they must have deliberately set could be achieved.

Characteristics

The characteristics of incubation are:

(1) Time
(2) Recurrence
(3) Tension
(4) Intimation
(5) Choice of the key "B," i.e., the significant "B" in the equation, $A + B \rightarrow C$
(6) Delivery of insight to the conscious as a new combination

The waiting *time* of incubation may be short or long—a few minutes or many years. This time may be spent in alternative effort, or in relaxation, or rest. Meanwhile the question keeps *recurring* to, or even nagging, the mind, in such form as "This might solve it" or "This is pertinent, I'll look it up" or "If I could only do this it would mean real success for me." The *tension* is proportional to motivation, being a complex of need to solve, drive for the reward, and, in part, the urge that keeps one trying to solve a puzzle or to recall something forgotten.

The other characteristics mentioned are noted at the time of insight. *Intimation* is reported only by some observers, as a feeling that insight is due to arrive. The new relationship given by the insight represents a search and a *choice*, made in the waiting period. Somehow, incubation hunts down the key "B." The *insight may flow* from incubation in a natural way when deliberate work is resumed on the problem, or it may appear delicately on the fringe of consciousness, or come to the fore with shattering impact. But, however spectacular it may seem, it soon fades and is lost, usually forever, if not seized and made fast.

The incubative process has been called a well, a bank, a mail box, etc. It has been called unconscious work by Hadamard and Poincaré, scanning by Flesch, joinery and fusion by Lowes. This may be called the "what and where" of the work. The "how" of the selection of B is unknown. There is an interesting hypothesis as to why the good combination is transferred to the conscious, namely, that the unconscious, like the conscious, experiences pleasure or elation when the good combination is struck, just as in deliberate conscious work there is pleasure in progress and solution. An *echo* of this emotion reaches consciousness and is then followed by specific insight.

Intimation

This echo is the intimation reported by some workers as the premonition, tenuous and fleeting, that insight is about to appear. This subject has been most extensively considered by Graham Wallas. It comprises a considerable part of the famous Chapter IV on "Stages of Control," in Wallas' "Art of Thought," as well as the beginning of the following chapter on "Thought and Emotion."

Wallas defined intimation as "that moment in the illumination stage when our fringe consciousness of an association train is in the state of rising consciousness which indicates that the fully conscious flash of success is coming." But in fact Wallas recognizes several types or facets of intimation, which are evidenced by the quotations and discussion to follow.

(1) Wallas says: "A high English civil servant described his experience of intimation to me by saying that when he is working at a difficult problem, 'I often know that the solution is coming though I don't know what the solution will be.' " This is in accord with the preceding definition.

(2) Wallas writes to this effect: "Many of the best thoughts, probably most of them, do not come, like a flash, fully into being but find their beginnings in dim feelings, faint intuitions that need to be encouraged and coaxed before they can be surely felt and defined." Then the intimation might be, not a feeling that insight is coming, but a realization that it is there to be noted. This is more truly descriptive of the psychological event: as when one sees something out of the corner of his eye, and turns his head to observe it closely, so the insight floats into the fringe of consciousness, and after a while one realizes there is an intruder on the mental scene, and allows it to come into focus.

Many references and comments have close relation to this, such as (a) Hadamard's statement that discovery may mean thinking aside—to recognize something on the fringe; (b) Ghiselin's remark that the real work may be going on in the background of the mental scene.

(3) In Chapter V, Wallas declares, "A poet who desires to retain an emotionally colored intimation for a period long enough to enable it to turn into a fully developed and verbally expressed thought, will find that it is extraordinarily hard to do so." Here, for intimation read insight. In other words, intimation is not a feeling that insight is ready to appear, but realization of a focusing difficulty for the insight itself.

(4) Again from Wallas' Chapter IV, Vincent d'Indy often had, on waking, "a fugitive glimpse of a musical effect which—like the memory of a dream—needs a strong immediate concentration of mind to keep it from vanishing." Intimation is here the *memory* of a not fully conscious insight that must be forcibly recalled.

All four of these have in them a factor of *recognition of importance*. Intimation is this factor, plus a tenuous insight, or as alternates, the feeling of insight coming, waiting, or escaping.

Theories

In the $A + B \longrightarrow C$ equation, it is incubation that hunts down A and B and synthesizes C. Three chief theories have been put forward to account for this mechanism. The first theory is, that when the problem is reattacked, the mind is rested. The second asserts that the unfruitful combinations have been forgotten and now the good ones stand out to be clearly perceived.

These can be dealt with together.

(1) If the unfruitful associations faded, some process must have selected the fruitful combination and determined that the others *were* unfruitful (mental *activity*, not mere fading).

(2) Insight often comes quite suddenly, and when no active work at all is being done on the problem (rested mind, but no reattack).

(3) Insight often comes only after a very long time, when (a) it would reasonably be expected that *both* good and bad combinations would have been forgotten, and (b) the mind would have been rested, and tired again, a large number of times.

(4) Repeated attack often fails to achieve insight, which only

arises, spontaneously, after the problem has been shelved, or even abandoned (i.e., reattack fails, answer obtained without it).

(5) Often a pattern is formed and maintained, to await a new, completing fact discovered much later.

(6) Often solution involves material not actively considered in the conscious work (e.g., chance discoveries).

These considerations foreshadow the third theory: that the work goes on in the unconscious, where the pieces of the puzzle supplied in the preparative stage are fitted and tried with other resources that the mind already commanded.

Poincaré said that inventive work could be fully conscious, or it could result from insight preceded by incubation. In the latter case, "to the unconscious belongs not only the complicated task of constructing the bulk of various combinations, but also the most delicate and essential one of selecting those which satisfy our sense of beauty, and consequently, are likely to be useful."

By far, the most generally accepted of these theories is the idea of unconscious cerebration. The large percentage of chemists in Platt and Baker's article, and of inventors in Rossman's book, who favored this view, will be recalled. Poincaré, on the notable occasion already mentioned, lay unable to sleep, and became "a spectator of some ordinarily hidden aspects of his own spontaneous creative activity." For us, the debt incurred by the person from Porlock * was repaid by whoever served the black coffee to Henri Poincaré.

---

* In Coleridge's own account of the genesis of "Kubla Khan," he writes: "In the summer of 1797, the Author, then in ill health, had retired to a lonely farm house between Porlock and Linton. . . . In consequence of a slight indisposition, an anodyne had been prescribed, from the effects of which he fell asleep in his chair at the moment that he was reading the following sentence, or words of the same substance, in 'Purchas's Pilgrimage': 'Here the Khan Kubla commanded a palace to be built, and a stately garden thereunto. And thus ten miles of fertile ground were inclosed with a wall.' The Author continued for about three hours in a profound sleep, at least of the external senses, during which time he has the most vivid confidence that he could not have composed less than from two to three hundred lines; if that indeed can be called composition from which all the images rose up before him as *things*, with a parallel production of the correspondent expressions, without any sensation of consciousness of effort. On awakening, he appeared to himself to have a distinct recollection of the whole, and taking his pen, ink, and paper, instantly and eagerly wrote down the lines

Unconscious Activity in Incubation

In summing up the papers at an interdisciplinary symposium on creativity, Andersen wrote:

> "The variability of treatment of the unconscious among these chapters ranges from complete absence to extended discussions.... Such emphasis as is given is focused on positive, organizational, truthful functions of the unconscious in providing innovations."

Freud emphasized the aspects of the unconscious he elicited in the treatment of disease. But the unconscious is there also in health, and it is more than a dark-cellar hiding place. "Consciousness by itself does not seem to be able to produce things of beauty, truth, and harmony, or at least not to do it so well as when it can draw on the so-called depths of the unconscious, the truth within the self."

This truth must be guarded with symbolism in a hostile, harshly evaluative culture. In a permissive atmosphere, where new ideas are encouraged and willingly heard, it can emerge diffidently, but even then, only in quiet moments of detachment from the busy life —at breakfast, or shaving, or strolling unhurriedly along, or working with assurance of no interruption. Then ideas come freely, without apparent effort. The effort went before.

It is difficult to see how the role of the unconscious can be denied. There is the overwhelming testimony of historical insights in the arts as well as in science. There is universal personal experience. The unconscious has at its command more than the conscious. Recoveries of memory by psychoanalytic and hypnotic methods make it appear that the unconscious never forgets anything. It has at its command not only the forgotten or repressed, but also material that

---

that are here preserved. At this moment he was unfortunately called out by a person on business from Porlock, and detained by him above an hour, and on his return to his room, found, to his no small surprise and mortification, that though he still retained some vague and dim recollection of the general purport of the vision, yet, with the exception of some eight or ten scattered lines and images, all the rest had passed away like the images on the surface of a stream into which a stone has been cast, but, alas! without the after restoration of the latter!"

never was conscious: peripheral and subliminal observations. Eidet-ics—the name is given to persons capable of unusually vivid mental images—recall the smallest details of a picture after it is removed. So can many non-eidetics under hypnosis. Faced with a problem, the mind searches banks of memories until there is a flash of inspiration when "a remembered pattern matches the pattern of the situation before you." To this end is plumbed Ghiselin's "richness of what has been called the depths of the mind, in which apparently all the experience of the organism is in some way re-tained, even an incalculable multitude of experiences that never reached the threshold of awareness at all."

Rogers, in writing of creativity, has emphasized permissive atmos-phere, openness to experience, and tolerance of ambiguity. His views are important for incubation, during which the elements seen by analysis as related to the problem are juggled in mental play until, "from this spontaneous toying," the hunch arises which pro-vides the solution. It does not matter that thousands of possibilities are manipulated to derive but one or two fruitful ones.

Hutchinson * has taken a somewhat radical position on incuba-tion in creativity, by dividing creativity into preparation, *frustra-tion,* achievement, and verification. He has interpreted the frustra-tion stage as deeply serious:

> "In order to gain some idea of the bewildering variety of reaction of which the creative mind is capable when faced with genuine frustration, we must see the matter against the background of a whole science—the science of psychiatry . . . the intuitive thinker is often in a state of problem-generated neurosis or its lesser equivalent tension owing to the practical block set to the immediate fulfil-ment of his creative desires. At bottom, therefore, we are dealing with situations manifesting conflict. . . . Such con-flict occasions the same sort of personality readjustment as is seen in the thwarting of any common life interest . . . the individual . . . tries to forget his ambitions, to cut them off from awareness. But these dynamic groups of

* E. D. Hutchinson, "How to Think Creatively," copyright 1949 by Pierce & Smith. By permission of Abingdon Press.

ideas, forming a repressed 'creative complex,' still control the things he sees, determine his moods. The hidden enterprise bobs up in hydra-headed forms producing sometimes melancholy, anxiety, fatigue, sometimes inflation of the ego, sometimes overidealization of purpose. In extreme cases, even a 'conversion' of the emotions of the repressed system into bodily symptoms may take place. Mild hysterical or neurasthenic symptoms are common. These play up and down the whole gamut from possible disturbances of action, perception, and memory to the most serious functional disorders."

The present author's position views the unconscious activity in a more conservative way, replacing the idea of frustration by a kind of problem-solving anxiety state of mild degree. When the preparative effort slackens to a stop, the material is pushed into the unconscious, as with an unresolved psychic conflict. Thus the means and energy to continue action in the unconscious are available. There develops a mild anxiety state which, like any other worry, recalls to the conscious mind from time to time that here is an unresolved *question* (rather than conflict). In addition, this anxiety, while tense, is accompanied by a pleasure that the task exists: "This melon is mine to cut."

Only rarely is frustration so intense as Hutchinson makes the general case. Especially is this true so long as the creator has personal freedom of action. However, frustration of creative impulse may become involved with frustrations of the general psychic life, and it then acts as Hutchinson describes. For example, the frustration of creative impulse may come from the actions of others in relation to the creative worker, if for instance there is conflict with his economic needs or his family life. The simple need to make a living may drain the energy and time needed for another, creative purpose. A supervisor may not allow an individual to work in the direction in which he is impelled. A wife may be unprepared for the sacrifices she must make to allow the creation to proceed. These frustrations are interpersonal, or social, forces, and do not arise directly from the creative process. They may blend with problem-frustration. But while pure problem-frustration is in a sense a wholesome force tending to solution, it is generally agreed that interpersonal and situational frustrations are definitely harmful to the creative effort.

It would seem preferable to put the emphasis in incubation on the drive to achieve solution and relieve the nagging of the creative complex. This drive supplies the energy for manipulating and scanning new combinations and assemblages. It should be remembered that, besides solution, the problem-anxiety may be relieved by thinking of a new and promising preparational avenue, an alternate goal, or a brand new idea on a different line; or, of course, by complete abandonment. The frustration concept ignores the cases where frustration is lacking, such as the occurrence of creation by chance stimulation; of creation aside from principal purpose; and of solution after so long a time in months or years that true mental abandonment is at least a practical assumption.

Thinking in terms of cybernetics, one can imagine transmission of the insight only along a channel that is properly insulated from worry, interruptions, and petty annoyance. There must be no short circuit along the path of communication.

Dr. L. L. Thurstone,* a psychologist who developed many of the best modern tests of ability and personality, has come closest to characterizing incubation, and to planning the study of this elusive process:

> "... the fundamental problem is to discover the nature of preconscious thinking that always precedes the moment of insight in problem solving. ... It seems a plausible hypothesis that creative talent is determined in a descriptive way by the rapport that the actor has with his own preconscious thinking. This rapport can be studied experimentally. ... Consider, for example, a long list of names of objects of all kinds and a code consisting of two or three rules by which a digit can be assigned to each word. Let the digits be one, two, three, or four, and let the rules be so set up that only one digit applies to each word. A sub-

---

* L. L. Thurstone, "A Psychologist Discusses the Mechanism of Thinking," in "The Nature of Creative Thinking," copyright 1952, Industrial Research Institute, Inc.

ject might be shown these words one at a time, and he would be asked to guess which of the four digits applied to each word. When he guesses wrong, he will be told the right answer, and then he will be shown the next card. There will be no repetitions. After a while he might say that the word elephant might have the number 2, but that he does not really know why he thinks so. He may protest that he is merely guessing, and yet it would be found that he is getting more right answers than would be expected by chance. By chance he would get only one fourth of the words correct. As he progresses through such a series, he may become dimly aware of the rules, and yet he may not be able to state them. Suddenly he may discover the rules, and after that all of his responses would, of course, be correct. In this type of experiment one studies the proportion of correct answers in the trials before the moment of insight. Some people actually show a considerably gain in this preconscious learning, whereas other individuals show no gain beyond the chance level until suddenly they get insight when they see the rules that apply in the game. One hypothesis that might be investigated is that inventive people are in this sense in better rapport with their own preconscious thinking."

This type of work by Heidbreder and Bouthilet will be described later, and it will be seen that Bouthilet came close to accomplishing Thurstone's visualization.

Experimental Evidence of Incubation

Experimental work has been done which is in line with Thurstone's discussion. Vinacke states that "an individual may be able to act in a manner showing that he has attained the concept, without awareness, i.e., he can successfully identify specimens of the class without being able to verbalize the concept."

Rees and Israel show how this works. They asked for anagrams from thirty examples, where the first fifteen examples presented had but one solution and were of the type NELIN, NEDOZ, SDLEN. Although the last fifteen examples had multiple solutions and were of the type KLSTA, or DLSCO, subjects had acquired set and solved them as 3,4,5,1,2 anagrams. But six of the ten subjects had no conscious idea that a uniform arrangement was involved. Other experiments also demonstrated sets established in this way.

Leeper comments: "Even when the subject comes to realize that there is a 'system' involved, it appears that he frequently develops the generalization and uses it for a while before he is able to recognize consciously what he is doing. For instance, the subject notices that the anagrams are getting 'easier.' If he seeks the reason for this, he may come to realize that he has been using a particular pattern, or a certain area of association, or whatever."

A major attempt to study intuitive thinking experimentally is found in the University of Chicago thesis (1948) of Lorraine Bouthilet on the "Measurement of Intuitive Thinking." Her purpose was to show that rapport with preconscious thinking led to improved performance on her experimental problem even before the solution was consciously explicated. The problem chosen was of the type used in studies of concept formation, and it was this literature especially that was reviewed. The work on concept formation, Bouthilet says, gives (1) evidence of unexplicated understanding of a rule, and (2) the methods used to get that evidence.

In the experimental work, subjects were shown a list of words in a learning set. Opposite each key word in the left-hand column was placed a correct answer. Subsequently, in a test set, five words were placed opposite the key word for a multiple-choice arrangement, and the matching word was to be marked by the subject. Each test set included the preceding learning set, with the correct response now mixed up with four other words, and twenty additions. Scoring was of correct choices on *new words*. Correct choice was a word containing only letters found in the key word. There were twenty subjects, and after twenty series, the experiment was stopped for subjects who had by then not yet discovered the rule.

The data have been condensed in Table B-2 of the Appendix by the present author. The most important observation is that one-third of the subjects scored significantly high even before they "knew" the rule and demonstrated it by scoring perfectly. There was a definite group of solvers who had very high scores in the run-before-last, and another group, who jumped directly from non-significant runs to perfect series. There was no significant difference between these two groups in the number of trials needed to solve the problem. The first class averaged significantly high even in the second-from-last series. It is as if the unexplicated answer were slowly dawning, or as if flashes from the already informed preconscious were getting through with more and more success.

The Bouthilet experiment may provide a method of selecting subjects with the "preconscious rapport" of Thurstone. It would be interesting to locate and work intensively with a group of subjects of Class 1.

Personality Aspects

What kind of personality incubates well? One that can live easily with, and communicate with, the unconscious. This is basically a consideration of creative personality (Chapter 9) but a few comments are appropriate here, to emphasize the importance of affective as well as cognitive elements. The significance of motivation has already been assessed. There are in addition many creative traits: flexibility of mind, tolerance of ambiguity, perseverance, discernment, self-confidence, and others. Three curious ones have been mentioned as possibilities: parsimony, by Flory; gullibility, by Thurstone; retained capacity for childlike wonder, by Knowlson. One can add, from Rogers, poorer integration of personality. This follows from the retention of the ability for childlike wonder. The creative man must have *all* his concepts more fluid. He has no frozen guides in life, though some are a little firmer than others. He must have better rapport with the capricious unconscious. Yet he must have determination to persist to get his insight, and then the faith to sell it.

For discussion in particular, the parsimony trait mentioned above makes much sense. A man brought up in a frugal home environment is subject to two powerful influences tending to break down fixation. Everything in the home is scanned on the basis that it represents a definite cost and must get multiple use, to wear it out and avoid waste, and to prevent an unnecessary purchase. The present author believes the frugality of his own home environment was important in this way, and can cite an example of especial interest.

Several years ago, casually reading a technical journal, he came upon an item to the effect that a great share of the money spent for bar soap perfume was lost by evaporation through paper wrappers. This tremendous waste (literally millions of dollars) nagged his mind, even though it was in no sense a research problem of his. The first answer obtained was a confession of failure to solve, namely, to let the perfume escape, but use it by keeping bar soap, or the wrappers, in the linen drawers as a sachet. The second answer was better. It came one night while the author was working in the library, and actively concentrating on Edna Heidbreder's first paper on concept formation. The solution, an excellent example of thinking aside, was: Wrap the bars with aluminum foil, which is impervious to vapor loss.

This instance is significant in several directions:

(1) The thinking aside.
(2) The sudden, worthwhile insight without active preparation.
(3) The motivation as a nag from a basic personality trait to avoid waste.
(4) The effect of home training on creativity (to be discussed later in more detail).

Other things being equal, it follows that, to study new uses of a by-product now going to waste, one should appoint the chemist with the tightest fist. The expansive man won't care about the loss, but the waste will *hurt* the parsimonious man. The expansive ego creates differently. Roosevelt, an expansive man, thought up the lend-lease version of give.

To digress a moment, two special facets of creative personality have been visualized so far in this book:

(1) The problem must match the man's superior factors.
(2) The problem must match the man's basic personality pattern.

Aids to Incubation

One can elaborate preparation with even remote structuring when necessary. One can aid insight. But how to help incubation? It has already been said, use liked symbols, and reinforce motivation. R. R. Updegraf, in "The Subconscious Mind in Business," advises deliberate, periodic scheduling of checks on the progress of incubation. In the process of such checks it will be the creator's task to develop his skill in judicious priming, which rekindles interest, and adds new associations.

Basically, this means accepting the idea of unconscious work in incubation, and planning to use it. For example, recurrence can be made deliberate by scheduling a review. This review is prepared with the material of the Preparation chapters in mind. It utilizes symbols as well as words. Having in mind the problem and preparative material, the basics are set up in a pleasing array on a large card. The goal is pointed out, and a gap is evident, waiting for the insight to be filled in when attained. The factual material, and various restatements of the problem in words and symbols are suitably arranged to provide an attractive *pattern*.

The purpose of this pattern is to focus in one unit the explicated need, the unfilled gap, the preparative variations, and the desired insight. As an example, Figure 6-1 shows a pattern for ideas for a new product by a lamp manufacturer. The development of some of the items in the pattern was done by still other techniques (p. 173).

The unification is intended to aid incubation, and serve for optimal review of the project for reactivation. Even if this is complex, the unconscious can readily hold it all. The review should sharpen the semi-eidetic image the unconscious possesses, and promote rapport with the conscious. Experiments show how such a representation in space can often be recalled from memory *in toto* under hypnosis. Teeple felt that, during incubation, the unconscious has before it all tables and diagrams, but can approach a deeper concentration.

Additional to the review is priming—supplying material which it is thought may be pertinent. Patrick quotes a poet: "If I had a feeling for a poem, I would read something that would keep the suggestion going and carry some sort of living relation to me."

Much experimental work is priming. The worker completes the preparation stage and starts some experiments. The results of the experiments (1) provide the occasion for review and reappraisal; and (2) at the same time provide new associations to be fed into the hopper. It is part of the power of the experimental method that its practice of necessity entails both of these factors.

In laboratory work, while one does not know the answer sought,

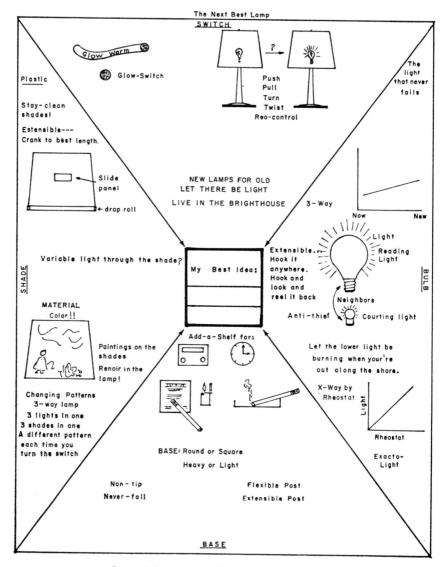

Figure 6–1. Pattern of ideas for a new product.

there are thoughts of some good experiments—in themselves insights. The experimental work proceeds to give minor insights which help to plan the next experiments, while one is in the incubation stage so far as the principal goal is concerned. The results of the experiments go into "the deep well."

In this fashion, a worker was searching for a new cold-waving formula. Then one day a value was significantly high, and he asked why, and began to grope for *that* answer, because by restructuring, it had now become the answer to the original goal. How much higher the value could be pushed, and how to lower it, were determined by the familiar variations of laboratory science. Adequate insight followed to produce a new, nationally marketed product. In this case, the important moment was to say, "This value is high, and examining its variation may answer the problem."

Management, in dealing with its creative people, should understand the need for incubation, its function of search, and its characteristics of time, recurrence, and emotional stress. The unconscious work must go on to attain the insight which is the goal of management, as well as of the creative man. The Creative Lodge, discussed in Chapter 13, is a place for polypreparative work and primed incubation.

Chapter 7 will consider the stage of insight—the aim and high moment of the creative process.

7. INSIGHT

"Insight is the Father of invention far more indisputably than necessity is its Mother."

Insight is the word used for problem solution by the Gestalt psychologists. It is the answer to the problem posed, the fruit of the preparative labor, the new combination, the birth of a new idea. It is also the prelude to proof, to verification, to the fabrication of what is to be communicated or displayed for public acclaim. Commonly used synonyms are illumination and inspiration. These, however, tend to refer only to insights "out of the blue." But there are other insights that follow resumption of solution-directed effort. They may be partial or total.

Insight is the distinguishing mark of creative work. To the recipient, it is new. "Thinking is different after that moment than before." To be valuable, naturally, an insight must also be socially new, at least in the current framework of the creator's culture.

Insight is a common experience, a pleasant experience, and a sought experience. It is of daily, even hourly, occurrence in the small affairs of life. It is itself a pleasure in intellectual work. It is sought, at moderate effort level, in games, puzzles, and reading. You hide a ball for your dog to find, and are pleased when he does so. *His* joy is evident in every line of his body and provocative toss of his head. On the serious side, the triumphs of insight, from school days on, are remembered for life.

Insight ministers to the ego ("I have done this thing no one else until now could ever do"); to the sublimation of sex; to the hope of economic profit; to the hope of appearing well before one's fellows in communication; to the sense of the esthetic, especially the desire to unify or simplify or correlate; and to the altruistic, if there be worth for mankind in it.

Other experiences are analogous to insight. Ribot mentions:

"... a long forgotten passion reveals itself through an act; a sudden resolve, after endless deliberation which did not seem able to come to a head." The total experience of wanting to recall something and being unable to do so; of feeling the resultant tension; of going about other things; and of having the desired memory pop into the mind with accompanying elation and relief—this is a recapitulation of creative experience, except that nothing *new* is produced.

Rogers has commented on the separateness one feels when insight is gained. Then one must communicate, and win social approval for the insight, in order to remove the separation.

There are two basic types of productive thinking: when the solution falls to direct frontal assault, and when it arises spontaneously in the mind. There is insight in both. Insight enters thinking very broadly, from simple problems to the most complex. A creation of scope usually consists of one major insight and many minor insights gained in the realization step. The scope of major insights depends on the mental force of the creative thinker. The accompanying emotion is also variant, depending on the size and reward-potential (rather than importance) of the insight, how long the problem has been an anxiety, and the temperament of the worker.

Perceptual problems may be solved practically at a glance. At the next level, in simple situations of reasoning, potential answers are quickly ticked off, and the correct one is at once recognized the first time it occurs. Here solution is reached with the first attempts made in the preparative stage. If the problem is more complex, incubative processes enter, and ideas recur, in modified form, until solution ensues. If the problem is difficult and complex, much preparation, much incubation, and much time lead up to major insight. The above are the poles of solution-seeking, from the easiest to the most difficult tasks, with a continuous variation between them.

When the concern is with a difficult problem, the stages of the creative process occur; but then, too, there are different levels of effort. In an example of Vinacke's, an artist commissioned for a portrait does a workmanlike job, but with "a minimum of free organization of experience and of autistic involvement." There is insight here, if the product is to be worth professional effort. But there is less insight, in this ordinary practice of his profession, than the artist finds in a subject that catches his fancy, challenges the imagination, gains emotional involvement, and culminates in the decision to go ahead.

Even in quickly obtained solutions, at a moderate level of mental effort, the creative stages occur. One can recall fleeting irritations, momentary satisfactions, as the work proceeds. An idea G, under manipulation as a potential solution, is modified to G_1, laid aside for a short time, found to recur as G_2, and then minutes later as G_3, when a quick, consciously performed twist produces G_4, the answer sought. Rapid, vigorously prosecuted exchanges occur between the material in the center of mental activity and that in the peripheral zone. The peripheral zone constantly changes, and each new entrant is quickly scanned for value in relation to the centrally focused material and the controlling purpose. In this method of direct attack, whether an original or a resumed effort, the creative process is telescoped, and stages are merged and even subliminal. The type of mental activity is that described by Patrick, when publishable poems were produced from a fixed stimulus in a matter of a few minutes. The play, from Conscious to Periphery to Unco (unconscious) and back, is free and open and too fast to follow.

Despite these similarities of process, there are differences, too, between getting solution by direct attack and by spontaneous rise. These differences are in the nature of the problem and the nature of the worker.

The more difficult the problem, and the more important the insight, the more likely is the solution to arrive suddenly and spontaneously. The *breakthrough* comes by spontaneous rise. On the other hand, a given area or territory marked out to be exploited yields to planned assault. (Here the important insight is the decision to mark out and exploit, which may have been of the spontaneous type.) The breakthrough type of insight comes by sudden arrival because it is not susceptible to logical attack, and can gain consideration only in a relaxed mental state or in dissociated thought. Such insights include:

(1) A discovery which *apparently* runs counter to established natural law (paint shadow with color).

(2) A discovery which must violate perceptual, cultural, or emotional fixations. This is the "why, of course" type of idea which everybody knows but nobody has yet thought of.

The rejection of these by reason is automatic because they obviously violate basic acceptances which the worker has integrated into his mental life to facilitate his living. Only in reverie can one say, what would happen if that which I believe to be true were actually not true? Or, suppose A and B were both true, rather than, as they apparently are, mutually exclusive. Fleming, like all bacteriologists, had it built into the warp and woof of his professional outlook that spoiled plates are washed up and done over again. But one day he said, "The mold on these plates produced a killer of bacteria; I can use that"—and penicillin was born.

The psychological makeup of workers inclines them toward a characteristic dependency on one or the other of the systematic and the intuitive approaches. The deliberate reasoner likes to go step by step and to change variables in a closely controlled manner. The more intuitive worker plays with the variables, changing several at once, until a sudden insight bridges the gap as the result of unconscious integration. Most men use both approaches. The intuitive worker must use the stepwise method to verify his conclusion, while discovery comes to the reasoner type in a reflective moment. They differ in the way they *seek* to gain the initial, or guiding, or major insight.

For some creative workers, intimation as previously discussed may forecast the arrival of insight. The insight arrives with definite emotion, but of varied strength, from a mild "aha" to an explosive *"eureka!"*

Persons differ in the span of concepts A and B that they can handle, and still permute them. Part of this may come from ability to handle extremely labile or changeable images packed with diverse content. Great generalizations have come when a large content in A from many separate segments of knowledge, was joined with a similar B, to yield a new grasp of a whole field.

Most often, it is in periods of rest and relaxation, or dispersed attention, that insight occurs. The degree to which this is true in the literature reports of creative experience is impressive. In Table 7-1 are collected some famous examples, to give an indication of the weight of evidence.

TABLE 7–1. CONDITIONS OF INSIGHT.

Person	Time	Place	Form	Discovery
Wagner [1]	—	Bed	Dream	Rheingold theme.
Coleridge [2]	Day	Chair	Dream	"Kubla Khan."
C. Bronte [1]	—	—	Dream	Images of incidents.
Poincaré [1]	Night	Bed	Wakeful observation	Fuchsian functions.
Poincaré [1]	Day	On foot	Striking idea	Analogy to non-Euclidean geometry.
Hamilton [3]	Day	On foot	Striking idea	Quaternions.
Darwin [4]	Day	Carriage	Str. Idea	Natural selection.
Berliner [4]	4 A.M.	Pullman	Idea	Potash mineral treatment.
F. E. Ives [4]	Morn.	Bed	Vision	Halftone process.
Hadamard [5]	Night	Bed	Sudden awakening	Mathematical proof, in new direction of thought.
Beethoven [6]	Day	Carriage	Dream	Musical canon.
Blanchard [7]	Day	Riding	Sudden idea	Special lathe.
Longfellow [8]	Night	Before fire	Sudden idea	"Hesperus." Wrote some, retired, got up, wrote more.
Aquinas [9]	Eve.	Royal dinner	Sudden idea	Clinching argument.
Tissot [7]	Day	Church	Daydream	Painting: "The Ruins."
Wesson [4]	Day	Church	—	A principle of circulation in pipes.
Kropotkin [4]	Day	—	Sudden organization of mass of data	Mapping of Asia.
Goethe [3]	Day	—	"	Plan of "Werther."

References, in bibliography:
[1] Dashiell	[4] Platt and Baker	[7] Porterfield
[2] Gerard	[5] Hadamard	[8] Hart
[3] Beveridge	[6] Ghiselin	[9] Knowlson

When so many in diverse fields make the same report, it may well be believed that there is a real method here to be learned and practiced. That method is, provide periods of quiet which clear the channel for insight. The kind of "quiet" differs from person to person. Morning, night, day-dreaming, resting, sleeping, traveling, working along a related, or even an unrelated path—all are factors. Another is recreation.

The communication of the result to the conscious comes when the conscious mind is relaxed—at church, at rest, in play, even in sleep. Knowlson commented that sleep is dawn to the unconscious. For some persons, the problem anxiety is relieved in sleep, by dreamed direct solution, just as a personality frustration reveals itself in dreamed symbol-stories.

In other cases, of course, the communication comes rather quickly, after work on the actual problem is re-instituted. Often, too, it comes when work is in progress on something unrelated.

The manner of relaying the result may be ethereal. An insight is very often like a fleeting, forbidden, sexual thought that escapes, in Freud's terminology, the censor, into the stream of consciousness, and is immediately repressed, or, being ribald, ignored. The unconscious presents its synthesis diffidently. It may not be in central focus, it may be a momentary, skittish passage. It must be seized. This is the importance of rapport: access is easier; the call for attention is more insistent.

At times, again, insight batters down the door, forcing the tribute of a physical gasp to its sudden, remarkable clarity and quality of fitness.

One may use an insight for some time before it is consciously explicated. This is shown by several reports of work on concept formation. On one occasion, the present writer enunciated a new approach to a problem in a conference, and only realized the value of the idea after he heard his own voice say it. It is quite common that the full implications of an idea dawn only slowly.

Insight is often achieved by group activity, during discussion of a problem. Each member of the group contributes a part of the solution. This action is more likely to be useful in hammering out an effective program or determining a course of action than in solving a scientific difficulty. Nevertheless, the sum of the group effort still crystallizes for one man; for insight is a lonely thing until communicated.

The precipitant of insight has been considered especially by

Hutchinson: "As far as I can determine, the agent which actually occasions the insight is superficially an accident having its locus in the field of unrelated pursuits which occupies the thinker during his period of renunciation of the problem." When the means at hand are exhausted, the mind is casting around for anything and receptive to "almost any plausible aid." The accidents are of two kinds: catalytic ones, not used in the creation; and pertinent ones, incorporated directly in the product.

The analogy of precipitation is a good one, and it is especially interesting to make the comparison to a supersaturated solution of, say, sodium thiosulfate. The addition of a minute crystal of this salt, or an isomorphic relative, initiates profuse precipitation of crystals, and the seed crystal is incorporated in the crystalline product. A particle of dust will also initiate crystallization, but will *not* be integrated in the precipitate. The separation of the crystal (idea) comes with evolution of heat (emotion). The crystallization can often be induced by mechanical action—just as ideas have come to many creators while walking or riding. The preparative work serves to supersaturate the mind with the material, so that an accidental stimulus can act. Supersaturation is comparable to overlearning, said by many to be useful for creation: the information is more readily available for recall than when mere learning has taken place.

As an example of one type of accident, an old woman entered a café, and became the prototype of Arnold Bennett's "The Old Wives Tale." For an instance of the other type, something in Heidbreder's article, or in the library surroundings, precipitated for this writer the idea of the foil-wrapped soap (p. 80). In connection with the idea of precipitants, the bizarre creative stimuli employed by some of the great creators may have served as sensory cues, motes inducing creative precipitation. Carlyle needed silence and tried to construct a sound-proof room; Proust achieved one; and Emerson would at times leave his family and rent a hotel room to get a quiet place to work. Freud chain-smoked. Kipling could not write creatively with a lead pencil. McKellar writes: "The act of working in a place one finds congenial for work provides for a sensory input of cues that have in the past provoked thought, sustained endurance, or perhaps been fruitful in evoking original ideas. The effect of such stimuli cannot be ignored, particularly in any explanation of *sustained* creative thinking."

In psychoanalysis, the analyst may feed to his patient a word or association or idea (an entirely accidental stimulus so far as the patient is concerned) known by the analyst to be related to buried material. Around this—to the patient accidental—stimulus there congeal associations of import for progress in the therapy. Just so, Hutchinson states, a chance stimulus precipitates insight.

How is any particular insight manifested? Insight has been widely studied in animals, especially chimpanzees. (One, called Sultan, even achieved the rating of chimpanzee-genius.) Evidence of insight in chimpanzees (research by Yerkes) showed:

Sudden *transition* from trial and error to success—correct response.
Good *retention* of correct response.
Transfer of response to modified situations.

In general, in insight these characteristics may be noted:

Newness.
Brevity.
Suddenness.

Insight is the distilled essence of much mental activity. It reaches directly to the heart of the matter and expresses it in a nutshell. The creation comes as a ten-word résumé: in poetry, a title or a first line; in music, a theme; in painting, a decision for a scene to do or a technique to use; in science, an explanation of puzzling data. Consider the brevity of the following:

Change the exhaust gas.
The moon falls too.
Use a match box as a support.
Rotate the patient.
Foil-wrap soap.

The insight is new to the person experiencing it. It must also be new and valuable to his culture to attain the rank of a worthwhile creative achievement. Newness may be in subject, content, materials, or technique.

Content: Monet, dark = closely spaced different colors.
Subject: Freud, sex in almost all motivation.
Material: Perkin, mauve dye.
Technique: Joyce, "Ulysses."

The insight shows great compression, but is at first bare. While it is being examined, as one would look at different facets of a diamond, sometimes ideas tumble faster than one can record—and some are lost. In the examination, the implications are seen. The breadth and variety of these depend on the faithfulness of the preparative work.

Sometimes, after a little, the shine wears off an insight, and one begins to realize—isn't there an overtone of being fooled?—it is dross and not gold. It really doesn't explain very much; it involves too many exceptions; or when refined, it is just unimportant. Since the esthetic beauty of this A + B combination was spurious, it is necessary to try again.

If one were to examine a finished work, and express the core of it in ten words, that would be the insight.

An apparent, but not actual, exception to the rule of brevity is when the insight is an ordering of a complex pattern. But in the insight this pattern is seen as a unit, and by comparison with the earlier diffuse complexity possesses a beautiful symmetry also deserving to be called "in a nutshell." So Darwin and Wallace telescoped huge volumes of work.

Classification of Insight

Duncker has classified insights as *total analytic, total synthetic,* and *mixed.* Total analytic is direct preparative progress to the goal. Total synthetic is sudden reorganization when not actively working on the problem. The mixed type is sudden reorganization in a period of resumed work.

Hutchinson has classified insights as using, or not using, the accidental precipitant.

There is insight by:

Pure creative tendency.
Chance.

Completion of a pattern long formed but missing one ele-
ment (B).
Direct preparative labor.
Full creative process.

By pure creative tendency, a man accustomed to create will see
something done, in a situation entirely new to his experience, and
say, "They could do it better this way." He sees a truck stuck in an
underpass, and says, "Let some air out of the tires." The creative
man creates not only in his own field but in other fields where his
good factors can operate. He is habituated to reject stereotypes and
seek the unusual or even remote answer. He is stymied only in fields
where his factors, especially of verbal or spatial character, are weak.

Chance creation is different; it comes most readily in a man's own
field. The examples of chance creation are myriad. They are discoveries that arise aside from the worker's main purpose of the
moment. In this they differ from a new fact that suddenly completes
a pattern to provide a solution long sought. An example of such
sudden completion was the "sanded" cotton of Bloede (page 32).
Examples of chance discovery are Galvani's twitching frog legs, and
Oersted's magnetic needle deflection by an electric current. There
is in science a large history of the role of chance in the setting off
of insight. W. I. B. Beveridge has collected more than twenty-seven
instances. Rossman records quite a few others. This is one of the
strongest arguments against the closely planned project: the big insight may well come by chance; the planning will inhibit recognition of the chance.

In "The Art of Scientific Investigation," Beveridge declares: *

"Probably the majority of discoveries in biology and
medicine have been come upon unexpectedly, or at least
had an element of chance in them, especially the most important and revolutionary ones. It is scarcely possible to
foresee a discovery that breaks really new ground, because
it is often not in accord with current beliefs. Frequently I
have heard a colleague, relating some new finding, say
almost apologetically, 'I came across it by accident.' Al-

---

* Reproduced by permission of W. W. Norton and Company.

though it is common knowledge that sometimes chance is a factor in the making of a discovery, the magnitude of its importance is seldom realized, and the significance of its role does not seem to have been fully appreciated or understood. Books have been written on scientific method omitting any reference to chance or empiricism in discovery.

"Perhaps the most striking examples of empirical discoveries are to be found in chemotherapy, where nearly all the great discoveries have been made by following a false hypothesis or a so-called chance observation. Elsewhere . . . are described the circumstances in which were discovered the therapeutic effects of quinine, salvarsan, sulphanilamide, diamidine, paraminobenzoic acid, and penicillin. Subsequent rational research in each case provided only relatively small improvements. These facts are the more amazing when one thinks of the colossal amount of rational research that has been carried out in chemotherapy.

"The history of discovery shows that chance plays an important part, but on the other hand it plays only one part even in those discoveries attributed to it. . . . It is the interpretation of the chance observation which counts. The role of chance is merely to provide the opportunity and the scientist has to recognize it and grasp it."

The introduction of floating soap is a famous example. In mechanizing the manufacturing process, hand-operated hickory stirring rods called crutchers were replaced by a mechanical crutcher. One day a forgetful workman let this machine run over his lunch hour. Somehow, conditions of time and speed were right so that the framed soap floated. The factory had no inkling of this, until orders started coming in for more of "that floating soap." The way it had happened was analyzed, and Ivory was born.

The following interesting illustrations are taken from Beveridge:

W. H. Perkin, 18 years old, could not obtain quinine by oxidizing allyl-o-toluidine. He thought of trying a simpler base, and made the first aniline dye when he chose aniline sulfate. Had not his aniline contained as impurity some *p*-toluidine, the reaction could not have occurred.

Before his discovery of penicillin, "Fleming was working with some plate cultures of staphylococci which he had occasion to open several times, and, as often happens in such circumstances, they became contaminated. He noticed that the colonies of staphylococci around one particular colony died. Many bacteriologists would not have thought this particularly remarkable, for it has long been known that some bacteria interfere with the growth of others. Fleming, however, saw the possible significance of the observation, and followed it up to discover penicillin. . . . The element of chance in this discovery is the more remarkable when one realizes that that particular mold is not a very common one, and further, that subsequently a most extensive, world-wide search for other antibiotics has failed to date to discover anything else as good. It is of interest to note that the discovery would probably not have been made had not Fleming been working under 'unfavorable' conditions in an old building where there was a lot of dust and contaminations were likely to occur."

According to Cannon, Pasteur was led by chance to his method of immunization, and it was an accidental observation by a lab assistant that ultimately resulted in the discovery of insulin.

As another example, Victor Meyer, in lecturing to his classes in chemistry, was accustomed to show them a color reaction of benzene. One day the demonstration failed. For most, this would merely have been embarrassment, and no doubt it was an embarrassment to Meyer too. But he also sought the reason for failure. He found that the benzene used in the unsuccessful test had been synthesized from pure benzoic acid. The benzene distilled from coal tar that he usually used must then contain something else that gave the color reaction—and distilled at the same temperature as benzene. The discovery of the heterocycle thiophene followed. Benzene is C_6H_6 and boils at 80°C. Thiophene is C_4H_4S and boils at nearly the same point, 84°C.

It was of these events and others like them that Poe, in "Marie Roget," wrote, "Experience has shown, and a true philosophy will always show, that a vast, perhaps the larger, portion of the truth arises from the seemingly irrelevant." Irrelevant as the fogged plates of Becquerel; or as the clear plates of Fleming; or as the little volume of left-over gas of Cavendish.

It was of these events and others like them that Pasteur said, "Chance favors only the prepared mind." To this one may add, prepared by heredity to possess the necessary factors, and prepared from childhood in the development of those factors, and in the disposition to create, and prepared by the furtherance of success to think boldly, and prepared by saturation in the subject to note and understand *any* unusual event or result.

Direct preparative labor may provide a desired answer. In a complex or difficult problem, this may come in a final resumption of work after the occurrence of the full creative process. Then the answer is mixed analytic. If the answer arises spontaneously, it is mixed synthetic, as in Darwin's synthesis of the survival of the fittest explanation.

Thus, the answer to a difficult problem is insight. It comes after preparation and incubation. It has many ways of coming, including the deliberate, the shocking, and the elusive. Indeed, insight is a maiden, often not easily importuned, but yielding to strategic neglect, and beautiful in surrender.

The present writer has distinguished eleven types of insight. The list, which may not be exhaustive, is given in brief form, and in some cases is a recapitulation of earlier material. The first three in particular are characterized by sudden appearance.

(1) The response is to sudden chance stimulation on a problem not under active attack, perhaps even never considered. This kind of thing may happen quite often, as when one looks up a journal article in the library. The attention strays to the article following. It stimulates an idea remote from the initial purpose in going to the library.

(2) The idea arrives as a "side thought" analogous to Hadamard's "thinking aside." It is the sudden realization of the answer to a problem while doing something else.

(3) An unexpected event, perhaps in experimentation, is correctly interpreted, as when Perkin said, "If this color is so intense, it can be a dye." The unexpected result may be in the form of a very slender clue. Assume that some experiments are made, even

without strong expectations. One result triggers the mind to progress, even though its relation to the direction of progress may be most tenuous.

The next four types of insight possess a large element of deliberate effort.

(4) The answer comes from a continuous sequence. There is the problem, and the work on it, and the solution.

(5) The answer comes on resumption of effort. Having done preparative work, and allowed time for incubation, some free time is taken for deliberate exploration for the answer. Soon, the fruitful idea comes.

(6) In this case, following preparation and due incubation, a train of thought directed to solution is initiated from the unconscious. This differs from (5) in the impetus of reattack, and from (2) in that one is not suddenly surprised with the answer, but starts thinking and quickly develops it. It is as if the solution were nearly ready, and the unconscious wished to gain rapport to finish the job most expeditiously, needing, perhaps, conscious aid to put the last stitches in the tapestry.

(7) Insight is by total coverage. A deliberate plan is made to cover all of a certain area and obtain the answer. Here, another and different insight preceded the planning. That was to perceive and delimit the area of study, and specify the methods to be used.

Four other types of insight are of special nature.

(8) A relay insight recognized as such. Here, some material is discovered which is at once recognized as especially pertinent. In scientific work, for example, one determines what would be a good experiment to try. It may or may not work. This insight differs in being an especially happy combination rather than the answer itself. The type is particularly prominent in literature and the arts. Tissot, in his mind's eye, saw figures moving in the ruins of a cathedral, and explicated the idea: That should be a good subject to paint. A lyric poet may be impressed by a scene, and feel that his description of the locale will make a good poem, after he has modified the details so ... and so ... and so. A writer may become acquainted with a strong or unusual character, and decide that he should be

put in a story. Such occurrences and decisions have been vividly described by Richard Wilbur and Dorothy Canfield.

(9) A very common kind of insight occurs when a mass of material suddenly emerges as a pattern, or several ideas fall together into a unit or orderly arrangement. The new thing is the *ordering* of the ideas.

(10) In this type, one obtains as an insight a particular aspect of a more general case. But only gradually, as effort continues and the particular insight is worked with, does it dawn that "the general case of which this is a particular example is true, too, and it may be stated in this way. . . ."

(11) In this case, an insight is utilized in the progressive work for some time before it is consciously explicated as the principle upon which one is operating. The occurrence of this phenomenon in concept formation studies has already been mentioned (pp. 76-79).

Some Aspects of Insight

Insight may come through any of the senses: visual, auditory, olfactory, gustatory, kinesthetic; or even as a dream.

Insight may tend to come at special times. Kleitman found that the human body goes through a daily cycle of slightly higher and slightly lower temperatures. The mind appears to be creative when body temperature is high. Correspondingly, there are creative people who are most effective when their temperature peaks at night, and others who are most effective and have their highest body temperature in the morning. Some have a high temperature plateau all day. Ernest Hemingway and Katherine Brush liked to work in the morning; John O'Hara and Helen MacInnes at night.

There is also some thought that there may be especially creative days. Hutchinson quotes an author's remark about inspiration to this effect: "Sometimes I have a very strong suspicion that this is going to be a lucky day." To this may be added Dimnet's interesting statement, ". . . we humbler people have our intuitions, our times for feeling on the crest of a wave, for thinking our best and doing our best." Creative workers, especially poets, writers, and musicians, have complained of dead periods when they could not work, and rejoiced in vital periods when they could not stop creating.

The present writer has obtained certain evidence that there are recurrent, especially creative periods of time. This evidence is a personal record of insights, and its presentation will require the reader's indulgence to introduce a personal note. Early in his study of creativity, he began to record insights in detail, and to note also the time, place, and attendant circumstances. A complete record of insights was kept over the period from July 19, 1954 to February 23, 1955. In subsequent analysis they were divided into five types, as follows:

(1) Single-shot, relatively complete, gadgety ideas.

(2) Special methods to develop creative thinking.

(3) Organizations of material into classes, units, or logical order.

(4) Ideas representing progress on the job of industrial research on protein fibers.

(5) Miscellaneous—mostly on other aspects of creativity than methods, and comprising some of the material in this book.

A total of 161 insights were recorded by date over the stated period of 220 days. For some of the 161, the record of attendant circumstances was incomplete, but 115 were distributed as to time of day in this way:

Morning	39
Afternoon	50
Evening	26

The most significant distribution referred to the day of the month. The recorded insights gave the distribution shown in Table 7–2 from July 24 to February 23, a total of 156 insights:

TABLE 7–2

Interval	No. of Insights
1st–4th	20
5th–8th	15
9th–12th	21
13th–16th	18
17th–20th	13
21st–24th	38
25th–28th	20
29th–31st	11 (15 *)

* Estimated value if this interval were also four days.

The only large departure from the expected 20 is, by inspection, the value 38, and by statistical analysis the probability that this divergence is not a real difference is less than .01. The days from the 21st through the 24th seem to have been especially creative. Certain ideas that came in this period had especial scope for the writer. For example:

August   21: An exceptionally useful individual and group creative technique of broad scope, cf. Chapter 11.

October   21: Incubation = anxiety state.

November 22: Foil wrapping for soap bars.

March   24: Smother theory of desensitizing mercaptans (given before Toilet Goods Association, December, 1959).

Aids and Blocks to Insight

Aids and blocks to creativity in general, for both individuals and groups, will be discussed in the later chapter. But certain comments are pertinent here. Insights are easy to lose, easy to spoil, even easy to forget as to their atmosphere of occurrence.

It is to be emphasized that awareness for insights must be cultivated. A big idea may cross the mind like any stray thought. One might visualize Fleming coming into the laboratory and looking at some Petrie dishes and saying to himself casually, "That breakfast coffee was too sweet," and in the next mental breath and at the same intensity, "The mold produces a killer of bacteria." If now the conscious mind seizes this thought, there will be insight and elation —and penicillin. It is at least possible that the stream of consciousness might continue with, "A nuisance. I'll have to throw these out and do them over." In fact, with other bacteriologists who had made Fleming's observation, the thought obviously did so conclude. Ferren said:

> "... how many times has preparation been inadequate, how many insights have we failed to accept at the time of insight, how many insights have we bungled through lack of courage or simple labor? A peculiar virtue, besides patience, is demanded of the creative worker: it is alertness toward the possibility of being surprised."

Regarding the attendant circumstances of ideas, the present writer tried to go back over old research notebooks and tabulate the time and circumstances of the various ideas which were written out and developed there. But it was found that these details could not be recalled. They have to be put down at the time they happen, just like any other significant data of whatever kind.

The simplest way of promoting insight, often overlooked, is to afford it the opportunity to appear. Other definite aids are known, including the many aspects of polypreparative labor. Discussion is probably the most powerful means—so much so that one professor said, "Even describing your problem and your thoughts about it to a marble statue should be of tremendous benefit." For free discussion among kindred spirits who have parallel or mutual interests, an attitude of helpfulness is necessary, and a critical atmosphere is certain to hamper, because of unwillingness then to contribute spur-of-the-moment thoughts. Flippancy also hampers. In creative discussion, the judgment is in abeyance, and the imagination soars. Critical appraisal comes later.

Knowlson gives the following "Laws of Inspiration":

(1) A period of tense thought should be followed by a change of subject or a period of mental inactivity.

(2) Insight is governed by a process of intellectual rhythm. There are dull periods, and those when ideas bubble.

(3) A new idea is partly dependent for its birth on the action of the right external stimulus.

(4) Analogy, consciously or unconsciously used, is a creative method of great value.

(5) When the mind has a set to discovery, its energies may develop a conception aside from immediate purposes, or make a chance discovery of a different nature.

(6) Think for yourself before you saturate yourself too much with the ideas and opinions of others.

Students of creativity list these conditions for incubation and insight:

(1) Interest in problem and desire to solve it.
(2) Absence of other problems crowding it out.
(3) Large store of pertinent information.
(4) Information worked over, systematic, well-digested.

(5) Sense of well-being.

(6) Sense of freedom from interruption.

(7) Absence of obstacles to functioning of the mind (worry, feeling that reward will not be attained, unsympathetic supervisor).

(8) Application of direct stimuli of evocation: reading, discussion, and oral or written presentation of material.

(9) Provision of opportunities of quiet for emergence of insight.

Beveridge details the following unfavorable influences: interruptions, worry, competing interests, mental or physical fatigue, too constant working on a problem, petty irritations, and distracting types of noises.

One of the best discussions here is that of Arnold, who distinguishes three basic classifications of blocks: perceptual, an inability to see the new implications behind observations; cultural, an inability to break free of the ingrained beliefs everyone has; emotional, an inability to break free of hampering personal fears and attitudes. These blocks will be discussed further in Chapter 10. The first two are the fixations of Duncker and other Gestalt writers. All three are covered by the one word—routine. Routine perception, routine living in a given cultural matrix, routinely personal emotional reactions, immediate and ingrained—all stand in the way of creating and appreciating new combinations.

Concluding Discussion

Management in maintaining and developing the business has a continual need for important new insights of its own and from its creative people. They must be recognized and used. It is important to credit and reward each originator, and equally important, to see that these insights get full development. Energy is far better expended in such development than in attempting the direction and control of the creative work leading to the insight. In many cases it is preferable to reward the originator with a bigger problem, and more freedom, and more status, rather than with a bigger group, which draws off creative thinking to replace it with administrative thinking.

In the handling of especially creative people by management, certain viewpoints regarding age and volume of specialized knowledge are cultural blocks. The fixations that block insight are not strong in a man new to a field. He denies them "because he doesn't know any better"—and creates. A worker's biggest discoveries often come when he is new to a field. In the usual case, this is when he is young. But chronological age may be less important for creativity than is generally supposed. It may serve just as well to be young in a field as to be young in years. Often a man known to be creative will blossom anew with striking ideas if he is deliberately forced, by himself, the circumstances, or the company, into a new discipline, not necessarily related to his old specialty. Companies keep moving their executives marked for promotion, to give them needed experience. They should make specialists of their technically competent but low-creative men. The high-creative men should be pushed into brand new fields from time to time, because they are more valuable as creators than as specialists.

In addition to the internal blocks mentioned above, there are blocks of external resistance in the creative path. Among the worst of these are the many so-called "killer phrases" employed like arrows to shoot down winning ideas. These phrases work precisely because they sometimes make such excellent sense. They can be used correctly only with the greatest caution, and they are poison to creative insight. Some examples are:

> "That doesn't belong to our department"
> "Somebody tried something like that years ago"
> "It's not practical"
> "Let's get back to reality"
> "The payoff is too small"

Important insight is: the absolutely new as sum from old.

Aids are: let it appear, watch for it, write it down, be satisfied with and act on a partial answer, with the assurance that more will then develop.

Having insight, it seems elementary to realize it to the full. Yet often this is prevented by interruption, or the pressure of day-to-day matters of negligible importance. If time is taken, and opportunity afforded, the reward is rich. For much of the material in the preparative labor will be integrated or utilized in development, either directly or in side thoughts. This is verification.

8. VERIFICATION

We have said that discovery is the art, verification the science. Also, verification is the toil. It is the action that follows the green light. The big decision has been made: it is a time of multiple small decisions. It is a time of realization.

The insight is purely personal in the satisfaction and the elation it brings. The verification is the valuable thing given to the world. The pure germ of the idea is usually not acceptable, be it a work of art or literature, a visualized machine, or a hypothesized coordinating principle of natural phenomena. Work is needed—the "nine-tenths perspiration"—to give valuable form to the thing conceived. Without this, the communicated contribution to society, there can be no valid and lasting credit.

Many insights of value are lost through failure to verify. For one thing, a creative man has many more insights in a lifetime than he can possibly verify. Their loss is inevitable. The hope is that those which each man chooses to bring to fruition are his most significant, and that his judgment in this regard will be true.

With insight will usually come a flow of supplementary and supporting material. It is necessary to give these thoughts time to appear, and to get them recorded—not necessarily organized—or much will be lost. Like a good showman, the unconscious will present the striking feature of the basic insight first. It is necessary to draw attention and gain rapport. But it is also necessary to stay and see the show.

Insight is brief, and nonspecific, a product of the unconscious, and purely ideational. Verification is specific, and is concerned with physical matter, numbers, equipment for experiments, paints, canvas, a typewriter. It "demands discipline, attention, will, and consequently consciousness." Poincaré's insight was, "These functions are similar to non-Euclidean geometry," a brief and general idea. The verification was specific equations, selected by deliberate effort, and worked through to prove the insight. The brief insights listed on page 91 need specific material and equipment to verify them.

The production of a finished creative product has this time-line:

Insight: The idea in a nutshell, and the immediately rising, surrounding material.

Verification: Elaboration to a rough-finished development, and revision.

The material that comes immediately with insight is a gray zone between insight and verification, and is here assigned to the former. The division is a matter of time, emotion, and scope. As a part of insight, the material may be an extensive rearrangement of most of the preparative work. Or it may be an immediate expansion of the base idea developed at the emotional peak of insight: a short poem, a foundational outline of a big work, a hypothesis and a series of points in its favor or a way to check it. But then, further expansion, experimentation, planning, and review are verification. If for no other reason, they are verification by virtue of the time factor itself. Verification may require years before the revised and polished end product is finished and ready for public presentation.

When the initial flow of material is safely on record, there follow two things: judgment as to whether in retrospect the insight has value; and if so, decision to go on with it or let it abort. Naturally, if the insight concerns the creator's main stream of activity, the decision will probably be to follow it up. This decision may be of vast scope for the life of the individual worker. For example, Hamilton declared himself ready to verify the quaternion insight during the remainder of his life. Gibbon, surveying the ruins in the city of Rome, saw in vague outline and framework the "Decline and Fall"—a verification of which took him seven years.

Size is important. A brief composition of any type may be completed in the insight stage. Then verification is revision. A larger creation is achieved when the total insight is followed by:

(1) Elaboration.
(2) Minor insights.
(3) Minor complete cycles of the creative process to overcome local blocks.
(4) Revision.

A major task, after the big insight, may break into a whole series of projects. As the work of verification goes along, these are soon in various stages of completion. For purposes of discussion, let it be assumed that realization of the major insight has been found to require the execution of four sub-projects. For example, a new chemical reaction is discovered—the major insight. It is then decided to work in four directions aimed to produce four papers, applying the reaction respectively to aliphatic, alicyclic, aromatic, and heterocyclic systems. Each of these then becomes the matrix of a separate creative attack. As effort continues, one task is in the preparation, one in the incubation, one in the insight, and one in the completion stage. In this way the verification runs the gamut of all creative thought.

In preparation, Search is King. In verification, Reason is King. Verification is the day of judgment, of logical analysis, of acceptance and rejection, of fulfilment of promise. Verification is more self-dependent. There are arrangement and utilization of material already in the mind, whereas in preparation, there was restless searching for outside material to be brought into the mind.

The principal divisions of verification to be discussed are elaboration and revision.

Elaboration

With the decision to follow up comes the labor of defining the insight, delineating its scope and limits, determining what it means and what it does not concern. Reason enters, to deduce implications, corollaries, and methods of elaboration.

Invention and expansion of the means of proof are usual requirements of the process of verification. In art and literature this is filling in the bare outline visualized originally. In music it is variation of the theme, orchestration, counterpoint. In science it is planning and doing experiments and programs. In the course of this work come many minor insights which may still derive their flow and energy from the shortly preceding major insight. Impasses arise which require minor repetitions of all the stages of the creative process to unblock them.

Rogers has elaborated the emotional states found in the stage of verification in the first three points below. The other two are added by the present author:

(1) The familiar elation of insight.

(2) The anxiety of separateness, which is a sudden, anxious realization that one has penetrated the unknown and stands there alone.

(3) The (consequent) urge to communicate the creation, and thus bring others up to the frontier and destroy the separation. This is the drive of the verification stage, but it is accompanied by

(4) The anticipation to astound with the accomplishment even in the act of communication.

(5) The disappointment of failure to achieve the full insight.

Nearing the stage of full development, or in the stages of critical review of the work, there is often discouragement that the full beauty of the initial vision has not been reduced to that reality which others can appraise.

This last is not unnatural. The creator may actually have equalled his original insight. What he cannot do is repeat the newness, and re-experience the discharge of emotional energy, that cast a halo around the first perception. He can only do that by seeking new insights. This he will do because, in Rogers' phrase, there is a "tendency for a man to actualize his potentialities," and because there is hope that the disappointment can be relieved by a new insight to be verified with better success.

A strong probability in the verification stage is that the fullness of input in the preparation stage will determine the output of detail *resulting from* the insight. Taste and logic have enabled the worker to seek out and supply many pertinent facts in the preparation. It is the relation and arrangement of these that elude him. When he gets the key, the facts take place and drop into a pattern. The more significant details that he has recognized and worked over, the more complete the pattern. In well-done preparative labor, you not only increase the chance of insight (because you make more certain of having A and B), but also enhance the quality of insight through the number and range of the secondary ideas that follow. The "CNB" method to be described in Chapter 10 compels skilled preparative work, and insures breadth of material brought to consideration, thus serving to add extra quality to insight when it comes.

Many writers, especially Beveridge, have made the emphatic point that logic and the classical scientific method are not much used in the act of discovery. This is partially because these techniques are so devoid of emotional content, partially because they are so inapplicable to vague imagery and its rapid transformations in creative manipulation. They are useful in developing the models of search. But it is in the verification stage that logic and reason come into their own, to deduce consequences, detect and plug loopholes, and point out the source, need, and nature of supporting detail, in any line of endeavor.

One would say, "If I do this experiment to prove my insight into reaction X, I must rigorously exclude oxygen. I shall look up the methods and apparatus for doing this in Jones' book."

Again, "If I paint this picture, I must put in some detail to indicate the intended period. Let it be the architecture of the house seen in the background."

Again, "If I write this short story, in which the detective solves his case through an expert's knowledge of nuclear physics, I must insert a detail early that will prepare the reader for and convince him of this ability. Let him attend a lecture by an eminent physicist, and in later conversation ask a question so exactly to the point as to suggest full understanding."

This is the type of elaboration that enters into verification. The insight is first of all a bare outline, a distilled essence, and as such is clear only to the recipient. But in communication, he must explicate material needed by the outsider, who lacks his background to the insight.

Elaborative work has been studied in cases where the different stages leading up to a finished creative product are available. In art, sketches preliminary to the final painting are available in many cases. In literature, notebooks and various preliminary drafts have been studied. Development is perhaps easiest to follow in science, where papers written over the years show the enlargement and modification of the original ideas, as the man follows the lead of his discovery. Pasteur, for example,

(1) First used bacteria to separate optical isomers.

(2) Proved bacteria did not arise by spontaneous generation.

(3) Showed bacteria caused disease.

(4) Showed attenuation could prevent disease, two famous cases being anthrax and rabies.

The *way* of elaboration is style in music, writing, or painting. In scientific experimentation, the development is according to the scientific taste of the worker. The study of *creative works* transmits understanding of these intangibles to the student, and serves to enlarge his own personal development of them. The study of the *way of elaboration* employed by the masters is also an important, and neglected, aspect which should be given as an organized presentation to the serious student in any field. A course for a chemistry department, difficult to prepare but fascinating to take, would be: the methods used by leading chemists to develop their ideas, with detailed examples from the original literature.

By elaboration, the work is brought to completion in rough-hewn form. It is then ready for the final planing and polishing of revision.

Revision

In revision, the completed creative product is edited and polished. The sketch becomes a painting; the first draft becomes the publishable book; the series of experiments becomes a paper. Judgment and a skilled critical faculty are of especial use in preparing the first-finished product of verification for communication. Usually the first product needs cutting down. This is hard, because practically all of it is dear to the creator, even in his disappointment at failing to fulfill his vision completely. Furthermore, when he begins the critical review, the mind burgeons into further creative activity. As the material is gone over, new insights are attained, new problems are glimpsed, and tentative thrusts of preparative thought in the direction of the new problems are made. It is just as difficult to keep out creative motivation in the critical revision, as it is to throttle critical judgment during the generation of new ideas. There is mental oscillation between the poles of the creation-criticism polarity, which is really an aspect of the self-outer world polarity that is the concern of all psychology.

The degree of revision employed by creative workers is highly variable. Mozart and Weber developed their compositions in the mind, and wrote them down in final form. Shakespeare seems rarely to have changed a word once written. Dostoyevsky did not revise. The revisions of these workers were mental. Many good speakers talk from notes in a form that could be taken down and published. On the other hand, the manuscripts of many writers show extensive revision, in some cases so much that a fair copy was possible only to the originator. One writer, preparing for all eventualities, divided his page vertically in half. He wrote first on the left side; the right was for the next draft. In many workers, ideas develop slowly. Their finished thought emerges as does the statue from the block of marble, and the intermediate stages are equally unimpressive. This was true of Beethoven. His first musical thoughts were often unimpressive, and did not forecast the grandeur of the finished work to come. This development has been traced in his notebooks. In such cases, revision is interwoven with genuine additions. Some parts which are added are bits of business, but some are new insights expanding the original, major one.

Product Analysis

The literature of creativity may be divided into studies of heredity, personality, the creative process, and the creative product. Only the last has an independent existence to the senses without interpretation. The creative product may be auditory, as with the teachings of a philosopher or religious leader, the performance of a singer or musician. It may be tangible: the thing itself, a painting, a sculpture, or a model illustrating an invention, or needles of a new organic compound. The largest part are printed records of the creations, like books, scientific journals, and music.

Creative products have been studied in connection with biography, and to delineate style and taste, and for comparative and historical purposes. Much more should be done to study and classify them in relation to creativity.

As a beginning, J. M. Rhodes' University of Arizona Thesis, 1957, divides creative products into

(1) *Art:* (a) ideoplastic (abstract) and (b) physioplastic (copy of nature).

(2) *Science:* (a) pure and (b) applied.

Study of even this preliminary classification vis-a-vis Guilford's creative factors, for example, should be helpful in finding what factors correlate with each type of product. The question is, what leads men to produce work of a particular one of these four types? Anne Roe has indicated more verbal fluency for theoreticians in *pure* science. Artists have an especially effective space factor. May it be that an artist's clarity of visualization influences him to undertake more *abstract* versus more *concrete* products? Is it a question of relative retention of eidetic ability, with greater retention influencing reproduction of the so clearly visualized physical world, and lesser retention influencing abstract work?

The work done along the line of analysis of creative product—i.e., analysis of the verification stage of creativity—is sparse, but such work should be attractive because when it has been well done it has received favorable and wide attention. Lowes' analysis of Coleridge's work in relation to his earlier reading is a case in point. Another is the derivation of Shakespeare's clusters from his works. A parallel study of Mozart's clustered musical phrases would be most interesting. The study of accretion and revision in Beethoven's notebooks is another case. In "Age and Achievement," Lehman has studied quality and quantity of creative product versus age, and reached some most illuminating conclusions to be discussed later.

As stated, much material exists in literature, in the form of successive drafts, and revised drafts, awaiting analysis. In science, the development, modification, and deduction of consequences, of a theory, or application of a method or reaction in different directions, should be studied from the point of view of the creativity aspects of the various steps. Nothing direct of this type exists. There is a little of it to be found in biographies—they are usually more concerned with analysis of the man than of his creative products.

The Next Task

One aspect of the final creative stage of verification is the delineation of the next work to be done. This develops during elaboration and revision in at least three directions:

(1) Side-thoughts deriving from rich preparative work and comprising insights in directions aside from the original intent and main purpose.

(2) Visualization of the definite boundaries of a territory uncovered by the major and minor insights. The boundaries mark out an area which the worker has the skill to cultivate and respecting which he has the certainty of worthwhile results and successful achievement. In industrial research work, after a breakthrough, a group meeting will outline such a territory and assign the work to individual members of a team effort to complete the tillage. The breakthrough is the big insight, and the boundary marking the second one. Unfortunately, there is less of the creative in the subsequent tillage.

(3) Glimpsing the next problem, and some explication of the needs of the preparative attack to be launched against it.

Verification and Management

A great deal of the material typed up in industry in the form of reports and memoranda represents simply, verifications, i.e., communications of insights to management by company personnel. And management's work deals mostly with personnel matters, and with decisions about their verifications. The realization of the company's research effort is found in the reports from the research department, which are elaborations of insight.

The aids management can bring to verification are: a record of creative utilization of creative work presented in well-rounded, realized form; and good provision of the appurtenances of verification in the way of surroundings, equipment, and secretarial help. As a matter of fact, in industry, aids to verification (and preparation) are provided in profusion. It is aids like freedom and opportunity for quietness, which minister to the interior stages of incubation and insight, that are neglected. The reason is that it is easier for the organization to give the physical aids, however costly, than the permissive, control-loosing ones needed by incubation and insight. The aids industry gives easily are directed to the concrete functions of preparation and verification; there is little or no aid for the interior stages. Some hard thinking and courageous action are required here. The needs are known. They must be implemented to provide opportunity for incubation in the same way that an electron microscope is bought for preparation, or a computer rented for verification. But provision for incubation and insight is a lot harder, and takes a much smarter manager. As a point of departure for thought, let the Creative Lodge of Chapter 13 be considered, or modifications and improvements of it.

A profusion of verification tools is not necessary for big insight. A few beakers and jars and chemicals may serve, or a battery and some wheels and string, some permissive atmosphere, some challenging problems, some promise of recognition—and a creative mind.

Unfortunately, most industrial "research" work is not the whole creative process, but is rather verification, done by verification-teams, on somebody else's idea later boundaried by management. The profusion of verification tools merely reflects this fact.

* * *

Summary

So far along the road, the discussion has been directed to the creative process as a whole, and its particular parts, and their dynamic interaction. Next will come a consideration of creative personality; then, how to put creativity to work, including individual and group aids, testing, creative climate, and currently vital topics of discussion that touch the field.

Dimnet has specified the meaning of the art of creative thought in this way:

> "... minor intuitions often come in clusters, or in a quick succession, but most often without any apparent connection. When we are dreaming awake, or under the influence of music, their number is so great that no calculation can approximate it. We then squander them freely. Yet, we know their value, for, sometimes, they develop into protracted trains of thought, during which we realize that our brain is doing its best work, yet doing it without taxing our cooperation. This is what we want to reproduce after the spell has been interrupted, this is what we call thinking, and the mention of an art of thinking means to us chiefly the possibility of recreating at will a similar state of mind."

At this point, the present author summarizes the creative process as follows:

The consensus of earlier workers in the field has divided the creative process into stages including usually, *preparation*, unconscious *incubation*, illumination or *insight*, and *verification*. One type of insight is simply that of perceiving the problem. Here, the concomitant emotion is interest, and the verification is the decision to attack, and the consequent preparative work. Frustration builds with the degree of fruitless effort and the visualized reward of achieving solution. The period of incubation ensues, a true mild anxiety state when frustration couples with the prepared models of search to form a "creative complex." Insight—the perception of solution—comes with joy, and then comes the anxiety of separation in the area of the new discovery. The task of verification is now that of producing a piece of work suitable for communication, since only this can relieve the separateness and earn the reward. The labor of verification brings into sight new problems, and the cycle begins again. Chapter 9 will discuss the creative personality that is concerned with this process.

9. THE CREATIVE PERSONALITY *

With the coming of the Space Age, the question as to what constitutes the creative personality has been raised with increasing frequency. This question involves many ramifications and problems. These include how to define the creative personality, which personality attributes and values are related to creativity, how to identify the creative personality, what contributes to it, and, indeed, whether there is such an entity at all. The research done so far in this area has provided some information on these questions and has raised still others. The emphasis in this chapter will not be upon presenting a comprehensive review of the research literature, but rather upon presenting material which can provide some clues to and some understanding of this subject.

Personality: Some Basic Concepts

There have been many attempts to define personality. When one considers a specific person, whether creative or not, certain factors become evident—factors which if considered as a whole may best describe what is meant here by "personality." An individual begins life with a certain amount of "equipment" provided by heredity. From then on, however, he is constantly striving to learn the rules of the environment in which he finds himself. He exists not in a vacuum but in an environment, in a culture. Involved here is a need to learn how to interact most effectively with others, and this is a continuing process. There are stresses and strains which beset the individual as he develops, with resultant problems of adjustment. Personality, as considered here, involves among other things interests, motivation and values. Briefly it may be defined along lines conceived of by Anderson (1959) as "one's rate of psycho-

* This chapter is by James F. Lawrence, Ph.D., National Director, Assessment Services, Richardson, Bellows, Henry & Company, Inc., New York.

logical growth in social situations." This concept involves change and development, and indicates that we are not dealing with an end product. Rather, an on-going process is involved. No two people have the same personality, but there appear to be many elements which they can have in common. In considering the personality of those who are capable of solving difficult problems—of being creative—we are looking for common elements.

Some Characteristics of the Creative Personality

It is agreed by all who have worked in this field that the creative personality consists of a constellation of traits. It is further agreed that certain conditions are required for the development of creativity. Maslow emphasized that mental health is a necessary prerequisite for creativity. A healthy person can let himself go. He is free to be creative because he is not too concerned about his own inner conflicts. He can enjoy himself and be spontaneous. He can take a chance and try approaches which would be impossible for those lacking in mental health. Maslow's theory broadens the concept of the creative act to include not only the hard aspects of thinking which result in, say, transistors, power plants, and research designs, but also those elements which might be characterized as an inspiration, a flash, and a peak experience.

It appears that creativity is fostered and is most evident when, in a sense, one's imagination is permitted full expression without being restricted by rules and regulations, either internal or external. Anderson (1959b) has said that creativity is concerned not only with object productions but also with positive human relations. Social creativity, and indeed all forms of creativity, can be fostered by a "propitious environment" which permits maximum growth. There is a strong element of learning in the development of creativity within an individual. Creativity can be fostered or restricted depending on whether the rules of life's game permit or inhibit originality. If it is wrong to be creative, or different, then it is difficult for anyone to have new ideas, to have a "spontaneous experience"; in effect, what is developed is a dull and unimaginative person. If it is right to be spontaneous, to express one's own ideas, then the individual in his personality development will have a fighting chance to be creative within his own limits of ability. A creative person is free to think, to be creative, because he is not inhibited and his unconscious is not cluttered by restricting stereotypes or by rote school book answers.

Related to the necessity for mental health in the creative personality are hypotheses by Rogers (in Anderson, 1959). These reflect the need for psychological safety and freedom, without which, in at least some degree, mental health is not possible. Creativity, or "constructive creativity," is explained in terms of internal or external conditions which involve the individual and his environment. Included among the constructive elements are: openness to experience (lack of rigidity), satisfaction with what is produced, and the ability to let oneself go, to "toy with elements and concepts." Even more important in the fostering of constructive creativity are such environmental conditions as psychological safety (acceptance of one's potentialities, elimination of external evaluation, and a true feeling of understanding) and psychological freedom which involves permissiveness, not in the action sense of the word, but in the thinking or symbolic sense.

Rogers, in his discussion of psychological safety, emphasized several important elements which can be found in the general environment of the creative individual. These include his acceptance in a climate free of external evaluation and with a sympathetic regard for his findings, even if they are not immediately useful. It is important that the creative individual not be restricted, but it is equally important that he should not *feel* restricted. He must feel that those responsible for his environment display toward him attitudes of permissiveness and acceptance and provide for him complete freedom of *symbolic* expression. What is being described here is in large measure what has been called the "research atmosphere" —the climate necessary for maximizing creative potential, whether in an industrial, medical, academic, or other setting.

Rogers has further indicated that, to be creative, one needs to develop "internal criteria" of judgment and evaluation. In effect, the individual has to make his own judgment as to whether he has created something that is satisfying to himself, that is a reflection of himself, and that can truly be labeled as his own. This is not merely a question of whether the product pleases the reader, the consumer, or management. It must, at the same time, please the one who created it. This concept does not in any way imply that the creative individual does not take into account the world around him and the opinions and attitudes of those with whom he comes in daily contact. It is related, however, to the feeling that attracts many into a given profession, and is the reason why in large part they continue in that profession. Whether it be engineering, medicine or chemistry, the creative individual must feel that "this is my handiwork."

It is important to note that Roe (1960) has commented upon the existence of certain internal and environmental factors that prevent full utilization of creative ability. This material can be considered as a corollary to the concept that mental health is necessary to creativity and that there are concomitant environmental factors of psychological safety and psychological freedom. Included in her discussion are such factors as emotional maladjustment, insufficient training in problem solving, inadequate development of curiosity, conflict between time available for one's career and for one's family, and inability to stand on one's own feet. The educational system under which the potentially creative individual is being trained may all too often place considerable value on the rightness or wrongness of a particular answer, on conformity to a given set of curriculum standards, and, as a result, discourage the inquiring mind. It may be difficult for a budding scientist, working with older associates of great renown, to present his own ideas, to disagree with the "experts" and to fight effectively for his concepts. A scientist who is intense and hard-working, capable of spending long hours on any given problem, may have little time for his family. Parenthetically it can be stated that although the question of economic security is not unique in the life of the creative individual, it can be an element that would act to dilute creativity. Money, security, position, status and the like can become effective counterattractions that would serve as detours or road blocks. The "hunger" associated with achievement for its own sake can be converted into such prosaic channels as the country club and the executive suite.

Roe (1958) has also presented a series of hypotheses which relate to the development of the creative individual. These hypotheses have not been fully tested to date, but they are presented here because they are both interesting and challenging. She believes that a person becomes what he is and chooses the career he does because of early attitudes in the home. What he is interested in doing has much to do with his career choice. If he is not permitted to develop interests in areas which call for creativity, then there is a strong possibility that the world has lost this potentiality. The problem as seen by Roe involves not merely the development of creativity but, even more important, how it can be prevented from being inhibited. An individual cannot be located for work in the scientific field if, from the outset, he is not interested in science. It appears that many potential scientists never enter its various fields because their lower socio-economic status did not provide them with the home atmosphere that permitted them a choice. A potentially creative individual, in short, may leave high school and end up pumping gas because he was not aware of other horizons, other areas from which he could make a career choice. It is assumed, then, that the home and its climate have much to do not only with interests but also with specific choices of a profession. Roe may be interpreted as suggesting that if an individual is creative, if he has developed an orientation which is not toward people, then in the home the climate may have tended to emphasize concepts, ideas, books, and achievement rather than the feelings of individual and interpersonal warmth. In the light of studies by Hagen (1959) and others, it is difficult to say whether this hypothesis and others of a similar nature can be accepted without further qualification or specificity.

In considering the "general emotional climate" of the family as described by Roe, several elements stand out which are worth taking into account when focusing attention on the development of the creative personality. There is the degree to which the family is concerned with the child and his career. This ranges from strong emotional involvement or concentration on the child, through considering the child as just a member of the family, to downright indifference. (See Figure 9-1.)

From these emotional attitudes there flow behavioral reflections that include overprotection or smothering, over-demandingness, rejection, neglect, acceptance, and love. The family, for example, might set extremely high standards of academic performance for the child. At times, such standards can be too high and the child

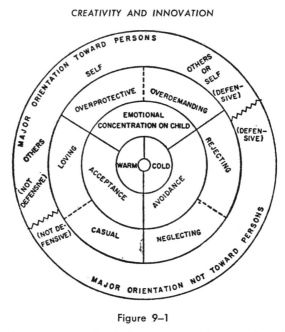

Figure 9–1

(After Roe, 1957, p. 216, as modified). Reproduced with permission of Dr. Roe and *Journal of Counseling Psychology.*

cannot hope to meet them. Although he is the center of attention, he may be considered as having let his family down. Hence he is rejected, just as he would have been accepted had he succeeded. The family climate, under other circumstances, might be of such a nature that there is a strong emphasis on relationships with people. Such emphasis is not necessarily in terms of parties or social affairs; it might make itself felt through family discussions of problems that involve people. Examples of these might be important questions of the time, such as racial integration, development of satisfactory school systems, housing, labor and management relationships, international affairs and the relationships between nations and their peoples. Roe would postulate that where in the developmental stage the emphasis was upon people and the relationships between people, then the occupational choice of the child in terms of the future would be people-oriented and would include, among others, such careers as physician, social worker, or personnel officer.

Hagen, in studying these hypotheses concerning the influence of family atmosphere on occupational interests and career development, concluded that only one of Roe's predictions—regarding the effect of the "casual family atmosphere"—appeared to have any empirical significance or could be verified. This study, of course, concerns itself with but one aspect of creativity—career choice—and does not consider whether, in fact, the individuals within a given career area are creative. Although it may not be possible as yet to demonstrate the accuracy of these theoretical constructs, which postulate a strong link between the experiences of childhood, the atmosphere of the family, and later occupational choices, there is enough face validity or "common-sense-ness" about them to conclude that "family climate" is a factor, even a strong factor, in the development of the creative individual.

A mentally healthy person is not defensive. He is not restricted intellectually by stereotyped concepts which are frequently fostered by a dull environment—by an environment which holds back the creative. He is thus capable of flights of imagination. It has been said that the creative tend to be less cautious about protecting themselves. In effect they do not have to limit their inventiveness, they are not afraid to be frank or to come up with an idea that is novel. Along lines already commented upon, Harmon (1956, 1958) believes that the creative individual must be able to manipulate ideas—his own as well as those of others. Creativity in such a framework would depend upon building from the old, on continuing from there, and on appropriate selectivity from the information that has been stored by the individual. There must, however, be an effective social climate which provides the opportunities for training and for the development of motivation and innovation.

Thomas considers three characteristics to be necessary for creativity, namely: flexibility, sensitivity, and motivation. Flexibility involves openness of mind. Here the individual is not satisfied with mere labeling or with pigeonholing and organizing ideas into "logic-tight compartments." Sensitivity permits him to note many things as he views the world around him—things not usually noticed by others. Motivation, as defined here, involves inquisitiveness—a restless urge or a drive to acquire knowledge. In many ways this is the most important element in the personality of the creative individual and one that is not easy to describe. In a research laboratory, the element of inquisitiveness can be illustrated by the scientist who is never satisfied, who is interested in finding out why certain factors appear to be connected with a frequency that is better than chance. The creative individual also has the capacity for teamwork, and he is well-trained and intellectually well-disciplined. Teamwork in the research efforts of today is needed because of the complexity and specialization found in the various fields of science. Thomas is convinced that the creative person, of necessity, must be well-trained in his field of endeavor so that he can depend upon a strong background of experience in producing solutions to complex problems. Another vital aspect of creativity is imagination, related in many ways to flexibility and the manipulation of ideas.

Although the above elements are different and distinct, they appear to be closely interacting, each contributing to and gaining strength from the other.

In describing the personality of the creative individual, many of the authors already referred to—and others whose work will be mentioned later—have ascribed to the creative individual traits presented under the following headings: (1) In relation to others, (2) In job attitudes, (3) Attitudes toward self, and, (4) Other characteristics. The listing which follows is not intended to be all-inclusive. It does, however, cover those traits which, in the opinion of the present author, appear to be most significant.

(1) *In relation to others:*
    (a) Not a joiner.
    (b) Few close friends.
    (c) Independent.
    (d) Dominant.
    (e) Assertive, bold, courageous.
    (f) Little interest in interpersonal relations.
    (g) Independence from parents.
    (h) Independence of judgment, especially under pressure.
    (i) Conventional morality.
(2) *In job attitudes:*
    (a) Preference for things and ideas to people.
    (b) High regard for intellectual interests.

     (c) Less emphasis on and value in job security.

     (d) Less enjoyment in and satisfaction from detail work and routine.

     (e) High level of resourcefulness and adaptability.

     (f) Sceptical.

     (g) Precise, critical.

     (h) Honesty, integrity.

     (i) Ability to toy with elements—capacity to be puzzled.

     (j) High tolerance for ambiguity.

     (k) Persistence.

     (l) Emphasis on theoretical values.

(3) *Attitudes toward self:*

     (a) Introspective, egocentric, internally preoccupied.

     (b) Openness to new experiences.

     (c) Less in need to protect self.

     (d) Great awareness of self.

     (e) Inner maturity.

     (f) Great ego strength, strength of character.

     (g) Highly responsive emotionally.

     (h) Less emotionally stable.

     (i) Less self-acceptance.

(4) *Other characteristics:*

     (a) Spontaneity, enthusiasm.

     (b) Stubbornness.

     (c) Originality.

     (d) Adventurousness.

     (e) High excitability and irritability.

     (f) Compulsivity.

     (g) Impulsivity.

     (h) Complexity as a person.

     (i) Anxiety.

When the traits listed above are considered carefully, it is evident that there are some which are in many ways contradictory. In dealing with a structure as complex as that of the creative personality where there is an element of uniqueness, it is difficult enough to describe even the major facets of such an individual's make-up. Inconsistencies can therefore be expected depending on the groups studied, their educational backgrounds and training, and on the environment in which they labor.

Knapp in his study of college-level science majors, as opposed to majors in non-sciences, obtained results which can be interpreted as illustrating some of the theories already presented. In the main, the science majors came from rural areas and from lower-and middle-class families. They appeared to be more reserved in their relations with others, to be relatively unimaginative in the area of structured human relations, and to be better adjusted and freer in handling their emotional impulses. The science major appeared to be non-aggressive and to avoid the emotional intensity involved in direct relationships with others.

Guilford (1960), in his extensive studies in the area of creativity, has emphasized the intellectual aspects of the creative individual. He has taken this position not because he believes that this aspect is the sole—or even the primary—one, but also because in large measure intellectual abilities determine what a "scientist is *able* to do." What is of great value here are the ratings of intellectual factors as given by scientists themselves. Although it might have been expected that the ability to adapt a familiar object to an entirely new use would be ranked first, this ability ranked fifth behind such factors as: arriving at original solutions by abandoning conventional techniques, looking beyond the obvious, and recognizing the basic relationships involved in a problem before its solution. In his work, flexibility was also referred to as an important element in creative thought—involving in part the ability to restructure problems to produce a diversity of ideas. Chapter 12, "Tests for Creativity," covers in some detail the tests used by Guilford in his study. They are therefore not discussed further here.

Identification and Measurement of the Creative Personality

In outlining the several theories regarding the creative personality, reference has been made to methods by which they have been or could be tested. As another *a priori* measure of creativity, it has been suggested that the kinds of behavior believed to accompany creativity could be determined by judgmental processes. Here judges are asked to list behaviors they believe to be characteristic of the creative act, or which are a necessary part of creativity. Further, when there is specified agreement on some of these behaviors, ratings of individuals can be obtained to indicate the presence or absence of such behavior when they are dealing with a creative act.

Sprecher utilized this approach in setting up an experimental form to get at "possible characteristics of creative research scientists." He asked that (1) items be marked as characteristic of the creative research scientist, not characteristic, or not important; (2) that items characteristic of the creative scientist be ranked; and, (3) that items not characteristic be ranked. The results, based on a small sample, are not conclusive. The technique itself, however, is one that appears to be worth pursuing further. This approach was utilized by Sprecher to verify his hypothesis that creativity involved ideas, work habits, and opportunity. It is evidently not just a question of thinking of a creative person as one who has new or novel ideas. It is also a question of his being able to get the work done—of obtaining "closure," as it were.

Over the years, various personality tests have been utilized as possible predictors of creativity. In most instances, they have been validated against criteria known to be characteristic of creativity. As a result, several interesting and useful predictors of creativity have emerged. Perhaps the most ambitious undertaking of this nature was that of Cattell (1960b). He obtained biographies of historic personages noted for their inventiveness and creativity. Utilizing the Personality Factors he had himself developed, he was able to utilize bibliographical material to arrive at a description of the creative individual. (The 16 Personality Factor Tests, developed by Cattell, are discussed in some detail in Chapter 12.)

The description of the creative individual arrived at by the use of bibliographical material contained such phrases as: "withdrawn," "internally preoccupied," "highly intelligent," "lacking in humility," "inhibited," and the like. Although this aspect of Cattell's work provides some clues regarding elements to be found in the creative personality, in addition to starting points for hypotheses to be tested further, the most challenging aspect of his work in this field has involved the administration of these tests to exceptionally productive research scientists in physics, biology, and psychology.

After examination of the data thus obtained, he constructed a combined personality profile. This profile describes—for this group at least—the creative individual.

The purpose of such a study was threefold: (1) to compare the personality of the research worker with that of the average person; (2) to compare the personality with that of someone of equal intelligence who had made a name for himself in administration or teaching; and (3) to determine how the personality of such a research worker compared with that of a creative, innovating, constructive individual who had attained eminence in such radically different areas as literature or the decorative arts.

The results are both interesting and significant. The personality of the researcher, as compared with the average man, shows the scientist to be withdrawn, internally preoccupied, more intelligent, more dominant, and more inhibited. The scientific groups so measured generally appeared to be quite similar. In addition, there was much similarity between the research groups and those in the administrative and teaching fields. The researchers, however, were more withdrawn, "less emotionally stable, more self-sufficient, more bohemian, and more radical" than the successful teachers and administrators. The scientists and the artists, finally, can be considered on the basis of these results as belonging to the same family group. Under these circumstances Cattell concluded that the various types of creative individuals considered were similar enough, notwithstanding divergencies between fields, to indicate that there *is* such an entity as "the creative personality."

Others have utilized tests of personality to obtain a picture of the creative individual. Among these was Bloom (1956), who examined good and poor problem solvers to determine the crucial elements that made them different. Variations were found in terms of how they tackled the problems, how they analyzed the material, how they brought significant material to bear, and how they used a systematic approach in arriving at solutions. Of equal importance, however, were the differences in terms of the confidence the groups had in their own ability and in their desire to solve the problems. Personality, then, played an important part in differentiating between the two groups.

Interests and attitudes have frequently been found to play an extremely important role. This was borne out by Saunders when, using various novel tests, he examined dimensions of the creative personality. Among his tests were several involving interests. In studying engineers in five industrial organizations, he found definite differences between the several types of engineers. For example, the research group *per se* had the highest interest in "ideas" and the lowest interest in the economic area. Sales engineers, on the other hand, had the highest interest in the economic area and the lowest interest in "ideas." In further studying personality *per se,* several questionnaires were used in an attempt to verify such hunches as: "The more talkative individual is to be found in the salesman group, while those in the strictly research group would like to think more." In the test designed to tap the latter area, items such as "Are you inclined to analyze the motives of others?" were included. The strictly research group scored in the predicted manner although, interestingly enough, scientists in an industrial setting seemed to be rated higher when they were able to express themselves and present their ideas in an effective manner.

Projective techniques have been frequently utilized to assess the personality of the creative individual. Such techniques are based in large part on the theory that what someone sees in ambiguous or vague figures, such as inkblots, is a reflection of his own personality. Roe has made extensive and effective use of projective techniques in determining what elements are involved in the personality of the research scientist and in studying the relationship of personality to vocational choice and career success. She has studied various groups of researchers, among them eminent research biologists (1951). The study of the latter involved the collection of life history data, a careful review of the biologists' published work, and a discussion with the researchers as to the sequence in which his work was developed. In addition, three psychological tests were administered to each subject. Two of these tests were projective in nature: the Rorschach and the Thematic Apperception Test.

The Rorschach is the classical and famous "inkblot" test which has been effectively utilized in determining how well an individual can handle a completely unstructured situation in which no "right" or "wrong" answers are involved, and where free use of the imagination can be tapped. The Thematic Apperception Test consists of

a number of vague pictures concerning which the subject is asked
to develop a story. These stories can be presented orally, or they
can be written out. The pictures are semi-structured in nature and
are vague enough to permit use of the imagination on the part of
the subject. The stories and other data obtained allow the psychologist to explore such areas as inter-personal relationships, motivation, possible emotional conflict, and the like. Since this particular
study emphasized quality and extensiveness of information, it was
of necessity limited to twenty research biologists. Utilizing the
group form of the Rorschach, it was also possible to sample university faculties in biology for comparison group purposes.

The results of this study are quite interesting, reflecting characteristics which are consistent and which would not be found in
adults picked at random from the general population. The research
biologists were able to perceive aspects of a situation which are not
usually commented upon. They were, in short, more sensitive. Although they did not appear to become involved in deep emotional
relationships with others, such relationships were at least smooth.
Not basically aggressive, neither were they the type that could be
pushed around. They were definitely interested in trying to find
out what makes things tick, but not necessarily in changing things.
The research biologists were not very outgoing in the social sense
of the word, and they exhibited strong intellectual control in handling interpersonal relationships. As a group they appear to be
more objective than most, and exhibit good judgment. In comparing
the research biologists with a total of 188 university biologists, a
similar pattern was found. In this latter group, however, there was
somewhat less intellectual control.

Barron (1956), as part of an extensive program designed to identify individuals who consistently performed creatively or with originality, utilized the Rorschach, the Thematic Apperception Test
and a set of inkblots devised by himself. Indications of originality
or creativity were reflected in the unusualness of the kinds of responses given to the projective material utilized. By definition,
responses to be considered original would have to be uncommon.
They would appear, for example, perhaps only once in a hundred
testings. Such responses, moreover, would at the same time "be
adaptive to reality," straightforward, and not weird. The results of

this aspect of the study were not startling statistically. The strong impression was obtained, however, that in dealing with originality, one is faced with a complex problem, difficult to define and hence difficult to measure.

This particular study went on to evaluate several other hypotheses or hunches of the following type: that individuals who are original prefer dealing with complex problems; that personality-wise they are more complex; that they are more independent in making judgments; that they are more self-assertive; and that they do not hesitate to consider new and unusual ideas. Included among the tests used to investigate these hypotheses were the Barron-Welsh Art Scale (where a "preference for complex asymmetrical figures" earns the subjects a high score), a psychiatric interview covering the life history of the individual, and the Social Dominance Scale of the California Personality Inventory. This scale involves measurement of dominance in real life social situations. From the results of the study it would appear that people who are original prefer complexity; that they are more complex in terms of their personality structure; that they are more independent in their judgments; and that they are more self-assertive and dominant. Moreover, they are quite capable of becoming interested in ideas which are unusual, novel, and even at times socially tabu.

The Development of the Creative Personality

As can be deduced from the material presented thus far, many elements influence the development of the creative personality—both that which exists and that which is potential. Some factors may tend to stifle creativity that is burgeoning, while others may bring out latent creativity that has yet to be manifested. Among the relevant elements are those environmental factors that might well include the temper of the times, immediate environmental conditions, and even inanimate influences. These influences are not restricted to people in the immediate environment or to the individual himself. They may also involve the existence of appropriate equipment and tools.

Besides the emotional needs essential to the development of creativity and the need to recognize the individual as creative, other, physical needs must also be fulfilled. Thomas (1960) has indicated that individuals "will express their creativity to the extent that management provides them with the necessary tools of the trade." Since Chapter 11, "Creative Climate," covers this area in considerable detail, little will be mentioned concerning it here. Beyond the physical needs required for such a climate, however, there are other elements (some of which may be difficult to define) which go into the establishment of a "research atmosphere"—an atmosphere which is basic if creativity is to bloom in any setting. Included among such elements is the presence of other topnotch scientists whose work provides mutual stimulation, competition, and an opportunity for the informal "trying-it-on-for-size" of new and unusual ideas. It is also obvious that if the creative personality is as complex as it appears to be—and if one cannot come up with "custom-made" creative scientists fitting a specific mold—there must be tolerance, which will permit utilization of the unusual or different individual who is at the same time creative or potentially creative. In our culture there is considerable emphasis on "ability to relate to others." Some creative persons are not interested in relating in this sense of the word.

Several of the personality factors that have been found in the creative individual during the developmental stage have a strong environmental element, and hence they need nurturing. Although it would be unnecessary to guide a child through all his waking moments, certain factors can be kept in mind which could in effect maximize the possibility of creative development. A child needs to be allowed to develop autonomy, the ability to control his own destiny, to be able to make decisions affecting his own life. He needs to be encouraged to show curiosity and to learn to explore in order to satisfy his curiosity. "Clinical inquisitiveness" is a desire to find out *why* certain things appear to occur in conjunction with each other. A child also needs to be taught to value knowledge and learning.

Roe (1957, 1960) has covered this area quite well in her theoretical propositions regarding the effect upon the development of the creative personality of the culture in which an individual grows up, particularly as this culture affects his interests and attitudes. In this developmental phase, the various groups to which a person belongs or, more important, to which he does not belong, can affect his potential for creativity. By his very brilliance and interest in what is novel he may find himself regarded as a deviate and hence not acceptable as a member of groups that may characterize his particular school. As a member of a minority, or even as a single individual, he might well develop habits which could be considered non-social in nature. He just does not want to mix with people because at one time "they" didn't want him.

Today there is considerable concern over our school system and whether or not, in competition with the Communist world, we are training the scientists required of the space age. The attitudes of teachers as a reflection in large measure of the theories of educators, affect the potentially creative individual. If he is permitted to be different, fine! If, however, he has to conform, then there is a problem. Again, when it comes to curiosity—"Why, daddy?"— there is all too often a tendency to ignore the question, or, more important, to indicate that curiosity is not an acceptable attribute. Such elements affect the development of any individual; they can, and often do, make the difference between creativity and mere technical competence.

Another aspect of the development and growth of the creative personality involves the influence of other individuals upon him. In general it can be assumed that the creative individual usually functions, in at least some degree, in relation to others and that he cannot function for or by himself alone. This statement is related to concepts which have already been commented upon, which in general indicate that the creative person, as do others, needs to be loved, appreciated, understood, and recognized. New ideas, or new ways of looking at old ideas, frequently come from discussions between individuals. It is not important whether or not these discussions take place in a formal forum or workshop situation, or in the "bull session" which results when individuals of like interests get together. Creativity is not solely subjective in nature but rather the result of interaction between the individual and his world (May in Anderson, 1959). Social interaction, then, appears to be an essential element in creativity. All too often research efforts are limited by continuing with the same approach—an approach which in terms of the problem at hand is not applicable. A fresh viewpoint, a new approach, a simple answer frequently spring from discussions with others. This opportunity for interchange of ideas is a necessary element in the climate for creativity, or the research atmosphere. Such an atmosphere, further, provides a medium for indicating to the research scientist that what he is doing is appreciated. Since he has the opinions of others, he is not functioning in a vacuum, and is not solely dependent on his own criteria of accomplishment.

When working with creative or potentially creative individuals in the world of business, it should be remembered that we are dealing not with machines but with human beings—particularly with human beings who, in the best of all possible worlds, are still in limited supply. McPherson has indicated quite succinctly the elements that can be considered by management in a self-evaluation of their relationships with creative people. These elements involve such factors as: (1) providing or delegating freedom to the scientist; (2) providing an atmosphere where, for example, the scientist has something to say about his own areas of research, where his ideas are truly welcomed, where there is no arbitrary evaluation of his worth based solely on production; and (3) providing opportunities for the scientist to discuss his ideas with management. A creative individual can lose his touch, his sharpness, and become satisfied with a little less than the best, depending upon the atmosphere where he is employed. His ability to function as an effective member of a research team can be affected by supervisors or organizations in paying mere lip-service both to the concept of teamwork and to creativity. Simply pronouncing the words "teamwork" or "creativity" is not enough. The emotional atmosphere must truly reflect them. The tone must be set by supervisors and management.

It should not be assumed that the creative individual is merely being acted upon in passive fashion. The results of various research efforts and the theoretical propositions already offered indicate that environmental factors cannot be ignored as they have so often been in the past. This chapter has necessarily reflected this emphasis. The stereotyped concept of the inventor working by himself in a garage is the exception rather than the rule. A definite factor in creativity, however, is the individual himself, his ability, and his own activity or lack of it.

An individual is able to influence his own creative ability by his own behavior, interests, and needs. This has been demonstrated by

Bloom (1956), and it has been agreed by other eminent psychologists that such elements are not only relevant but even crucial variables in a person's performance. Scientists work extremely hard at their jobs. They are interested in achievement for its own sake, in accomplishment, although they do not ignore other rewards such as prestige and financial return. In a sense they are always searching for what is beyond the next mountain and they have the patience that is a necessary concomitant of such searching.

This inner drive appears to make the difference in the development of the creative individual. He does not stipulate for himself a 40-hour week, a definite time to eat lunch, nor allocate specific periods for recreation. The external factors that have been discussed assist in maximizing creativity and in providing opportunities for individuals to be creative. However, without the inner drive, the push, the "hunger," these factors would be mere tinsel and there would be no truly creative workers. These elements of drive, interest in work, and motivation appear to be the key factors which characterize creativity.

Summary and Conclusions

One is impressed by the thesis that mental health—as far as the creative personality is concerned—appears to involve a "looseness" which permits the individual to function without undue concern over what others think about him. This condition then permits him to consider freely the ideas that come to him, to toy with them as it were, and not be blocked in considering them because of rigidity or inflexibility. The creative individual can not only have a "new idea," but he can also appreciate such an idea and, more important, recognize it as such.

Yet with all the positive personality features associated with creativity, there are some which also can be considered as negative or as having a negative aspect. The creative person is an *independent* thinker and an *independent* doer. At the same time, in our culture it is not always easy clearly to define what is meant by this adjective. In being independent, one needs to avoid being objectionable and to learn to tolerate differences of opinion. Personal stumbling blocks can adversely affect creativity. If one insists on one's right to think as one believes, this can reflect the independence associated with creativity. At the same time, however, it could reflect "pig-headedness" and rigidity—possibly resulting in strong negative reactions from professional confreres and an associated damping of one's own creative efforts.

Neurotic symptoms of varying degrees can have a positive as well as a limiting effect on creativity. In the limiting sense they represent in no small part a draining of energy, a distraction, which may affect any of the elements that appear essential to the creative effort. It can readily be seen that excessive concern about whether one is right or wrong in taking a given course of action may result in indecisiveness and inaction. Yet the ability to function without too much concern for what others think or feel has strong positive aspects. The fact that in many creative individuals personality characteristics can be found that fit no set pattern—or are even paradoxical in their implications—reflects the complexity of the problem and the uniqueness of such individuals.

In considering the personality of the creative individual, much stress has been placed upon external factors. This is not because the individual himself is a non-crucial element in the total picture, but because external factors have much to do with maximizing creative potentialities and because such factors have all too often been ignored. Mental health is the result of reaction in an environment, and is not static. Hence our concern with factors that affect the development of the creative individual—including family and research climates. Creativity, then, can either be fostered or it can be inhibited. The creative individual is at his best when he can be himself, when he is able to entertain new and novel ideas and do something about them. He must feel it is not wrong to be different.

Various hypotheses have been presented regarding the essential elements connected with the creative personality. It seems clear that such a personality exists. As yet, however, only a few of the pieces of the mosaic have been put in place. In the developmental stage or, more properly in the early developmental stage, as a child, the child with potentiality for creativity can be affected by such factors as parental attitude and school atmosphere. In order to become creative, he needs to be curious and to learn how to explore to satisfy his curiosity. Overemphasis on the "school answer," insistence on conforming with approaches which were "good enough for grandfather" and other similar restricting attitudes on the part of parent or teacher can result in dullness and unimaginative conformity in even the most potentially creative child. The degree to which the members of the family are concerned about him, the standards of performance they set, and their own fields of interest as reflected in family conversations, are factors which apparently affect the personality and possibly the career choice of the child. The research atmosphere or the climate within which the potentially creative child later works as an adult, also affects his further development. If it is possible for him to express his ideas without restriction, if he is able to discuss his research problems with colleagues, if his role is accepted, then conditions are propitious for real fulfillment of early promise.

The creative individual reveals internal factors which are quite important and which are a reflection of his mental health. It is not only a question of an end product of his activity that is satisfying to others but, even more important, of his own satisfaction with what he has created. Involved here is confidence in his own ability, the perceiving of aspects of a situation which are not usually commented upon by others, frankness, flexibility, a restless urge to acquire new knowledge, a capacity for team work, the ability to manipulate ideas imaginatively, good work habits, and the ability to get things done.

The creative person is a hard worker, frequently placing his work and achievement above all else. He is more interested in ideas than in people. Several traits not already mentioned have been found in such people, namely: independence of judgment, particularly under pressure; assertiveness, boldness and courage; high level of resourcefulness and adaptability; capacity to be puzzled; openness to new experiences; and enthusiasm. Scientists themselves in rating characteristics of a good scientist included as their main choices the following: the ability to arrive at original solutions by abandoning conventional techniques, the capacity to look beyond the obvious, and the recognizing of basic relationships involved in a problem before its solution.

PART II

PUTTING CREATIVITY TO WORK

10. GROUP AND INDIVIDUAL AIDS

The preceding chapters have explored the creative personality and process, and related aspects of the knowledge of creativity. Many opportunities have been taken to suggest creative aids, such as to take time for and note insights, and to understand and utilize symbolization. Besides these, other creative aids will have occurred to the reader, either because they are implicit in the material, or as a result of thoughtful derivation from it. Examples are: develop creative traits, overcome blocks and fixations, prepare well and diversely, give the creative process a chance.

More direct application of this knowledge of how to put creativity to work will now be sought. One of the points to be emphasized will be not to hesitate to apply the principles of creativity. Many of these points are well established and generally accepted, but are just as generally ignored. There must be times of quiet for insight, a sympathetic willingness to listen, and a policy of adequate reward—these are acknowledged, and ignored, by management and by society in dealing with a creator. And indeed, the creator fares scarcely better at his own hands, permitting himself to be held back by inadequate preparation, failure to make opportunities for the creative stages, and unwillingness to develop useful traits.

In this chapter, ideas and procedures that have been developed by various workers to promote creativity will be taken up. They will have the form of group methods with formalized rules; organized knowledge of the blocks to individual progress; and check lists and other techniques used by individuals in problem solution. Group methods will be discussed first, then individual methods.

The present writer will add his own suggestion for individual and group furtherance of creative activity by an organized system. This scheme is adaptable for individuals and for small or large groups; it utilizes meticulous polypreparation, specific interest-priming efforts, opportunity for incubation and insight, and for credit and reward.

All participants have a chance to be heard, the shy and inarticulate as well as the forceful. Decision is not to all intents and purposes actualized before all the ideas are in, as is so often the case. The exploration of important side issues which may arise has its full place.

GROUP AIDS

There are two aspects to this subject. The first is group action to a creative end. The second is group sponsorship to teach creativity —usually to members who jointly practice the methods.

Group Creation

Before considering the strengths and weaknesses of the various procedures and techniques employed at the present time, certain basics in group operations directed to problem solving must be emphasized.

(1) The $A + B \rightarrow C$ process is solo, and occurs in the mind of one man. Groups may spark ideas, but only individuals *have* them. The function of the group may be to restructure A and furnish B for the man who enunciates the answer C. The group may then hitch-hike on C, modifying it to C'.

(2) In any group meeting, there is a limited time and idea space. The larger the group, the less free space per person. Since there is not enough freedom to accommodate all, the more forceful, rather than the more creative, personalities tend to garner this space. Since he lacks opportunity, the motivation of the person of low power but high competence suffers.

(3) The withering breath of criticism, directed against new ideas, is never completely controlled except in the individual mind.

(4) The group has best success when it has a leader who obtains space for minority views, and for less articulate men to express themselves. *There is no more important function of the leader.* Otherwise, the more forceful men, having already expressed their ideas, are impatient to proceed to judgment, and at once move in that direction. Groups lose a multiplicity of opinions in too rapid progress to judgment. They lose suggestions of shy members; they lose wild suggestions. Unlike the individual, they have no space for a

brilliant new suggestion once the stage of judgment and decision has begun.

Collaboration extending over years is very commonly found in most lines of creative work. Examples are Gilbert and Sullivan, Rodgers and Hammerstein, Mozart and da Ponte, Wordsworth and Coleridge. Sometimes the collaborators do the entire job together. Sometimes the task is divided into parts, and each collaborator does a part, though the give and take of their creative thinking is evident throughout the whole. With a team like librettist and composer, each brings a special creative skill—and these are the best examples of the genre of cooperation so far as creativity is concerned. In chemistry, much work is done by the collaboration of professor and graduate student, or supervisor and directed subordinate. In these training relationships, the junior should also be contributing to the creative thought, at least if his instruction is to be at all effective. In invention, co-authorship is very common, where the second man added something to implement or extend the first one's idea. Collaborative authorship of papers is commonest in chemistry, often running to four or five names, or even more. Sole authorship is commoner in the field of physics, and is the rule in mathematics and psychology.

Additionally, there are the many schools, or creative groups, that expanded outward from a creative and forceful initiator: the Lewis group, Kelvin's men, the Impressionist school, or the Greek Peripatetics. In these cases, each man brought a larger or smaller contribution, but uniquely his own, to swell the total.

"Not much, but still a little more,
Than what was in the world before."

Members serve these functions in group problem solving:

Energizer.
Information seeker.
Information giver.
Initiator-contributor.
Elaborator.
Opinion giver.
Evaluator-critic.

Harmonizer.

Expediter.

Encourager.

In recent years, certain formal systems for group creation, with organized rules, have gained prominence. The best known is brainstorming.

Brainstorming

The brainstorming method, already discussed briefly, has been developed and described by Alex Osborn in his important book, "Applied Imagination," probably the most widely used single text for creative thinking courses. In brainstorming sessions, a group of individuals, usually 5 to 12, develops ideas concerning a problem for a period of a few minutes to an hour, under the leadership of a chairman. The chairman announces the problem as succinctly as possible. The group then generates ideas, and in doing so subscribes to these rules:

(1) Criticism of an idea is absolutely barred.
(2) But its modification or combination with another idea is encouraged.
(3) Quantity of ideas is sought.
(4) Unusual, remote, or wild ideas are sought.

It is emphasized that a wild and apparently unworkable idea expressed by one participant may spark in another either the way to make it work, or a workable modification. The simple rules are also recommended for *individual* brainstorming of a difficulty.

The wild ideas, of course, are useful because they open up new directions of exploration. The value of this in working toward solution has been discussed at length in Chapter 4.

The chairman must enforce the rule to bar criticism; must thwart "idea selling"; must restrain the comedian. If the session begins to run down, he must stimulate with an idea or new direction of his own. He closes the session when fatigue comes.

Partial transcripts of brainstorming sessions have been published by Charles H. Clark in his book, "Brainstorming." A verbatim transcript was published in *Printer's Ink* * of a 45-minute session moder-

---

* Feb. 17, 1956, p. 28 ff.

ated by Willard Pleuthner on the problem of "having people in the office and plant be good personal salesmen for company products to friends, neighbors, relatives, and nearby store outlets." A total of 104 ideas was developed. The nature of these was: Give talks about the company to union members and office employees in business hours; direct different kinds of material to employees' wives; encourage employees to buy and use products, and devise means to make this consumption tastefully conspicuous; generally, make the employees happier, with reciprocation toward company products one implicit expectation.

The earliest comments in the transcript will be considered in detail:

> The first thought was *"talks* by salesmen."
>
> Items 2-4 were other "salesmen" ideas.
>
> Item 5, a new departure, was "show product in *Company President's* home."
>
> "Home" suggested item 6, send copy to *wives.*
>
> Item 7, a "wife" idea.
>
> Item 8, market research products to employees.
>
> Item 9, a "market research employees" idea.
>
> Item 10, a combination, Company President writes letter to employee wives.
>
> Item 11, Undoubtedly suggested by gifts of products in market research work, was to *give* new employees Company products.
>
> Items 12-13, "gifts to employees" ideas.
>
> Item 14, Give new products to employees first, by letter to home.
>
> Items 15, 17, 18, 19, 20 are "gift" variants.
>
> Item 21 is back to "presentation."
>
> Item 22 is "gift."
>
> Items 23, 24, 26 are, "brainstorm this very question with groups of employees."

So the session continued. Item 29 was "use wives of employees for tests," hardly new in view of item 9. Item 39 was another "President writes." Item 48 was a twist, "employees to use products as gifts on their part."

A few themes like Presentation, Company President, Wives, Gifts are established, and worked and reworked, sometimes repetitiously, sometimes to new purpose. This process is much like preparation, when new directions to study are uncovered and explored. In brainstorming, the more creative minds establish the new themes; the less creative minds develop combinations within them.

Very large numbers of people have brainstormed a problem at the same time by means of "Phillips 66 Buzz Sessions." The large group is divided into many small ones. These each elect a chairman, brainstorm the problem, and select their one best idea to be presented to the whole group. This adaptation of brainstorming was originated by President J. Donald Phillips of Hillsdale College to serve several purposes. The first is to use all the minds in a large group to participate in an attack on a problem. The plan here is to *get all possible ideas*. The second purpose is to pave the way for all to have the opportunity to take part. Many people are unwilling to speak up in a large group, nor is there time for all of them to do so if they would. The idea here is to *grant maximum participation*. A third intent is to *instruct large groups* of people at one time on the technique of brainstorming, and show them the possibilities. Many may never in their lives before have tried to assemble a list of ideas without concomitant criticism.

"Buzz Sessions" have also been used to develop questions for a question-and-answer session after a talk or presentation. Again, the small groups discuss for five minutes, and each comes up with the one best query it can produce.

In the aftermath of brainstorming, the ideas are scanned, in a strictly judicial session. The poor ideas are rejected, and the good ones selected and acted on. The basic of brainstorming, then, is to avoid trying to do the creative and the judicial at the same time, but rather to do them in separate sessions.

Naturally, brainstorming is a part of other creative techniques. The Hotpoint Company has reported use of some interesting brainstorming variants:

(1) *The Waste Not method*. The group is shown a plant discard —say a small packing box. Uses are brainstormed.

(2) *The And-Also method*. A suggestion is made. Each man fol-

lowing adds to it, saying, in effect, "Yes, and also this would make it even more effective."

(3) *The Tear Down technique*. This has been called brainstorming in reverse. The object of the conference is "to think of all the possible limitations or failings of the specific product" under consideration. Brainstorming rules apply. Afterwards, the long list of weaknesses is analyzed with a view to improvements and corrections.

The Gordon Method

One rather wide and significant deviation from brainstorming is that practised by William J. Gordon of Arthur D. Little, Inc. He organized a six-member design-synthesis group to invent machines. This group learned to work together with him as leader. At first, Gordon alone knew the real problem at the start of a meeting. At the beginning, he would extrapolate from the problem all the way back to the extremely general and abstract case of which it was a concrete and mechanical example. For example, wanting a new lawn mower, he would simply say, "The question today is separation." As discussion proceeded, he would watch for opportunities to narrow and guide it, meanwhile developing a vast association field to be channelled to the specific job when announced. Development in detail would then follow, the process requiring more, often much more, than three hours.

A particular meeting was detailed by Gordon in an article in the *Harvard Business Review*, November 1956. The goal was exceptionally general: "invent something which fills a real need." The discussion proceeded as shown in Table 10–1 (stages interpreted by the present writer).

The group consisted of the following men besides Gordon:

> A production specialist.
> A mechanical engineer designer.
> An artist with experience in electronics and
>   industrial engineering.
> A chemical engineer and sculptor.
> A private inventor and expert at machining.
> A liaison man between Gordon and the group.

TABLE 10–1

Stage	Specific Discussion
Preparation	Needs of modern man vs. caveman. Caveman did everything himself.
Narrowing	Do it yourself is modern man's attempt to achieve something concrete.
Restructuring	Design the optimum power tool group set-up to help him.
Insight	Apply "lazy Susan" principle.
Verification	Each "lazy Susan" segment carries a tool and its own working surface. Proceed to actual details and specific design, raising and answering objections along the way.

A single Gordon session does not provide opportunity for incubation; but often there are several sessions, at intervals, which do so. The other creative stages are evident, as noted by the present author.

Gordon emphasizes the need for freedom from criticism of comments made in the sessions. In their three-hour duration discipline is necessary to keep the ball rolling when only the leader knows the goal. He must be ready with help and encouragement, and be watchful to guide the discussion naturally in the direction of the desired objective. Fatigue helps some participants, to the extent that it loosens inhibitions. The goal may be revealed in an atmosphere of high excitement.

The procedure requires an exceptional leader. The group under Gordon has developed:

> A new type of can opener.
> A radically different gasoline pump.
> Improved fishing lures.
> A new razor.
> A new tooth brush.
> A plastic cup coating machine.

The idea of starting with basics far removed from the *specific* intent represents a new approach, similar, however, to the concept of polypreparation, and to the input-output process to be described below. Starting with basics is bound to enrich the associative material available for the problems.

The achievements of the Gordon method are practical inventions —a little too practical and a little too limited. The reason is that creative principles are violated. Opportunity for incubation is denied, in the first session at least. Opportunity to restructure the problem is scarcely available when five-sixths of the creative group do not know what the problem is. It should be possible, with practise, for the Gordon participants to know the problem and still begin the attack from a general point of view. Gordon himself believes that creation proceeds by an oscillation between involvement with the problem and detachment from it so that it can be scanned from a distance. Such alternation can only begin when the goal is known and the problem defined and grappled with by each individual.

The important features of the Gordon method are (1) finding certain rare leadership skills; and (2) starting with a basic concept —in the ballpark, but deep in the outfield.

Teaching and Developing Creativity

A number of companies have designed methods and training courses to enhance creative thinking by their employees. A continuing effort is that of the General Electric Company. Since 1937, men showing creative promise during the first months of employment have had the opportunity to join the company's creative engineering group. The methods of this group have been described by its leaders in the *General Electric Review* and elsewhere. Throughout the course, both theoretical and practical aspects are emphasized. In the first six months, knowledge of creative theory as viewed by Guth, von Fange, and Osborn, is presented. Homework problems deal with engineering fundamentals, with design questions of interest to the company, and with specific model work. The curriculum has ten elements: *

(1) *Orientation.* Course administration and history, policy, salary procedures, facilities.

---

* Reprinted by special permission, *Factory Management and Maintenance,* May, 1956. Copyright McGraw-Hill Publishing Company.

(2) *Creative philosophy.* Using Osborn's "Applied Imagination," plus lectures and reading, students see, hear, practice idea-building.

(3) *Engineering fundamentals.* Emphasis on physical laws of engineering, empirical equations, electronics, measurements, and control systems.

(4) *Unusual materials and processes.* Experts tell students about such things as radioisotopes and nucleonics so that these factors may be included in idea creation.

(5) *Useful basic components and devices.* Knowing how certain devices work (like thyratrons, thermistors) broadens the brain storehouse.

(6) *Company services and organization.* This tells how to use staff assistance from the patent, purchasing, and traffic departments.

(7) *Presentation of ideas.* "One of the weakest points of young engineers is their inability to describe effectively and to sell ideas, whether in writing or orally." This course gives practice in this area.

(8) *Human relations.* An understanding of human relations and some of the techniques of handling people are woven into the course.

(9) *Homework problems.* About 15 to 20 hours of each week. Aim is to get at least eight workable solutions to each problem presented.

(10) *Model-building project.* This 5-week project completes the first phase of the course. In a way, it is like a thesis for a master's degree.

In the second phase of the course, lasting 18 months, the development of ideas to final form is studied and practised, according to this sequence:

> Recognize
> Define
> Search
> Evaluate
> _____
> Select
> Make preliminary design
> Test and evaluate
> _____
> Follow through.

There is constant association on the job with creative senior engineers. Emphasized are such tenets as, get eight solutions to the problem; use the input-output technique.

The "input-output technique" puts the problem in the form of a dynamic system comprising input, output, and specifications. These are generalized, and questions are asked about all three in such a way as to suggest variant approaches to answers. As an example, if an improved electric clothes dryer is the problem, the input is electricity, the output dry clothes; or by finer analysis, the input is electric heat, the output is evaporated water, or water vapor. The specifications are according to the objective, which might be a faster machine. Can the output solve the problem directly? Let the evolved water vapor be conducted over an indicator which switches the machine off when the vapor reaches a predetermined low concentration. Thus, in this method, the output is utilized as a new input aimed toward the specified objective.

In the AC Spark Plug creativity program, the man is first tested, then given the creativity course, then tested again. In the creativity test, the man has 80 minutes to answer 25 questions split into 5 groups, including the familiar "uses or improvement of a common object," or the "consequences of a described situation." The subsequent course includes:

> History and objectives.
> Judicial vs. creative thinking.
> Factors affecting creativity.
> Factors promoting or inhibiting creativity.
> Training the mind to think.
> Gathering data and developing hypotheses.
> Restating the problem and rectifying.
> Effect of effort, motivation.
> Values in self-questioning.
> Supervising creative people.
> Review.
> Re-test with new questions.

This program was developed by AC after top management was trained in seminars conducted by Professor John Arnold of MIT, acting as a consultant. The program uses Osborn's book, "Applied

Imagination," for its stimulation and excellent training exercises. The dual purposes are to maximize creativeness in the employees taking the course, and identify extra-creative men. These men are then judiciously distributed through the organization to catalyze progress on all fronts; some of them can be concentrated where progress has been stalled, or a break-through is needed.

The AC program is designed to distribute "creative supervisors," to quote the General Manager, Joseph Anderson. It would seem equally important, or even more important, to identify and distribute creative *researchers* the same way.

What have been the results of these programs? For AC, the average increase in number of ideas was 40 per cent. For GE, after training the men averaged more than double the number of patents of those who had not had the same training. The men have won more than a proportional share of company awards for individual contributions. (But it is necessary to point out that they were also preselected for creative ability.)

Many universities offer courses in creative thinking. One of the best known was Professor John Arnold's at MIT. Students learn the basics of creativity, with emphasis on the different kinds of blocks to be discussed below. For practice, students in one class designed equipment for the hypothetical Methananian people of a cold, heavy planet near Arcturus. This was described in *Astounding Science Fiction*, May, 1953:

> Arcturus IV is the fourth planet out from the sun α Bootis (Arcturus), 33 light-years from our solar system. It was first contacted by a member of the Solar and Galactic Explorers' Union on January 22, 2951. It is a large planet, 12×10^6 meters in diameter, having a mass of 60×10^{27} grams, and the acceleration of gravity at the surface is 11,000 centimeters per second squared. It is a distance of $1,800 \times 10^6$ miles from α Bootis and its sidereal period is 49.4 Earth-years. The length of day is 159 hours; the atmosphere is largely methane; and the mean temperatures range from -50 C° in the summer to -110 C° in the winter.

The Rutgers University program is of especial interest for group creativity. It has these facets: instruction and practice in basic research techniques; the creative process and its mental blocks and how to overcome them; and a group problem. One class chose solar energy. They subdivided this, and assigned segments to class members on the basis of individual skills. The intention was to read, think, confer, and fuse all experience toward solution.

The CNB Method

The present writer's somewhat radical proposal for a group creative method is termed the "Collective Notebook" or CNB method. It assumes a group of competent men who understand the purpose of the project and agree to cooperate. But this assumption is made also, for example, by the brainstorming and Gordon methods. The procedure is this:

(1) In the participating group, each man receives a notebook in the front of which is printed:
    (a) A problem of major scope.
    (b) A very broad-front presentation of preparative material along the lines of Chapter 4 on Preparation, including a variety of creative aids.

(2) Each man records in his notebook, one to several times a day, his thoughts and ideas on the problem, for a period of a month. Then each summarizes:
    (a) His best idea on the problem.
    (b) His suggestions for fruitful directions to explore in regard to the problem.
    (c) Other new ideas, aside from the main problem.

(3) At a specified time, each man hands the book in to the coordinator.

(4) The material in the notebooks is carefully studied and correlated by a coordinator who is creative-minded, and skilled in organizing and summarizing such a mass of material. He gives full time to this study, and prepares a detailed summary, which credits those especially deserving it. The willingness to commit a competent man to this full-time work is a *sine qua non* of the method.

(5) All participants can see all notebooks after summarization.

(6) A final creative discussion of any adequate length is held by all the participants, if desired.

It is submitted that this is the most powerful group method presently known, because it is a major, not a minor, commitment by the organization, and it is directed to a problem of considerable size.

In connection with our previous discussion of preparation, the reader has probably realized that there would be resistance to taking that much care with a problem. One of the big advantages of the CNB method is the deliberate decision to give the full preparative treatment to a problem of major scope, with the additional conviction that each worker will later enrich it with his individual experience. The preparative work is done by a team which includes a writer able to draft crisp statements and an artist or draftsman able to draw striking and communicative diagrams.

The participant finds this work done for him as he reads his notebook, but he also finds places left for him to fill in *his* preferred diagrams, *his* answers to stimulative questions, *his* comments on check lists. He is asked to record at least once a day. Most men will find it fun. They will be stimulated as they (a) note their own creative faculty and the way it works, and (b) are taken out of their little problem as a cog in a research team. *That* work is verification—but *this* is creation. The problem has scope to challenge. There is time for incubation, and for insight and its full realization. There is promise of recognition and implication of reward for exceptional performance.

The company gains: through this stimulation of the men; through the new ideas on the problem; through the new avenues of approach suggested; and through side ideas in other directions that are bound to be aroused.

The present writer has prepared considerable material amplifying this suggestion, but space does not allow its presentation now. It is hoped that this brief outline may arouse interest to try. These special points will be mentioned:

(1) Recording may take many forms, such as:
   (a) Ideas for solution to the problem.
   (b) Related or unrelated ideas.
   (c) Interesting facts, or recollections, or material read, that seem to bear in any way on the subject of the book, or

on any related subject the book-user has wished to introduce, as associated in his mind in some way with the
job at hand.

(d) New symbolizations, new analogies, or expressive verbal
terminology.

(e) New replies to the stimulative questions.

(f) The statement, "nothing to write tonight."

(2) The CNB allows personal application, to attack a big problem on one's own. The preparative work is done first, and not
skimped, and then recording is begun, day by day, and week by
week, or even year by year. Let the problem be as big as one dare—
a new artistic or literary departure, gravity, cancer. Pertinent material is watched for, and practise is applied to develop individual
creative skill. This will help on the daily job, while providing a
creative outlet aside from it.

(3) There are at least four kinds of stimulative questions that
can be used.

(a) *Simple and direct changes:* Will it help to double it,
reverse it, mirror it, use only a part, etc?

(b) *Enforced broad exploration:* What six qualities can be
enumerated which, if present in a thing, would make it
an instrument of solution of the problem? Or, list the
three improvements most likely to be announced in your
line of work in the next few years. Or, name four things
that a given product is like. Do these analogies suggest
any new product along the same line?

(c) *Off-trail hints:* What sound does it suggest? What taste,
what smell? In ideal form, should it feel smooth, soft,
warm, dry, slippery, etc?

(d) *Rousing remote associations:* Write down the three most
unusual properties belonging to three substances that
you know. How could each make a saleable product? Or,
can you think of a strong symbol that might be descriptive of your new product, like a lamb for spring, an hour-
glass for time, the Sphinx for mystery, a dove for peace?
As an example, an anti-caries toothpaste might use the
symbol of the shield of Richard the Lion-Hearted.

(4) One of the special creative aids that can be used with the

CNB method is *priming,* that is, stimulation with suggestive material given out at intervals during the month. This material is culled from the literature or prepared by company experts or consultants, and has the form of short, highly informative articles of *Reader's Digest* approach. If the CNB problem is a longer-wearing tire, the related subjects for preparation of a precis might be: examples of old rubber articles exposed to abrasion that have given notable service; the factors in wear, such as light, heat, tread design, inflation of the tire, nature of road surface; more basically, the nature of abrasion, how it is measured, how it has been improved in other lines, such as shoes, rugs, or bearings. These precis serve to furnish further preparative material, to stimulate flagging ideas and quicken interest, to "drop material into the well" and provide new associations, to re-energize incubation; hopefully, to supply a B for some individual's A, and evoke insight.

(5) Suggestion systems might employ a considerably modified CNB technique, using colorful, printed booklets. The presentation would be compressed and simplified; but again, careful polypreparative labor would try to start and aid thought. The booklets would be passed out to a large number of employees. There would be no undue pressure for their return. At the option of the employee, he could fill in just an idea, or add background. If the idea caught on, the subjects of the creative suggestion booklets would be changed from time to time, perhaps rotating new products, new methods, new savings, safety, etc. This is one of the ways to use very large groups to create new ideas.

The literature reports a number of instances of a notebook method to study creativity. Bahle asked musicians to compose to poems he supplied, and to record in a diary the creative psychology of this work. Eindhoven and Vinacke asked painters to record creative ideas while doing a painting over a period of time, but obtained poor response. In these cases the notebook was a side issue, and indeed, was so treated in the authors' publications. Catharine Patrick, in the work recorded in her paper, "Scientific Thought," gave unselected subjects a scientific problem, and asked them to record their thoughts about it in a notebook over a period of weeks, and finally offer their best solution. The problem was to plan an experiment to investigate the relative importance of heredity and environment. There was never any intent in this work to do any of the planned experiments, or to use the material any way except psychologically. But suppose, the present writer asks, there *were* such intent?

Pros and Cons of Brainstorming

After a continued interest over many years, and some deliberate scientific study, the advantages and limitations of the brainstorming procedure are beginning to appear. The preliminary remarks at the beginning of this section, on the basics of group creation, apply. They derive from deliberate studies of group problem solving.

Pro. First, it should be remembered that "brainstorming" is not a method for solving problems but a technique for stimulating ideas that will lead to problem solutions. Group brainstorming is a situation where this can happen under discipline such as might be absent in individual work. It sparks a good man's ideas, and *makes* him think under tension. There is a stimulating and vitalizing ego-satisfaction as the group launches into unknown territory.

Brainstorming works best on specific and limited but open-ended questions. It serves to supply a plenitude of ideas on a restricted subject when that is what is needed. The principle of reserving judgment in accumulating these is most important to learn, both for brainstorming sessions, and for individual creative thought. In this atmosphere, one learns to lose the fear of offering ideas.

With a limited definition, brainstorming is successful, more so than usual "conferences," in accomplishing its objective—a long list of ideas of more or less equal weight on a problem of modest scope.

Con. The criticisms of brainstorming come mainly where the method is extended beyond the scope indicated above. New combinations in advertising and business, where brainstorming was developed, are different from those in science or art in that few are foolish, many are good, several are almost equally acceptable, and judgment cannot really determine the best one—only trial. For example, let 100 names be brainstormed for a new product. Ten may remain in the final evaluated list. Who knows whether the one finally selected and used is actually better than another of the ten?

But in art, *one* color is *right*. In music, *one* note is *right*. In science, *one* conclusion is *possible*. In these hypothetical cases, brainstorming would have to turn up the needed *one;* the rest of the list would be valueless. The concern here is the possible fallacy of the many, that mere quantity of ideas is good in and of itself. This premise needs evaluation and study. It is of course true that forcing the mind to produce extra ideas ultimately forces it to search out extra directions of work also.

The group brainstorming procedure restricts the stages. It allows for little or no preparation or incubation, and in that alone automatically consigns itself to the superficial problem. This does not mean brainstorming is not useful. It does provide a way to build a list of things to consider, to try, or to aid in planning, that is more complete than one man could put together on his own. That is the most important function of brainstorming—a complete list.

Brainstorming does not provide for recognition and reward of the creator—a creative basic. A man will toss off a few names for a box of cereal without requiring credit. He will not put forth a major industrial invention quite so casually.

Taylor compared individual creation with group brainstorming in one of the few experimental studies of this method and found:

(1) Not surprisingly, a group can produce more ideas than an individual.

(2) But a group of individuals working separately can produce more ideas than when working as a group.

(3) The group working as individuals also produces ideas of higher average quality.

Individuals working alone produce more and better ideas. A significant departure derives from one mind. In group work, others then add the fairly obvious until a new, significant thrust in another direction appears. Then the pack takes off on the new trail, with further superficial and trivial additions. But it is also true that occasionally a remark or suggestion sparks the new-direction idea in a participant. This is probably more important than the obvious hitch-hikes.

Some believe that brainstorming may do harm by forcing out

premature, unformed ideas, which the proposer might himself have developed to something worthwhile, but in which the group in its rapid progress displays no interest, because they are half-formed and obscure.

A person alone is still freer in thought than one in a brainstorming group, despite the suspend-judgment, no-criticism rule.

Taylor and Jordan said of engineer training: After one or two brainstorming sessions, students "were overstimulated and had to be brought back to earth!"

In brainstorming, the newly formed group is not jelled. In a creative team, as in the Gordon technique, people know each other, learn to communicate through a common language, and soon understand the type of response others will give when a new idea or direction of thought is advanced. Such rapport is missing in the casually formed brainstorming groups.

Studies. Studies of brainstorming by an extension of Taylor's method are needed on the number of people in the group and the quality of ideation of the different numbers. For example, let 16 men ideate to problem A for 30 minutes as a group. Later, they ideate to problem B for 30 minutes as four 4-member groups. Later, they ideate to problem C for 30 minutes as individuals. Two other groups of 16 also attack the three problems, in such a way that the problems A, B, and C are balanced among the three approaches. The number and quality of responses, both individual and total, are tabulated. Such work would determine the consistency of the creativity of the men; would establish the identity of the most fluent ideators; and would determine the effects of larger groups and smaller ones, on individual production and total production versus purely individual work.

INDIVIDUAL AIDS

Several writers have discussed the subject of individual aids to creativity from the viewpoint of stimuli, including check lists as "idea needles," and blocks to creativity. The most general discussion of blocks, as three basic types, is credited to Arnold:

(1) *Perceptual:* incorrect interpretation of the physical world because of predetermined expectation. A spoiled plate is a spoiled

plate. The implications behind something one sees, which make it the truth but not the whole truth, are not even perceived.

(2) *Cultural:* conformity-pressure preventing free interpretation of experience. Another aspect is that established cultural outlook makes it nearly impossible to see certain developable values.

(3) *Emotional:* feelings attending the creative task. One is over-motivation, which fails to utilize all available clues and gives up vicarious exploration and efforts to be generic in favor of a quick solution. The worry and pressure of daily life are immediate blocks. Deeper are the blocks ingrained in the basic personality from earliest childhood, especially the fears and the attitudes adopted as need-satisfying behavior.

Clearly, the obverse of these blocks are favorable circumstances or aids, as shown in Table 10-2.

Table 10–2

Area	*Block*	*Aid*
Perceptual	Important point seen as obvious or trivial. Real problem in the situation not even recognized.	Ability to identify important point.
Cultural	Educated to use only the given and achieve one answer. Thinking by rules and cliches.	Ability to search for useful material to provide alternative answers. Ability to break fixed mental attitudes.
Emotional	Tendency to conform. Over-motivation. Personal fears and phobias. Distrust of associates. Going with the first idea you get.	Nonconformity. Fascination with problem.

By extrapolation, most of the favorable and unfavorable aspects of individual creativity can be brought under these heads. One example is the cultural block of functional fixedness, which denies the ability to see objects or to associate ideas and factors in new relationships. Another example is the emotional aid of creative tendency, gained from having been reared in a permissive atmosphere, and encouraged to create new combinations, some good, some bad, all accepted, with freedom to fail without recrimination, freedom to diverge without ridicule. There is the parallel aid of being permissively taught to allow time for the creative process to occur, time for care in preparation, time for incubation, time to realize insight. The cultural to a large degree determines the emotional, so that, given intelligence, a personality of the creative type and characteristics emerges. A willingness to be a nonconformist is fostered when creative action is encouraged, since a new combination is nonconformity *per se,* until successful communication "to gain acceptance of the general mind."

However, certain basics are not covered by the table.

One is the external block of society's reluctance to accept change. So much is this so, that many creators have failed to have their work accepted during their lifetime, and it has only been heralded at its true worth after their death. An example in music is Mozart, whose operas, now considered among the greatest, were not highly regarded in his own time. Examples in science are common. Work has been ignored, even refused publication. Mendel's study of inheritance and Tswett's study of absorption columns lay fallow a long time until resurrected. But they at least finally received credit. The fate of Waterston was different. He was refused publication, and gained no credit, for work which anticipated James Joule, Rudolf Clausius, and Clerk Maxwell by many years.

Great creators who gain rewards in their lifetime are fortunate to be in tune with the *Zeitgeist* of their era. Others wait for, or perhaps create, the *Zeitgeist* of the future, and have recognition only then. Wide recognition is in no way necessary for creation. But some recognition, if only by a small circle of associates, has practically always been present. The group provides feedback to the creator to help clarify, alter, or progress. From "Love's Labor Lost" and "Comedy of Errors," Shakespeare progressed to the great tragedies of "Hamlet" and "Macbeth." This growth came from many sources, including the feedback from what the audiences liked in earlier works, what his friends said, what his fellow playwrights were doing, as well as the growth of his own talent and experience.

Another basic is decline with age. Lehman has described this, and his studies show that the biggest achievements come in life's prime. But a great creator may still do better at 70 than most of his contemporaries at 35. His work at 70 suffers only in comparison with what he himself did at 35, and sometimes the decline is not great. But in general, with age there come:

> Work to elaborate the big achievements of earlier years.
> Hardening of fixation in the discipline, so that more and more is taken for granted, or seen as trivial, obvious, or axiomatic, unchangeable, and immovable.
> Life's goals achieved; lessened drives.
> Concern with details: affairs to tend, children grown to occupy the stage as individuals, wife with fewer household duties wanting more of husband's time, less time alone.

Favorable Circumstances for Creation

From the copious mention in the literature of circumstances favorable for creation, some items can be grouped for discussion, others will be given singly.

Tuska has proposed the equation of creativity:

(Surround yourself with favorable circumstances) $+$ (Exercise creative imagination) x (Apply effort $+$ .... $+$ Apply effort^n) $+$ (k, which is good luck) $=$ Creative Product of Social Value.

Personality traits favorable for creativity derive from upbringing, but they can be recognized and reinforced. The traits have been summarized as a questioning spirit, which combines associative and analytical characteristics.

A favorable problem is needed, matched to one's training, most effective factors, and deep personality inclinations. A definite commission is especially fortunate, since it provides a clear road to communication and reward. When a worker must uncover a problem as well as attack it, there is the extra need to sell as well as solve. The two greatest operas, according to Lehman's research, are "Aida" and "Don Giovanni." Both were composed on commission, with ample time for the composers to achieve masterpieces. (Still, it is curious that one was late in being completed, and the other nearly so—the ink was still wet on the Giovanni overture when Mozart conducted the premiere.)

Given the commission, to establish creative tension, time is needed for the creative process to occur. Time engenders a feeling of detachment, a comfortable freedom from physiological and psychological strains, from fatigue, worry, interruption, anger, and demanding competitive interests. There is high but not over-motivation, which time and detachment prevent. All this can be summarized as the favorable circumstance of *calmness*.

As the work proceeds, an initial stimulus is needed to trigger insight. This is Hutchinson's catalyst, which may, or may not, be incorporated in the creative product. This catalyst is most likely to be found in a man's preferred surroundings and atmosphere of creative work.

Too long experience and too narrow training are inhibitive; thus the intensive specialist is often found to have done his best work when he was new in his field, and merely to have elaborated on it in his later years. Broad training, on the other hand, is favorable, because it gives multiple directions in which to work, and the knowledge of where to obtain the necessary material in each case. Acute powers of observation help. This includes the ability to see something when it is there, *and* the ability not to see something when it is not there.

Besides *multiple preparation,* many problems permit *multiple solutions.* These should be explicated, so that work is done, not on the first, but on the best ideas. It has been recommended, for technical problems, to obtain answers in *multiple* areas: at least one in psychological, mechanical, chemical, and electrical fields. This can be illustrated by the following suggestion for practising and improving analogic ability: Take a common object, a pen, for example, and derive at least eight things it resembles, in the several fields mentioned. A possible set of answers is given in Table 10-3.

This kind of practice is useful because creation is a new combination, and because one aspect of creative skill is the ability to make a variety of associations to a commonplace object.

Note how "set" works here. The term *set* in psychology means a mental attitude, and in particular refers to adjustment to a group of specifications, and readiness to respond to this pattern. The command was, *make analogies to pen.* If the command had been *list possible uses of a pen,* responses would have been, a weapon, a probe, a sucker-up of spilled liquid, etc. This is different from the set and

TABLE 10–3

Field	Analogy and Explanation
Mechanical	A pen is like a pencil. Both write.
Psychological	A pen is like a man talking; material emitted may be sense or drivel.
Mechanical	A pen is like a nail. Both have fatter portion and sharp point.
Psychological/ Mechanical	A pen is like a sword. Both have point and handle—an obvious association from "the pen is mightier than the sword."
Electrical	A pen is like a flashlight; from the commercial penlight.
Chemical	A pen is like a chemical reaction. As the pen writes, the blank page is gradually converted to a report, just as refluxing gradually forms an ester from alcohol and acid.
Mechanical	A pen is like a probe. The point will go into a small space.
Psychological	A pen is like an author's mind. Both wait to produce the words of a book.

responses to the command, *improve the pen.* The set is in the verb, and has the force of a command to the mental scanner: *analogize, use, improve.* Set of this type has a bipolar nature in a creative person. He changes set easily as he searches for solution, but he does poorly at tasks which require inflexibility of approach.

A favorable circumstance is strong self-knowledge, permitting easy interchange between conscious and unconscious. The strong self can admit primitive fantasies, naive ideas, tabooed impulses, secure in the knowledge that it can correct itself.

Other aids are these:

Adversity. This has been a concomitant of many creative works, as an observed fact.

Furtherance. This means that success sparks success; then people give attention to the next creative presentation. Freedom to fail is gained—and that means space to dare.

Contact with great and original creative works. The largest profit here means to get a peep behind the scenes, on how they came into being, and the qualities of care and detail that make them great.

Consistency of interest and effort. Willingness to work. A positive emotional attitude toward the task.

Fascination with the task.

Saturation with the task.

Elucidation of one's best creative time, conditions of work, maintenance of creative mood and creative dissociation. Elucidation of how to find initiating stimuli, e.g., to walk, drive, ride, read, visit the theater, etc.

Self-confidence.

Feeling for beauty or harmony in material or in nature.

Recording. Lewis Carroll invented a "nyctograph" so that he could write down ideas that came to him in the night.

Action on ideas. The unconscious will stop producing if they are not used.

Intelligence.

Sense of humor, and especially enjoyment of intellectual play.

Broadening of experience, to give new directions of search to any problem that may arise. Useful for this are travel, study, and contacts with others in the general field of interest.

Travel. This favors creation by forcing times for reveries and for being alone in quiet surroundings.

Learning and practising to withhold judgment.

Explication. Making clear, brief statements of the problem or goal.

Minimum organizational barriers in doing a piece of creative work and selling it.

Model of search.

Working to a model of the desired creation, if procurable.

The difference between the last two items is that the model of search would be the impressionist formula as given on page 41, whereas the model to work to would be, for example, a painting in the category aimed for: a rural landscape, a seascape, a city street, or a portrait; it would be not to copy, but to study the other worker's technique and how he accomplished it.

One other aid needs research, and that is the use of mild drugs to aid rapport with the unconscious, or promote a tendency to dissociated thought. This idea should not be shocking. Such drugs are widely used already in the form of tobacco, alcohol, and coffee. But mild dosages of modifications of lysergic acid diethylamide might improve rapport with the unconscious; and intelligent use of a derivative of mescaline might serve to promote hypnagogic imagery and shackle the judicial faculty during a period of creative effort.

Unfavorable Circumstances

Rearing and education are among the biggest blocks to creativity. The failure of interest, permissiveness, and encouragement in the home environment is a heavy handicap, especially as this is reinforced at school. The problems in education will be discussed in Chapter 15. Suffice it to mention here the feverish activity favored in today's schooling; the learning methods of memorizing to reproduce at examination time, and of using all that is given, no more and no less, to obtain a single and unique answer; and the study of literature with the critical factor high, the analytical one active, and the creative one throttled.

Weisskopf has considered the various influences in childhood that affect intellectual malfunction and may affect creativity. The child may inhibit progress or growth in order to punish the parent or himself, or to maintain an infantile level of gratification. Guilt feelings, which arise with the acquisition of sexual knowledge regarded as wrong to have, or as having been obtained in an improper way, may threaten general cognition and intellectual progress. Alternatively, failure in an investigation of sexual matters may inhibit intellectual attainment in general. The child learns to avoid failure; he simply does not compete. The child may also hold back so as not to show superiority, and so gain love and ward off aggression. Such protective stupidity may become an automatic block. There may also be blockage of whole idea systems. This is common in adults. In a famous case, involving failure to use proper antisepsis, doctors persecuted Semmelweis because they could not admit to themselves that they had murdered patients.

Through formal education, one may know too much even to give consideration to a certain avenue of approach. This is the reason for the admonition to question basic premises and dicta. Long experience in a field and a habitual way of doing things operate similarly. From these influences are generated such creative blocks as technical overconformity and worship of reason, as opposed to the free, creative way. Related to these blocks are fear of error and failure, which may destroy hard-won security, and fear of ridicule.

Overmotivation can be as bad a block as lack of interest or laziness. Starving animals are found, experimentally, to be less successful in negotiating a maze to obtain food than those merely hungry. Overmotivation, combined usually with too much pressure, means too much speed, and that means:

Too much narrowing of the field.

Giving up the vicarious trial and error which ultimately yield the true feel and texture of the situation.

Loss of opportunity to be generic.

Choices made by attempting to use more information than is really there, for example, by generalizing from a single instance.

Refusal to use even the information available, because of intolerance of ambiguity or too literal interpretation generated by the need for speed.

Loss of opportunity for reflective thought.

Other blocks to creativity are a desire to avoid self-evaluation, and inability to make oneself do what is necessary or take the extra trouble needed for a really good job.

In business, promotion from within has been declared a hindrance to creativity. Each man who moves up has been trained by those above him in the hierarchy. Traditions and ways of thinking are firmly ironed in, and if they are not, the man's progress suddenly stops. This difficulty is counteracted to some extent by hiring men from different schools in different sections of the country and with various backgrounds.

Also in industry, creativity is hurt if a man is removed from a favorable creative climate; or if administrative duties or everyday life pressures and anxieties mount; or if creative disclosures are filed without trial. Men may also be discouraged from creating by the prevalence in the company vocabulary of the numerous "killer phrases," already alluded to. These have been widely listed, and some in addition to those mentioned before are:

"We tried something like that years ago."
"That's ridiculous."

"That's too radical."

"Let's form a committee to consider it."

"That's contrary to policy."

"Has anyone ever tried it?"

"It won't work!"

"That's too obvious to be considered." (A new idea is often something that everybody knows but nobody has yet thought of.)

"We could never market that."

"That's superficial."

"That's interesting, but we don't have the time .... or manpower."

"Tell me right now—what's the potential profit from it."

"That's not the kind of idea we expect from you."

Most of these can be guaranteed to work, but the first is worth all the others.

Specific Aids to Creativity

Practice. The deliberate noticing of resemblances, or explication of relationships, is an ability that can be practiced in several ways, and, perhaps, cultivated. This is important for creativity because such new combinations are innovation. One method was mentioned above, namely, to take a common object and write down eight things it is like, including several different areas of thought. A second is to observe, as well as invent, unusual uses of verbs, such as time *anneals* to grief. A third method is to discover analogies as one experiences things in daily life. Examples are:

> Hot coffee: bracing as mountain air
> as flattery
> as good news
> as praise.
> Lift the lid: from fatigue
> from anger
> from repressed wrong.
> Kite in the wind: lifts like the heart to praise.
> Ticking of a clock: pulse ticks your life away.

Practicing this way, relations are the same as: the apple—falls; the moon—falls; the universe—knit with a single force.

Another practice is listing ideas or associations while withholding judgment, the keystone of the brainstorming method, of Schiller's advice to open wide the gates, and of the spectator behavior of Heidbreder. During creative scanning, one should learn to watch for criticism and squelch it until it is needed.

Check lists. Check lists are a special case of the promotion of associations. In general, they are lists to tick off against a clear visualization of the problem in the hope of sparking a solution. The list may use such concepts as, make it bigger or smaller, add or subtract, multiply or divide. Most check lists are either lists of verbs to set up in turn as correlates between two problem-centered nouns, or they are a list of nouns to be related to a given verb-and-noun condensation of the problem. It will also be true that when an idea clicks for one of the items in the check list, the $A + B \rightarrow C$ situation has occurred.

To show how this works, let a few examples from each of several check lists be given, and then applied to a particular case. Complete lists will be found in the appended references.

Osborn: Adapt, modify, magnify, minify, substitute, rearrange, reverse, combine.

Reiss: Make it look like something else, animate it, take it literally, make it a parody or imitation (so-called "cute" formulas).

Mortimer: Give it convenience of form, time, place, quantity, packaging, readiness, combination, automation, selection.

Flesch:

What am I trying to accomplish?

Have I done this before? How?

Could I do it another way?

Use more, less, all, none, one, two, several, part.

What if I do the opposite?

What if I do nothing?

Von Fange:

What about shape, size?

What if reversed, inside out, upside down?

What else can it do?

What can be left out?
What if carried to extremes?
What if symmetrical? Assymetrical?
Can it be safer?
Can it be cheaper?
Slide instead of rotate?
Can it move? Can it be stationary?

In addition to these problem-directed lists, *Reiss* has an excellent special list for finding needs or problems:

What's your pet peeve?
What troubles, bothers, tires, bores you?
What gets you wet, cold, dirty?
What do you like to touch, smell, see, hear?
When do you wish you had an extra hand?
What do you often put off, forget to do?

These are useful, and can work this way: What troubles you? A pen running out of ink? Give it a reservoir. What gets you dirty? Firing the furnace? Feed it by machine, heat with a furnace burning gas, use coal covered by sealed paper.

It will be noted that in many of these items, the key word is a verb. Verbs are correlates which denote relationships, and they also determine set. Therefore, as the list of verbs is ticked off, the set or attitude toward the temporarily rigid part of the thought is changed. Suppose the problem were to increase the circulation of a magazine. Then circulation-magazine is set up. Make it (the magazine) bigger? Increase the format, or add more material so it is thicker. Make it smaller? Reduce the format to pocket size. Divide it? Have one section for men, another for women, call it "His and Hers" magazine, and publish it so it comes apart, and each partner can read his half. Thus the set switches from verb to verb of the check list.

In order to show further the relationships among these methods, Example 2, page 29, of the A + B → C series will be considered: A (a basic need is a safer match) + B (cellulose may be impregnated to fireproof it) → C (impregnate half the matchstick so the match burns out sooner).

This can be set up for check-list attack as follows (see Figure 10-1):

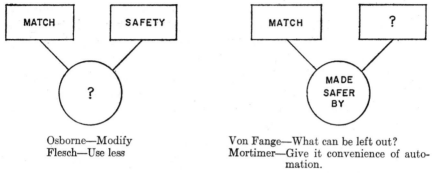

Osborne—Modify
Flesch—Use less

Von Fange—What can be left out?
Mortimer—Give it convenience of automation.

Figure 10–1

Let (?) be the solution, *burn out sooner*. It is required to reach the solution by substituting the check lists.

Using Osborn's list, one arrives at modify the stick; using Mortimer's, at the convenience of automatic early extinction; using Flesch's, at use less = burn less; using Von Fange's, at what can be left out, one-half the burnable stick.

If this looks contrived, it is only because it is. But the principle illustrated is *not* contrived. The associations stimulated by the mechanical set-up range far and wide until something clicks. The lists are only needles, and the mind uses them while keeping implicit the above detailed analysis of what is going on. Each question in the check list is twisted around until it applies in some way to the problem. Thus the check lists serve to promote associations, but there are other ways, too.

Promotion of Associations. The methods to promote associations to the problem all have a random approach.

One is to thumb through Roget's "Thesaurus," and jot down key words which may serve to spark association chains. The selection of words related to the work in hand will extend the associations beyond those that would come from the words one would readily think of himself. A chemist in the cosmetic field might glance through the entries for hair, coiffure, shampoo, spray, lacquer, bleach, dye, tint, and so forth. It should be remembered that (1) many of these are available to the unconscious in the clusters, yet (2) this conscious work may serve to start new directions and stir things up.

Another technique is to jot down descriptive words or phrases. Later, each is applied with a specific product in mind, trying for free associations to give improvements, of whatever kind, in those directions.

In attribute listing, the properties and qualities of an article or product are called to mind and listed. This becomes a checklist, a step-wise mental set modifier. In going through it one considers what useful changes could be made at any point.

As an example of attribute listing, a man's shoe will be considered. For purposes of this discussion only four important attributes will be discussed. The chief components of the shoe are the sole, heel, upper, and shoestring. Each of these will be analyzed as regards its purpose and modification.

Sole. Purpose—to wear well, protect from water, heat, cold, abrasion. Material—leather. Modify leather by waterproofing. Change it by using another material with improved water-resistance and wear (Neolite). Alter appearance by pigmenting sole a contrasting color. Improve it for the original purpose by weather-sealing to upper, and by automatic arch adjustment.

Heel. Purpose—to give natural feel in standing and walking. Material—leather. Change leather by using another material like rubber with improved resilience and safety. Alter appearance of heel by pigmenting. Improve it for original purpose by personalizing, with correct heel for each customer easily put on by salesman at point of sale.

Upper. Purpose—to protect toe with hard shell and foot with softer but still firm covering. Material—leather. Modify leather by softening or by baking an enamel-like, scuff-resistant, permanent-shine finish on the upper, particularly the toe. Alter appearance of upper by pigmenting (most are black or brown, use an in-between shade). Improve upper for original purpose by changing its height or by metalizing the toe shell for safety shoes.

Shoestring. Purpose—to hold shoe on foot. Material—cotton. Modify cotton by impregnating or reacting it to lengthen wear life to that of the shoe itself. Change by using plastic or synthetic fibers, or by using hooks, buckles, snaps, elastic member in upper construction, or (as in casual shoes) nothing. Alter shoestring appearance by making round or ribbon, and by pigmenting. Improve for original purpose by lightly elasticizing the cotton string.

The Hotpoint method of listing defects of a product may be applied individually, and broadened, to list both merits and defects. Then follows analysis, to remedy defects, and reinforce the meritorious spots.

A still broader technique again starts with a product, but digs deep, and asks, what does it basically do? The mouse trap kills mice; the clothes dryer evaporates water. From here, the Gordon method can be applied, thinking about removal or separation, and progressing gradually to the mechanical and specific. Or, from the basic point of view, another direction is the input-output analysis. Both methods are attempts to shake off fixations, and achieve radically new ways of accomplishing the objective. The mind starts with this:

$$\text{Wet Clothes} \longrightarrow \text{Dry Clothes} + H_2O\uparrow$$

and free-associates, using the Gordon method, or the input-output analysis, as a framework or model of search.

Naturally, not all of these methods appeal to all workers; to some, none will appeal. The more deliberate thinkers may have a greater tendency to use them in an attempt to force new associations. The writer of this is by inclination an intuitive thinker, with the normal practise of hard, variable preparation, and commission of the lot to the unconscious to unscramble. But he has found it possible to develop both new ideas and promising directions of work by these methods of forcing association. However, the ideas may be remote from the problem in hand, according to Knowlson's fifth principle (page 101).

The method of forced relationships bears resemblance to the foregoing, and it has been refined in several directions by various writers, including Whiting and the present author.

In the listing technique, a list of starting ideas is made, then each is exhaustively considered in relation to all the others. In the catalog technique, the Yellow Pages or a Sears catalog are thumbed through, and the items selected or ideas generated are exhaustively associated. Whiting's proposal is to fix one pole by deliberate selection—the technique of the "focused object." In practise, as Whiting describes, the fixed pole is a problem-related noun. Another noun is selected at random. Associations are sought. When that vein has been worked, another noun is picked, and so forth.

If two nouns which are names of objects are selected at random, and the choices are happy ones, and the mind is on a creative track, then the range of associations is wide indeed, and an astounding spectrum of ideas develops: some nonsensical, some whimsical, some of the nature of advertising slogans, some useful or useless gadgets, some inventions, occasionally not already made by somebody else. The author can use the whimsy; the advertiser, the slogan; the industrial researcher, the invention. With practice, it is possible by this technique to invent, virtually to order, ideas or combinations that are new and useful—provided there is no specification of the field they are to be in. The only specification is:

"Make a useful new combination."

In using the method of association to a pair of nouns, the present writer employs special means to control the associations before letting them go farther afield. Thus, consider *paper* and *soap:*

Adjective: Papery soap = Flakes.
    Soapy paper = Wash'n Dry travel aid.
Verb: Paper soaps = Tough paper impregnated with
     soap and usable for washing surfaces; has
     been used for shampoo.
    Soap papers = Booklets of soap leaves.

Verb-
 correlates: Soap ...?... Paper
     " wets " in coating and impregna-
             tion processes.
     " cleans " (suggests wall-paper
             cleaner.)
     Paper ...?... Soap
     " wraps " and saves perfume.
Foil in place of " wraps " " " more per-
             fume.

The words themselves are manipulated in various ways. Each in turn may become an adjective, then a verb. This *manufactures* unusual verbs which modify set.

When one has run out of verb-correlates, the more tenuous associations of Whiting's method are developed. As a further example of his method, let the lamp-clock pairing briefly considered on pages 81-82 be extended. The first ideas to come to mind are:

> lamp-clock or clock-lamp
> clock lamps, i.e., lights
> lamp clocks, i.e., is turned on by a timer.

Then, a clock has many parts. Give the lamp parts, swivel it, let it be movable up and down, fix the bulb in the lamp on a long reel cord so it can be pulled out and anchored where desired, i.e., build in an extension. A lamp gets hot, arrange a clock to turn on a heater in the morning a half hour before the alarm. Or let it turn on the thermostat. A lamp can carry different-colored bulbs, let clock have different colored faces from time to time. A clock is for time. Let the lamp carry a calendar, and a weather predictor. A lamp has bulbs of different power, including a 3-way. Let the clock have a 3-way alarm bell, soft . . . loud . . . LOUD, which ring successively. A lamp may have adjustable bases and heights; give these attributes to a clock.

When this sort of free association to a problem runs down for one pair, then, according to Whiting, if your business is clocks, you start out on clock-*pen*. But if it is lamps, you continue with lamp-*porch*. Using the latter, put an all-weather lamp on the porch, or install a driveway light or a lamplight in the yard. A porch is a small attachment to a house. Give a lamp a porch. It can be a tray, or better, an extra little light offset and independent from the big light of the lamp. Keep the little light on at night, or when you are out, or for courting.

To quote the monarch from "Anna and the King of Siam"—"Et cetera, et cetera, et cetera!"

Heuristics. The routine use of heuristic methods has been mentioned before. A few are: the technique of close comparison of neighbors; the $(n + 1)$th and $(n - 1)$th, or adjacent, cases; the examination of the simplest case; the examination of special cases; the search for a theorem to apply; the search for a modified structure to which a theorem applies; analysis until theorems apply to some of the parts; a rare recentering of the problem. Examples have been given in Chapters 4 and 5.

Another technique is to set aside the first, easily obtained ideas, get some more, and examine the entire lot later. This is personal brainstorming.

In the historical growth of the sciences, methods of discovery have been developed, which may serve as individual aids. They are especially well exemplified by some famous workers.

(1) *Newton:* the use of mathematics strictly as an instrument of investigation.
(2) *Faraday:* reliance exclusively on experiment.
(3) *Cavendish:* the use of care to achieve the highest possible degree of accuracy.
(4) *Mendeleev:* discovery through classification.
(5) *Pasteur:* discovery through micro-examination.
(6) *Pasteur:* the use of persistence to confirm a hypothesis not readily verified, but which appears sound.
(7) *Darwin:* validation by an overwhelming mass of systematized information.
(8) *Mendel:* discovery through the combination of classification and statistics.
(9) *Quételet:* discovery through the application of statistical methods.
(10) *Galton:* discovery through introspection.

Miscellaneous Methods. Lester R. Bittel listed 32 "springboards to good ideas" in the March, 1956 issue of *Factory Management.* Some are listed here, using Bittel's numbers:

1. Find your creative time of day.
2. Build up idea sources by travel, conventions, etc.
3. State problem carefully.
20. State ideas specifically.
11. "Accept the fact that much of what you do will be chaff." It is more wasteful to wait around for the one perfect idea.

21. Use all your senses.
24. Attribute listing.
25. Osborn checklist.
26. Input-output.
28. Record ideas.
32. Discuss problems with others.

The deliberate substitution of verbs in the statement of the problem to modify set is another method. A noun plus a verb sets up the problem. The verb establishes set. Changing the verb changes the set.

A good way to set up a problem for quick reference, to resume mulling it over at intervals, is to *make an ad of it.* Set up the question stripped of verbiage as if it were a question on a billboard ad, with a strong, symbolic drawing or diagram to point it up. For example, a pretty housewife, standing outdoors, sniffs an armload of dried-in-the-sun clothes and says, "I Wish The Dryer Did This!" This suggests, put *ozonization* in the dryer cycle.

The present writer has obtained favorable results with this method of assumption. Let one say, if I had a material which would do (1) such and such, then with it I could accomplish (2) this result, which would have (3) these consequences. In practice, a real material as close as possible to the hypothetical is thought of, and then attempts are made to arrange matters so that (2) and (3) come about. As an example: if I had a material which would impregnate cellulose and make it fireproof, I could impregnate the holding end of a match stick for earlier extinction and greater safety. I could expect fewer forest fires and fewer burnt fingers. I could even let the fire end burn a little more fiercely, because its extinction would be certainly controlled. Such materials might be phosphates for nonflammable impregnation, and a little nitrate near the tip to promote flame there.

External Aids by Management Action

Management's aids to creative employees will be given under "Climate" in the next chapter, but a few comments are appropriate here.

In large research laboratories, there is neglect of two most important aids to creativity. The *first* is inadequate use of free, creative discussion—the most powerful means of invoking insight. A creative discussion is a communication session, involving two or more persons, in which the purpose is to generate new ideas or combinations.

Creative discussions should be scheduled, for they are too important to leave to chance. Reporting sessions and decision sessions are scheduled at regular intervals at all levels of government and business organizations. These may or may not consider new ideas as they proceed. Creative discussions should be scheduled because then there will be more of them, and they will start with brakes (i.e., critical and judicial attitude) off. "Brakes off" is harder to achieve when a creative interlude burgeons in the course of a reporting or judicial session. It is possible to select groups for creative discussion in which the members spark one another particularly well.

Occasional participation in a creative discussion outside the area of direct responsibility is very stimulating to a research worker. A strong creative effort in one direction often will carry over its general impetus into the worker's own field.

The *second aid neglected* is in arranging for time and place for purely creative opportunity. The creative lodge discussed in the next chapter is a rather far-out extension of this thought.

In the setup of the modern industrial or government research laboratory, problems are attacked by teams. It is inevitable that a man's particular segment of a problem should occasionally become, or seem to him, petty, even stale and unprofitable. Efforts are indeed made to show him how his problem relates to the whole group problem, and beyond that to the company's business. As far as it goes, all well and good. But the man may have hit upon the truth. Perhaps he *is* engaged in trying to create something pretty small.

An occasional crack at something bigger may help. The best way to give him this chance is the CNB method already described. Another way is this: No better opportunity exists for a man to acquire B's to couple with A's already in mind than when he goes to a scientific meeting, especially a general one such as those of the American Chemical Society or American Physical Society. In advance of attendance, let section heads in charge of several major areas of study define carefully the background and specific need in one or two of their more pressing problems. There will be perhaps a dozen of these. A man chosen to go to the general scientific meeting receives, let us say, two of these in advance. He can begin incubating ideas about them, and thinking of people to talk to and papers to hear in connection with them. At the meeting, he tries to get some new facts or ideas to correlate with his two extra problems. Naturally, he must take care to gather all he can for his own problems and section as well.

Every man will enjoy such a challenge. Since it is in a way an expression of confidence in him, the psychological lift might be worthwhile even without an ideational by-product. There will, however, *be* worthwhile ideational production. A creative man possesses a whole group of well-formulated A patterns awaiting B closures, as earlier diagrammed. Meetings supply these. This writer differs strongly with that school which avers that useful material at conventions is only to be gained from "contacts" in the halls outside the meeting rooms. Hearing the papers is much more important— for creativity.

Selection of the Best

From the foregoing methods, the best seem to be as follows:

(1) Understand creativity in general, and your own way of it.
(2) Use polypreparation.
(3) Allow time for incubation, and realize insight.
(4) Record.
(5) Understand the different types of blocks, and how to overcome them.
(6) Practise analogy.
(7) Practise deferring judgment.
(8) Practise creative discussion.
(9) Create your own best check list.
(10) Use forced relationships.
(11) Improve verb vocabulary.
(12) Use heuristics.
(13) Make an ad of it.
(14) Know the common denominator of great creators in different fields—detail matched to concept.

11. THE CREATIVE CLIMATE

The business organization needs research and development, not for growth alone, but for life itself. In a competitive situation, for example, from one-fifth to one-half of the present business may derive from products which did not even exist ten years ago.

These new products are made by creative men—whose chief, perhaps only, products are ideas. They require creative climate for work. The characteristics of such a climate, whether in a university, a business, or a "school" of art or psychology, follow inexorably from the principles of creativity embodied in the creative stages and creative personality. Many aids to creative climate will be obvious from the nature of the individual and group aids already alluded to. But in organizations and, for our immediate purposes, in industrial research laboratories, there must be a compromise between the optimum creative climate and total organizational maintenance and discipline. For research, development, and engineering are big business in themselves. The phenomenal growth of this field appears in the following chart, published by Ewell (Figure 11-1).

In industry, technical workers depend upon management to operate the company at a profit, to provide capital and services, and to establish conditions under which they can do their creative work. But management's basic dedication is usually to *continuance* of the organization, while research's is often to *change* of the organization. Management usually wants the changes to be small, slow, and carefully planned. But the research laboratory must show creativity. Clearly, the extent of creativity must be limited. The problem is to establish a climate where even the limited creativity the organization needs will flourish. The nature of this limitation has been diagrammed (Figure 11-2) by Quinn in an article in the *Harvard Business Review* (March-April, 1960) to show the contribution of the industrial research laboratory to the business picture. Quinn shows how the three types of research—fundamental, development,

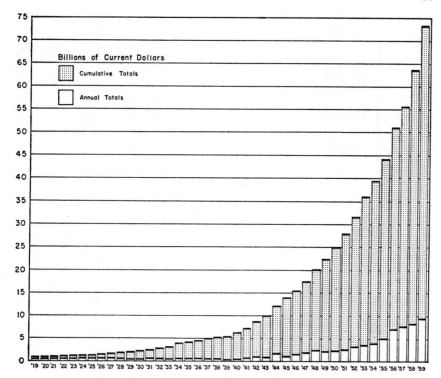

Figure 11–1. Cumulative expenditure for research and development in United States (from the year 1776 to end of each year indicated).

Updated for 1955-59 from chart originally appearing in *Chemical and Engineering News,* July 18, 1955, "Role of Research in Economic Growth," by Raymond H. Ewell, National Science Foundation. Annual totals in the Ewell chart are based on data from a number of sources, including Dept. of Defense, Bureau of the Budget, California Research Corp., "Science—The Endless Frontier" (Vannevar Bush, 1945), unpublished data from the National Science Foundation, and estimates by Ewell to fill in gaps. Cumulative for 1919 is a rough guess from fragmentary data, virtually all expended between 1880 and 1920, but extended to 1776 to make the picture complete. *Expenditures for the last five years exceed the prior cumulative total.*

and applied—produce a wide technology to be exploited in numerous, specific directions which all work toward the two basic company goals, public service and profits.

In this framework, men are selected who are competent and suitable. The tasks of paying them, providing plant, services, and favorable climate, and capitalizing results are the responsibilities of management. But aside from all the desirable or difficult qualities the selected men may have, their goal and management's is the

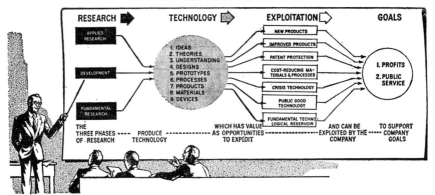

Figure 11–2

(From Quinn, *Harvard Business Review,* p. 70, March-April 1960. Reproduced by permission.)

same; and that is the reason they are there—to realize their creativity.

The area of their problem is defined first by the company's business, which the worker knew when he took the job. The broad region to study is management's decision. The particular area to attack is management's decision in consultation with research supervisors; this should include men who are riding the laboratory track as well as those who have switched to the management track. As an example, let the business be soap; the region, anionic surfactants; the area, redeposition of soil. At this point it is up to the individual creative researcher, and this is the time and place to give him his head.

Just what must the organization do to enable him to be creative? The basics are:

(1) Alternative goal
(2) Recognition
(3) Use
(4) Freedom
(5) Services
(6) Selection and Training

Admittedly, some of these are not organization-oriented.

Alternative Goal

The creative scientist in industry should be offered a clear, alternative road of progress to that of joining management. At the present time, the only general way to reward him is promotion to management ranks, often making a poor administrator out of a fine engineer or scientist. On his part, the temptation of the larger monetary and status rewards of administration prove too strong to resist. After all, both his average IQ and his average training are on the very highest level in our culture. It is natural for him to desert the purely creative ranks—to the real detriment of his company and society as well—rather than accept a second class future. The creative path must be made more attractive.

In industry, a second avenue of progress, the Senior Scientist concept, is growing, but slowly. A concept of this nature was developed by Benger in "Industrial and Engineering Chemistry" thirty years ago, and his was probably not the first. The growth is slow because the senior scientist is granted independence and pay virtually equal to management's. The grant is not made lightly, but several very progressive organizations have adopted it. A news item in *Chemical Week* discussed the Monsanto Chemical Company's "key scientist and technologist advancement plan" after ten years' operation. Advancement is comparable to the alternative administrative line of promotion. An exceptional senior scientist, Monsanto declared, might achieve pay equal to that of the company president.

Since the development of this concept is slow, it would appear to offer a definite opportunity for forward-looking management to step ahead of the field in its industry by introducing the senior scientist plan. Thus, it would assure that high creatives would create all their lives; and managers with high-judgment skill would be recruited elsewhere.

Recognition

The pride of creation demands recognition, whether a man is composer in a ducal court or research chemist in an industrial laboratory. For both, satisfactory pay is necessary. But the true coin of the realm is not pay, nor buildings, nor equipment, nor even golf courses. It is recognition and credit which says, the basic idea behind this achievement was yours, and all know it, and recognize the part you have played in it.

The importance of recognition follows from the nature of the creative process and personality. Recall that creation is individual. Remember the pride of the artist, since even Genesis says, "And God saw everything that he had made, and behold, it was good." Remember the joy of insight, and its aftermath of feeling: *I* have done this thing, and it is beautiful, and when I tell it, it will bring me food, family, and fame. A big component of *Eureka* is the anticipation of *Hurrah!*

From recognition of a man's creative work must inevitably follow the status and material rewards he seeks. The recent drive for professional *recognition* shows the importance of this, as evidenced by a 1959-1960 series of papers in *Chemical and Engineering News*. This interest is strongest in the industrial chemist, because the university professor has recognition as an educator.

The vital importance of recognition is indirectly emphasized in a thought-provoking article by S. L. Pressey in the *Scientific Monthly* on the development of precocious genius. He lists five key factors, four of which have to do with recognition:

> First are the "excellent early opportunities for the ability to develop, and encouragement from family and friends."
>
> Second is the chance to practice and work from the earliest years. This inevitably entails the recognition that what the child is doing is important, and that he is *able* to do something important.
>
> Third is association with the great, both in the particular field and in the world. (This comment was a reiterated point in the National Science Foundation and fifteen professional societies' Conference on Research Goals held Dec. 3-4, 1959.)
>
> Fourth is that ever greater success experiences build confidence by recognition even while they provide the spur to surpass.

Pressey says:

> "Mozart lived from early childhood in a world of musicians who listened to and watched one another, played

together, cooperated, competed, raised levels of aspiration, and were keen in criticism and encouragement. His musicianship brought acquaintance with the great all over Europe, including the Austrian emperor ... (and) the stimulation of many and increasingly strong success experiences—and his world acclaimed these successes. It is well recognized that frequent failure and continued frustration may debilitate personality and competency, just as a disease does. But the opposite also seems true, although it is not generally appreciated: Frequent, much-admired successes increase effort, build up psychosomatic vigor, make attempts more vigorous, and adequate, and better integrated, and build ability. The opinion is ventured that such 'furtherance' is as important a phenomenon as frustration, and that systematic research regarding furtherance might well be as profitable as research on frustration has been."

Use

A part of favorable climate is that results obtained be used. As imitation is the sincerest flattery, so use is the highest form of recognition. Indeed, the unconscious sources of creativity refuse to work without this pay. There is little joy in sterile insight, and little point in full realization of it during verification, if it will not be used. Management is probably not fully aware of how many follow-ups are prevented by this feeling. In particular, management should guard against a tendency to oversimplify which is commonly attributed to it by professional men. Researchers get very tired of hearing, "Oh, we tried that years ago"—especially when it isn't true because a new twist has been added. It is more helpful, as well as more creative, to adopt the attitude of thinking,

"What is new about this idea?"

rather than,

"What is old about the idea?"

Very important sessions should be held at low, middle, and top management levels all the time, just to ask the simple question,

"What can we do to exploit these recent discoveries of our Research and Development Departments?" This *use* is the big challenge to management. It is the time for imaginative interpretation, for extrapolation into all areas of the company's visible or visualized business; it is the time for bold, positive action. This is more properly management's job than overdirection or overcontrol of the research function.

Freedom

The creator must have freedom to create. He must live in a permissive atmosphere in which he can announce what he has discovered with assurance, if not of acceptance, at least of a sympathetic hearing. Despite hardship and obstacles, creators who have succeeded have found some audience willing to grant permission to try, and able to hear and praise intelligently.

This freedom, within limits, must be granted in the industrial research laboratory, though it is one of the hardest things for the organization to give. It is essential to the creative climate. The approach needed here is to bring the difficulty plainly into the open. That difficulty is research's need for freedom against organization's need to maintain control and management's need to have its finger on the pulse of all organizational activity. The research man must understand the management image and the limitations on the professional image of the industrial scientist.

Two favorable circumstances to be played up are:

First, in many ways the researcher already has more freedom than anyone else in the organization. Second, intelligent management curbs its desire to control research in detail by channeling this effort and energy instead into imaginative and creative planning, to utilize the creative research and development discoveries made.

The researcher has freedom to plan his attack, in spite of the fact that there is a smaller chance of eventual useful success for the company in his work than in efforts in other fields. He has freedom to a certain extent to pursue side issues merely because they have aroused his personal curiosity. He has freedom from immediate responsibility for turning out a definite piece of work on a definite schedule. The manager must have his plan, the advertiser his copy, the factory superintendent his cases of product; whereas the researcher is often asked only for an interim summary.

The industrial scientist is nevertheless subject to rather severe limitation of the scientist image of his boyhood and initial training, as of one who, suspending judgment in favor of facts, discovers truth, proves it, and reveals it. Stein has drawn a profile of the professional scientist in industry. As a scientist, the truth he discovers may be shared only within the company; his ideas are given to others, and the decisions about them are made by lay personnel. Before he is a scientist, he is an employee, who must accept his status position in a hierarchy, follow organization rules, and develop awareness of costs and finance. The "industrial professional" limits scientist; and "employee" further limits "industrial professional." He has also a social role in relation to company associates and the community, where social skills may give status over professional skill without it. All of this, unfortunately, is clear and simple argument for a man to leave the professional-scientist ranks for management. In research, he is limited in his creativity, he is limited as a scientist, he is limited as an employee, he is marked for a secondary social role. This is why the second avenue of the senior scientist must be opened.

The *Report of the Conference of Research Goals* has drawn a grim picture of industrial research freedom, which will tax management's ingenuity to mitigate:

"In our structured research programs, that is, in the sponsored research projects in the colleges and universities and in the directed research efforts of industrial and governmental laboratories, freedom is too often bounded by the objectives of the immediate program. In such an environment, the individual usually resigns himself to the directed program, rather than developing ideas of his own. Furthermore, the long leap may require years of painstaking effort, and even then it is more likely to fail than succeed. If it does succeed, it may not fit any of the objectives of a structured organization. If the project needs financial support, it is likely to be regarded as too far-fetched to be economically justifiable. All of these deterrents may perhaps be summarized in the statement that freedom and opportunity of a kind that will encourage the high-risk research effort usually run contrary to the objectives of organized and directed research programs, hence it is sacrificed on the altar of expediency."

Many writers on research emphasize that first among favorable conditions comes freedom of action. The nature of this freedom has this basic: to let the man fulfil as much of the scientist image as organizationally feasible, and to perceive in the distance on that road a worthwhile personal goal. From the beginning, the man understands there is confidence that he can succeed or make significant progress. From the beginning, he can select the method of attack, and assemble and launch the means to make it.

Overcontrol has two aspects: overplanning, and overreporting.

Modern science, especially in industry and government, is afflicted with *projectitis,* requiring of the worker a detailed layout of what he will do, from the concept of the project up to the final report. This is not an argument against planning, but against too great detail, and against the limitation of slavishly sticking to the blueprint, or that sacred cow, the Established Objective. General areas of work should be mapped out in open-ended planning. But as Kettering so often emphasized, the proper thing to plan with detailed care is the next experiment. It is the purpose and function of that experiment to say what to do next. These three things are to be remembered:

(1) Discovery is not, by its very nature, subject to the logic of *a priori* planning.
(2) Discovery very often comes by chance.
(3) Plans are not followed out anyway.

One of the hardest things for a mind attuned to logical thinking to digest is that discovery is not accessible to logic. But even a moment's reflection shows that logic must reject unusual new combinations precisely because the common ones are more reasonable. Discovery is achieved with the creative imagination!

In the history of large discovery, very many have come by chance, and this has been documented in Chapter 7. Pasteur said these chance discoveries come only to the prepared mind. Yes. But that mind was prepared by broad training in the art; and it was prepared by intense study of the immediate subject. Overplanned projects forbid, or discourage, such chance digression, and indeed, serve to prepare the mind *not* to see the discovery.

Regarding planning, an article in *Fortune* by Burton Klein of the Rand Corporation comments: "... the uncertainties of the future cannot be resolved by pretending they are certainties ... the belief that all steps required to bring about a major advance can be deduced beforehand is a postwar disease ... less than one quarter of all the aircraft developed since World War II ended up with the engines initially programmed for them."

Over-reporting, both oral and written, is an evil because it wastes time that could be given to creative advance. It is necessary to keep in touch with the progress that has been made, but a balance should be established, so that not too much time and effort are expended in going over the same ground in repeated oral and written versions of the same material. A reporting-aid service might be trained to help management in this area.

Given all the above, the specific task of the researcher is to produce insights and implement them by verification to achieve new technology. Insights require opportunity for the man to work in his own way to operate *his* creative process. He needs time for incubation and dissociated thought, quiet for insight, and freedom from interruption to work his insights out to full realization. This apparently picayune item, freedom from interruption, is more serious than it sounds. In the present author's experience in the business world, with the omnipresent telephone and people working in the same office, or coming in and going out, he has *never* found freedom from interruption. This is the reason for "Saturday discoveries." Workers often retire to the library to work out insights, as well as to write reports.

Insights are often best triggered by discussion. Opportunities for this should always be easily available. This is parallel to, and not a contradiction of, absence of interruption. Group discussions of the brainstorming type are helpful in the right atmosphere. They can be scheduled as needed, or even on a regular basis. Travel and attendance at conventions are useful. Travel has an important side effect in affording time to be alone. It focuses incubation, while the man is away from the office and provides much opportunity for dissociated thought while riding in trains, limousines, planes, eating meals alone, relaxing in hotel rooms. Through papers and discussions conventions also afford new, divergent associations, and serve to give men freedom from the necessary limitations of their industrial jobs.

A move worth considering by bold management is to build an "ivory tower," the purpose of which is, not for retirement from the world, but a retreat for incubative thought. In the world today there seem to be fewer chances for incubation and dissociated thought than ever before. The principle of "togetherness" is inimical to creation. Reflection is hindered by the open structure of the modern house—where a man has a do-it-yourself workbench but not a study—and the multiple means of home entertainment like TV and hi-fi.

This analysis of modern life, set off against the requirements of creativity, suggests the following. At appropriate times in a man's career, e.g., when he has just been assigned a new problem and has worked over the preparation as described in Chapter 4, let him go to the company's "Creative Lodge" in the country to mull over his problem. Here he is free from family and most other social obligations. He expects to be alone much of the time. The place is as quiet as Holmes' Diogenes Club. He uses methods, described in this book or elsewhere, which work for him. Priming material to start thought in new directions has been brought along for study; more may arrive by mail from the man's supervisor or the company library. The lodge itself has a select library.

Groups meet in the day or early evening for creative discussion of the various problems the men have at hand. These meetings are scheduled. The man whose problem is to be discussed prepares a brief summary of it for general study in advance, as in the case of brainstorming. The session is taped; thus the man whose problem is discussed can summarize the tape the next day. After the sessions follow recreation, cards, TV, conversation, and libation.

After a week, the creative worker returns to his job with new ideas and a fresh plan of attack. After one or two such trips, a man who does not benefit from them does not go back. A man whom the lodge especially helps may go back several times a year.

The idea of enabling, or gently forcing, a man to think about his problem and nothing else for a whole week is unusual. The purpose of the lodge is to force preparation, and provide the opportunity for incubation and reflective thought, and discussion to trigger insight.

Whether such major efforts as these pay off in greater creative success of the Research and Development Department is the gamble that is taken. If won, the extra success will carry a special bonus, which is the furtherance of success. A successful laboratory gets a reputation that attracts good men; the atmosphere of success breeds success. The creative men are emboldened to make the next step bigger, more daring, with full confidence in achievement. Success itself means many fine things for creative climate. It means tradition, it means challenge, it means that rare thing, *esprit de corps*.

Selection and Training

Selection and training are a part of climate, because men can be selected and then trained to match the degree of creative climate the company is able to provide. The more creative men are, the more they will need those aspects of climate which have been discussed above that are contra-organizational. The company first determines the level of creativity it can accommodate in its more or less authoritarian structure, and then selects a "company type" for its research as well as its advertising and production departments. As stated earlier, such climate as will encourage the limited creativity the organization needs is desired. Creativity needs vary with the organization just as other requirements do.

Highly creative persons seem unable to work in an industrial framework, with such notable exceptions as Langmuir and Carothers —who received very special handling. It is related that Langmuir was surrounded by a corps of people whose principal job was to see that he was not burdened with unimportant trivia. Naively, he never realized this. But judging by results, a Langmuir or a Carothers would appear to be well worth tolerating.

Recently, two articles, respectively by Elder and Kelton, have appeared which independently list almost the same qualities and

Elder	*Kelton*
Training	Knowledge
Desire to continue to learn	Initiative
Aptitude for industrial research	Attitude
Aggressiveness and ambition	Personality
Creative imagination	Originality
Good judgment	Good judgment
Accuracy	Professional integrity and honesty
Leadership	Leadership
Co-operative attitude	Co-operation
Optimistic Outlook	Publications, honors, societies
Ability to communicate	Ability to communicate
Growth to greater responsibility	Responsibility

attributes desired in a young researcher or engineer, as shown in the accompanying comparison.

Somewhere in these tabulations our creative man got lost. There are two defects in the lists. First, only one avenue of advancement for the young professional employees is visualized. Second, qualities not necessary for creativity, nay, even antagonistic to it, are emphasized. Creative men are not necessarily long on leadership, or judgment, or co-operation, and their desire for greater responsibility is mostly on the score of their art.

Unfortunately, the list is realistic. Danielson, in "Characteristics of Engineers and Scientists," shows that in a series of 75 supervisors of engineers, and scientists, only 17 listed creativity as a quality of the ideal professional employee. To advance our culture, the author submits that a greater emphasis of creativity is needed, even at the cost of adjustment of the organizational viewpoint. The above list of qualities for a creative researcher is like the following satirical management advertisement, from *Chemical and Engineering News*, which asks to eat the cake and have it too:

> "WANTED, TOP EXECUTIVE—Unusual opportunity for an imaginative (but not unconventional) planner who thinks quickly (but isn't impatient), acts aggressively (but ruffles no fur), and can get things done (through channels

without stepping on toes). Should have an A.B. in Business Administration (preferably from an Eastern University), but the equivalent in experience will be considered (for blood relatives of management). Applicant should have varied and broad background (yet be a specialist) and have a work record demonstrating job stability (i.e., without being a "job-hopper," he must nevertheless have acquired "a varied and broad background"). The man chosen will be a member of an executive committee (team) jointly responsible (he'd better fit in) for company policy."

Training programs of widely varied complexity exist to serve different needs. The interest here is only in the creativity aspect of training and its relation to the subject of climate. Education is needed in several directions. The problems inherent in climate for research and development should be aired and discussed with the young professional. He should understand management's function of decision and need for control, and know that his management understands the technical man's need for freedom and function of challenge of things as they are. Young men are not overly aware of the image of the industrial scientist plotted by Stein, and this should be made explicit to them. If done properly, the men are prepared to visualize and adjust to their industrial roles.

Another need is more positive in nature, and in its appeal will compensate for any disappointment in the preceding paragraph. This is, surprisingly enough, training in the principles of creativity. These are often neglected in school. Some men grasp them dimly, others fumble for years to learn what they might have received in a few brief sessions of presentation. In particular, the use of varied preparation is important, the appreciation of motivation, of recording insights, and allowing opportunity for their full realization.

The trainee needs instruction in this connection—that extensive reading in the library is not the panacea for all ills. He will have been well indoctrinated in the usual prescription for a new problem, an exhaustive literature search. This is often not the best approach. Rather, one should read enough to understand what the problem is, to learn to state it in several different ways, and to have available several methods as tools for his attack. Reading is no substitute for trying, and a researcher can know too much to try the right thing.

Some of the best short articles for the young professional interested in creativity to read are the references (Part IV) to Easton, Beveridge, and Murphy. The best books are by Hadamard, Beveridge, and Rossman.

Services

Climate to aid the creative process is fostered by providing many routine-type services. These services eliminate blocks to creativity, decrease interruptions, and remove those things which limit opportunity for reflective thought. An extended list of what the services are might be made, of which this is a selection:

Stenographic.
Library: relieve men of searches; do translations; circulate
    journals, books, abstracts.
Efficient files.
Accounting and clerical work minimized.
Analytical laboratory service.
Engineering and mechanical aid by specialists.
Pilot plant: segregated, delegated authority to operate.
Reporting aid.
Information from other departments well-circulated.
Easy procurement of materials.
Advice and help from consultants—routine.
Easy relations with universities.

An additional aid to success is to do what would be done with any other department. That is, *polish the product as much as possible*. The visible products of the research department are reports. They are the communication stage of the creative process, the repository and realization of the big and subsequent smaller insights attained in the established favorable climate. The reports should contain a summary for management—what to do and why; the conclusions for research colleagues without time for the details; the main body for the record and for the next man working in the area. Enlisting the aid of technical writers and editors to help get out the best reports quickly is a growing practice, and many reports are written this way that otherwise would never be written at all. This step is worthwhile because access to research reports of such quality that they promote the *use* of research ideas is bound to create good climate.

A final and important service is the fostering of general intellectual growth. Steps to broaden men's interest in and enjoyment of literature and the arts further the appreciation of these finished embodiments of creative skill, and impart taste in the selection of means to prosecute and lend finish to their own creative tasks.

Conformity

The problem of climate arises because organizational pressures operate to limit and to mold creativity. This is but one aspect of the larger problem of conformity, which stands as one of the most important blocks to creativity. We squelch our children with conformity and social adjustment in school, and give them another big dose in business. But creation is nonconformity *per se*. If one applies any logic at all, the organization should strive to make a man whom it desires to be creative, *less* a conformist than he is already. The creator has to be a nonconformist because every creation is an act of nonconformity.

The Foundation for Research on Human Behavior has given the following interesting information, showing the nonconformity of the research scientist. Tests were administered to groups which involved the willingness of subjects to hold to an answer they believed right in the face of unanimous group insistence on a different answer they believed wrong. Results are shown in Table 11–1.

TABLE 11–1

Subjects	% of Times Conforming with Wrong Group Answer
Female college sophomores	37
Female college seniors	32
Female college alumnae (Av. age 40)	22
Applicants to medical school	27
Male college sophomores	26
Senior, Honors, Engineering Students	22
Research scientists	16

Both creativity and conformity are needed; the one is essential to social stability, the other to social progress. The wholesome balance between the two is being upset by the rising pressure of conformity to organizations of all types in modern life. Part of this is very simply that increased population requires more, and more complex, organizations in order to develop the necessary cultural institutions.

Nevertheless, let it be remembered that the creative man who seems a little sandy in the fine-meshed organizational gears is fighting a battle for the very management that may look at him askance. He fights for all men, and for the free spirit of the western world, which has in large degree given freedom to live, and now seeks to maintain freedom to create. In modern life, in education, in status seeking, the pressure is strongly in the opposite direction, toward more and more slavish conformity. As this conformity-pressure develops, the problem of letting individual creativity flourish within the group confronts all men, demanding a creative solution. The number of scientists in the western world is relatively small. Quality must make up the lack of quantity, by letting each man be relatively more creative. Let us beware lest, within our vaunted freedom, we do not shackle creation more than the authoritarian state. There are these promises implicit in creative climate:

We will let you try in your own way.
We will recognize and credit your work.
We will use your work.
We will provide a satisfying goal to reward your creativity.

12. TESTS FOR CREATIVITY *

Investigators have devised and used a wide variety of specific tests for creativity. Until recently, most work was directed to having subjects answer questions on batteries of psychological tests directed to performance, and assessing creativity from the results. But modern work has swung heavily in the direction of assessing creative personality and creative behavior. The reason is, the responsive answers to the performance tests must be rapid, and necessarily at a low level of creativity. It has to be assumed that this creativity is similar to the concept of solution of difficult problems used in the rest of this book. On the other hand, personality studies are made in relation to the creative life-work of individuals, often famous creators, and such work may appear to have a sounder basis. There has been great activity in these fields, especially for the purposes of early identification of creative talent, and for purposes of hiring and then stimulating the talent in industry.

In testing, the construct of creativity may be thought of either as a unit, or alternatively as a composite of qualities or attributes that are related to each other in that they occur together. This is similar to the construct of beauty, where it is known that the beauty of an object can be subjectively assessed in toto, or else partially in terms of size, color, shape, texture, and form. But can one assess the parts, give each of these a numerical value, and add the values to arrive at an assessment of beauty? Both the "total" and the "summation of partials" methods have merit.

* Acknowledgment is made to Dr. H. A. Edgerton, President, Richardson, Bellows, Henry & Company, Inc., for consultation on and contribution to this chapter, although the author must, of course, assume responsibility for the form in which the material is here presented.

Study of Creativity by Solutions to Tests

Many of the tests devised by early workers have been revised and refined for present-day use.

Sharp used a group of tests of invention in 1899, including suggestions from ink blots.

Whipple, in the various editions of his Manual on general psychological testing, gave tests of imagination and invention, including suggestions from ink blots, writing sentences using given words, and inventing stories incorporating a given series or list of words. All of these are used extensively in modern work.

Chassell's work on "Tests of Originality" is classic, and has been much copied. She employed analogies, puzzles, word building, and completion tests. She asked for suggestions (economic prophecies) of original ideas for locomotion, heating, housing, and the like, and required details of a mechanical invention to turn the pages of sheet music. Her puzzles needed high space factor abilities. She also wanted associations to situations of exaggerated novelty such as these: What if water should contract in freezing? Suppose no more paper were ever available? Suppose the earth began to cool, how could man preserve himself? A subject was allowed 2.5 (!) minutes each to produce associations to such possibilities.

The list of ideas for locomotion may be compared with the "uses of a brick" test much used today. The responses to unusual situations is copied exactly in the famous AC Spark Plug Battery of creativity tests.

Chassell ranked her subjects by averaging the grades over the twelve tests she used, and then determined the correlation of this ranking with grades in the individual tests. She found the best correlations with final group rank were as shown in Table 12-1.

TABLE 12–1

Correlation with Final Group Rank	Test
1st	Analogy (hoe : gardener :: scissors : tailor)
2nd	Novel situations
3rd	Economic prophecy

Solutions to the mechanical page turner problem were interesting, and some very good. This seems to have been a true test of creativity, albeit rather heavily loaded in the direction of spatial skill.

Thurstone, in his work on primary mental abilities, developed many refinements, as well as additions, to these.

Welch applied certain tests to compare the abilities of professional artists and college students, with results as shown in Table 12-2.

TABLE 12–2

| | College Group | | Artist Group | |
	Mean	Std. Dev.	Mean	Std. Dev.
(1) Make sentences from a list of ten words (10 min.)	18.0	4.24	17.7	7.15
(2) Make capital letters with 3 straight lines, 2 st. lines, 1 curve and 1 st. line (3 min.)	6.7	1.83	12.5	1.93
(3) Write story, using 20 given words in order (3 min.)	9.1	3.15	11.4	4.09
(4) Make furniture from ten blocks (5 trials, 2 min. for each)	3.4	2.68	18.4	7.78

The list for item one was: fish boy waits catches the a long cold by from.

The list for item three was: stairs ocean chemistry song test mountain bubble dog lemon picture post blanket violin lamp nightmare steam leg window swamp stamp.

In the two verbal tests, there was little difference between the groups. The artists excelled where a well-developed space factor was needed.

In subsequent work, this time comparing artists, art majors, and other students in the same college, it was again found that major differences were confounded with a space factor requirement. In tests where this factor was heavily involved, the students in general scored poorer than art majors, who on their part did not differ in achievement from the professional artists. Probably, a good space factor led the artists and art majors toward their line of work in the first place, whereupon development and extension of the ability occurred.

Thurstone has discussed factors in connection with the study of creative thinking. Factors are basic human abilities that have been identified by mathematical analysis of extensive psychological testing. Obviously, a factor must be exercised during the battery of tests if it is to appear in the later analysis. If it is exercised in only one test, it is specific; if in several, it is group; if in all, it is a general factor. The most useful factors to study have been group. Many have been identified, but the ones that have appeared and reappeared and become commonly accepted are verbal, numerical, spatial, memory, reasoning, and motor ones. Each of these may show a variety of aspects, for example,

$$\text{Verbal } I = \text{Reading Skill}$$
$$\text{Verbal } II = \text{Word Fluency}$$

The very extensive Air Force analyses have been correlated to extract the factors shown in the accompanying list.

Very briefly, the factors are obtained in this way: 50 tests are given to 200 subjects and scored. The correlation coefficients of all the tests, taken two at a time, are computed. The operation of "factor analysis" is carried out on this basic table of correlation coefficients to show which tests tend to cluster in groups. This tendency must meet statistical tests to be called significant. *Then,* the clustering tests are looked at, and the common thread of a particular ability running through them all is analyzed out. If a battery of 12 tests had six arithmetic tasks and six verbal tasks, a verbal and a numerical factor might appear. But other factors could also appear, inter-relating some of the number with some of the word tasks, if, for example, the same kind of reasoning were concerned in both.

Workers in factor analysis have separated factors related to creativity, for example, ideational fluency. In his presidential address to the American Psychological Association, J. P. Guilford made a logical analysis of the problem of creativity and determined by analytical thinking that it is composed of certain elements:

(1) Sensitivity to problems: seeing needs, seeing the unusual.
(2) Fluency: of ideas, of associations.
(3) Flexibility: freedom from inertia of thought, adaptive set.
(4) Originality: uncommonness of response.
(5) Penetration: remote associations.
(6) Analysis: recognition of pertinence.

(7) Synthesis: closure ability.

(8) Redefinition: shifting of function.

Guilford then adopted or invented certain tests to serve as predictors of the presence and variation of these elements in a group of subjects. Some of Guilford's novel tests were: A new invention makes it unnecessary for people to eat; deduce consequences. Present some items, and the broad instruction to do something with each item.

FACTORS OF HUMAN ABILITIES

After Cranbach, cf. Ref. 36 (p. 278)

Carefulness	Perceptual speed
General reasoning I	Pilot interest
Integration I	Planning
Integration II	Psychomotor coordination
Integration III	Psychomotor precision
Judgment	Psychomotor speed
Kinesthetic motor	Reasoning II
Length estimation	Reasoning III
Mathematical background	Social science background
Mathematical reasoning	Spatial Relations I
Mechanical experience	Spatial Relations II
Memory I	Spatial Relations III
Memory II	Verbal
Memory III	Visualization
Numerical	

The subjects take the tests and the results are analyzed. The creative products are the questionnaire answers. They may be direct creation, as in the case of a list of "uses of a brick" for idea fluency. Or the products may be referred back to a personality trait, if the questionnaire (the physical paper product) should happen to be an example of the TAT, or a personality inventory.

If the result is direct, and concerned with creative performance, the product has the aspects of quantity and quality. In some tests, however, only quantity enters, while in others, only quality. The total *number* of uses of the brick is one important datum. The average *quality* of responses is another. The number is determined objectively by counting. Quality can be obtained by panel judgments and/or by counting the frequency of the responses in the questionnaires.

Tests invented to measure hypothesized items must be validated to prove by psychological techniques that they do so. One way of validation is to check the correlation of the tests against ratings of the subjects for creativity by supervisors, peers, class grades, IQ, etc.

Guilford states that the factors most relevant to creativity are those found in the category of divergent thinking. There are two exceptions to this general rule, that of redefinition, which is in the convergent thinking category, and that of sensitivity to problems, which is in the evaluative category. Divergent thinking involves various forms of fluency and of flexibility, as well as originality and elaboration. Redefinition is tested by such devices as camouflaged words, hidden figures, and object synthesis, in all of which a subject is expected to recognize more than one item in a unit in which one item is usually outstanding and another or others, are hidden in the original one. Sensitivity to problems is tested by seeing problems and deficiencies in situations in which none is apparent at first glance.

Guilford's tests for creativity stand up well in a number of different test situations which use different criteria. They seem to be one of the most stable predictors of success in situations in which creativity helps to determine achievement. The tests assume:

> All persons are creative to some extent.
> Low-level creativity has all the characteristics of composing "Don Giovanni" or the infinitesimal calculus.
> Studying creativity without preparation, incubation, insight, or motivation is the same as studying creativity with these elements present.

Having designed a large number of tests directed to the analyzed components of creativity, Guilford factor-analyzed the results, and was able to show the emergence of many of the predicted factors (fluency, originality, redefinition, etc.). The specific nature of some of the tests was as set forth in Table 12-3.

TABLE 12–3. GUILFORD TESTS AND RESULTS.

Test	Task Required for Item	Factor Related to Test
Sentence Analysis	List all facts or assumptions contained in simple sentences.	Analysis
Paragraph Analysis	Analyze paragraph into five basic ideas.	Analysis
Figure Analysis	Pick out objects jumbled together in drawing with lines in common.	Analysis
Figure Concepts (uncommonness)	Find features in common in pictures of objects. (Score as the number of uncommon responses.)	Originality
Impossibilities	List things that are impossible.	Fluency
Plot Titles (low quality)	Write titles for story plots. (Score is the number of low-quality titles written.)	Fluency
Plots Titles (cleverness)	Aim at cleverness of titles. (Score is the number of clever titles written.)	Originality
Brick Uses (fluency)	List different uses for a brick. (Score is number listed.)	Fluency
Brick Uses (flexibility)	Develop as many *classes* of uses as possible. (Score is the number of classes of uses listed.)	Flexibility
Number Associations (uncommonness)	List associations for given numbers. (Score is the number of statistically uncommon responses.)	Originality
Consequences Test (low quality)	List consequences of certain changes. (Score is the number of more obvious consequences.)	Fluency
Consequences Test (remoteness)	(Score is the number of indirect or remote consequences listed.)	Penetration
Match Problems	Take away matches and leave certain number of squares or triangles.	Flexibility

Quick Response (uncommonness)	Word associations. (Score is the number of uncommon responses.)	Originality
Word Transformation	Regroup letters in series of words, without changing order, to form new set.	Redefinition
Sentence Synthesis	Make sentence out of words in scrambled order.	Synthesis

D. W. Taylor had supervisors rate their men on a checklist of 79 statements about creativity, and on originality, quality and quantity of work. The men also took a group of tests. Statistically significant correlations were reported.

Taylor first collected 206 statements concerning creativity or originality on separate cards, and 44 judges were asked to sort the cards into 7 piles, which was to indicate a range from high to low creativity. A frequency distribution was obtained for each statement. Those statements with least standard deviation, which most judges agreed belonged in the same pile, were considered to have least ambiguity, and of the 206 statements, 79 were selected as having a low measure of ambiguity. These had both positive and negative orientation to creativity. The statements had such texture as:

By comparison with other people in such a job he is outstandingly creative.

He has little knack for thinking up new things.

He follows established procedures consistently.

Each of 103 participants was rated on the 79 statements by his immediate and secondary supervisors, between whom reliability was found to be 0.73. The same men were also rated by immediate and secondary supervisors for originality of work and quality and quantity of it on a different set of rating scales, set up specifically for this task.

The correlation between the statements ratings and the originality rating was (0.71) statistically valid.

The 103 men were given the following tests: (1) the *Strong*

Vocational Interest Blank, scored only on the Engineering Scale, which was most appropriate for this group of electronics engineers; (2) the *Terman Concept Mastery Test,* developed for use in studies with gifted individuals and composed of two parts, one called Synonyms-Antonyms and the other, Analogies; (3) Owen's and Bennett's *Mechanical Comprehension Test;* (4) the *Test of Productive Thinking* which was formulated by the Psychological Corporation to require listing of consequences of an imaginary situation; and (5) the *Test for Selecting Research Personnel,* developed by the American Institute for Research. In three sections it tests ability to formulate a problem, ability to interpret results, and ability to accept responsibility.

The significant correlations between the statement checklist ratings and the tests were:

Ratings vs Mechanical Comprehension	.29
" " Productive Thinking	.24
" " Personnel Selection	.36

It would appear that these tests would tend to select men whom industrial supervisors would rate as creative.

Besides these analyses of results of creativity tests, as such, creativity has been evaluated in these other ways:

Direct personality studies.
Ratings of creative workers for creativeness.
Behavioral analyses.

Testing for Traits of the Creative Personality

Much of Chapter 9 on Creative Personality is pertinent in the present connection also.

Certain methods have been developed to obtain information on the creative personality by studying average people, or groups engaged in creative activity like research, or famous creators.

Importance of Drive. Anne Roe used a case method to obtain dossiers on famous, creative scientists nominated by their peers. The groups were small, and in addition to the case histories, the men were tested with a carefully selected battery to evaluate space, verbal, and number skills. The Rorschach and TAT were also used. The accumulated data were searched, and yielded as significant items, first, the effects of home influences, and second, the common characteristic of intensive drive toward intensive prosecution of the lifework.

Bloom, at the University of Chicago, has especially commented on motivation. He studied problem solving in groups of good and poor problem solvers, and found that the differences between the two groups seemed chiefly related to motivation, desire to attack the problem, and skill in going about the attack. He felt that attitudes and emotions interfered with problem solving in one group and facilitated it in the other, and that interest and motivation were among the relevant variables in problem solving and achievement measures. He obtained a group of outstandingly creative chemists and mathematicians by nominations from panels of their peers, and he obtained another group of chemists and mathematicians who were not remarkably creative at all. Both groups had about the same amount of education and experience. The two groups were compared by means of 27 tests, only two of which showed significant differences between the groups. Bloom found almost nothing in the way of significant difference in their aptitudes, problem-solving abilities, and perceptual-cognitive habits. The two significant variables concerned the enormous amount of energy channeled into productive research effort, characteristic of creative individuals, and the fact that creative individuals appear to have difficulty in establishing warm, friendly relations with other people. This seems to be true, at least partially, because of apparent need to retreat from a world of people to one of ideas and objects.

All this may explain the dedication to work that Roe found among creative scientists, and it is undoubtedly apparent in the high schizothyme quality found by Cattell among creatives. In general, most researchers in the area of creativity agree that those individuals rated as being high in originality are at least somewhat introverted.

Cattell Test Battery. Just as Guilford has developed a complex battery to analyze creative performance, Cattell has devised a complete battery for testing creative personality. His work yielded the following conclusions, amply confirmed, but scarcely expanded, by the large volume of current work to evaluate creative personality.

(1) The same creative traits are found in creative men from all disciplines (just as they all use the same creative method).

(2) The most important traits outstanding in creativity are that the individual is

more schizothymic
more dominant
more inhibited (desurgent)
more emotionally sensitive (from overprotection in childhood)
more radical
more likely to show an exacting self-concept

The correspondence of these to much of the foregoing material will be evident:

$$Dominance = recognition$$
$$Ego = vying$$
$$Emotional\ Sensitivity = high\ drive\ or\ motivation$$

These were arrived at by analysis of results from subjects taking the Cattell battery, which yields a profile of sixteen traits. Many of these are complex psychological concepts needing too extensive definition for this space. But as a matter of interest, the profiles of the average man and the creative researcher are reproduced in Appendix F (p. 297).

Cattell also has applied the information from his work to famous people, by doing analyses of the biographies of famous creators, and identifying in their characters the special traits of creators.

Barron Projective Tests. Frank Barron, at the University of California's Institute of Personality Assessment and Research, has used projective tests in combination with performance tests and peer ratings. It is believed, logically enough, that the quantity and quality of unusual responses given in projective tests are a measure of originality, based on the fact that great productivity of novelty seems characteristic of those individuals who have made noteworthy contributions in their field. If, then, some people are regularly original in their thinking, this trait might be expected to stand out in examinations of responses to projective measures.

The criterion of an original response is usually established as uncommonness in the group being studied, including the individual being studied. Working with Air Force captains, Barron studied them in terms of uncommonness in *Rorschach* and *Thematic Apperception Test* responses, and in terms of nominations by their peers, and found that the more creative individuals showed independence not only on a scale set up to determine that characteristic, but also in a group pressure situation, in which an individual is given cues to indicate that his peers believe something in particular and then he is asked what *he* believes. Independence of judgment is shown when the individual negates false cues or cues that lead to an untrue conclusion. Later, Barron (1960) studied writers who were nominated by their peers as being particularly creative. He found that in a nonpressured situation in which subjects were presented with two identical circles and asked to tell which had the greater area, the subjects chose one circle about as often as they chose the other. When they were exposed to a majority judgment, however, they selected the circle opposite to the one they believed their peers had chosen!

In other work, described in the *Scientific American,* Barron discussed the Welsh Figure Preference Test, in which simple abstract line drawings vie for attention against more complex, and more formless, drawings which seem to appeal to the imagination to define, what is this? Barron found that 80 painters showed marked preference for the complex figures, which they termed vital or dynamic. Then, later, doctoral candidates, in the field of science at the University of California, who were rated by the faculty as relatively more creative, showed exactly the same predilection.

Barron found, then, preference for (spatial) complexity, an ability for uncommon responses, and independence of judgment. Examples are given in Table 12-4.

TABLE 12-4

Test	Common Response	Creative Response (uncommon)
Inkblot Shape	An ape	A baboon looking at itself in a hand mirror
Response to the stimulus-image, empty bookcases	A deserted room	The vacant eye of an idiot
Stimulus image, foghorn	Belch	Cry of despair of a great, unseen animal

In addition, Barron wrote this in regard to the concept of rapport with the unconscious:

"The creative individual, in his generalized preference for apparent disorder, turns to the dimly realized life of the unconscious, and is likely to have more than the usual amount of respect for the forces of the irrational in himself and in others.

"This respect consists in a faith that the irrational itself will generate some ordering principle if it is permitted expression and admitted to conscious scrutiny. To put the matter more strongly, I believe that the creative individual not only respects the irrational in himself, but courts it as the most promising source of novelty in his own thought. He rejects the demand of society that he should shun in himself the primitive, the uncultured, the naive, the magical, the nonsensical; that he must be a 'civilized' member of the community."

Behavior Analyses and Creativity Ratings by Supervisors or Peers

The technique of ratings by supervisors has had especially wide use, and was employed by Taylor in the work described above.

Buel, of the Pure Oil Company, used a method parallel to Taylor's, but without performance testing.

"Research Supervisors in the laboratory of a large oil company were asked to anonymously describe the most and least creative research men under their supervision, without recourse to a definition of creativity. The behavioral statements so obtained served as microdefinitions of creativity and were used as descriptive checklist items to rate personnel in a wide variety of research activities. . . . It was suggested that the items presented may be valid discriminators between relatively more or less creative persons in a wide variety of research areas."

A few of the behavioral statements were: Looks for new ways of doing things; fails to follow through on his own best ideas; has developed short-cut methods.

Sprecher conducted a study in which he had peers and supervisors rate engineers on creativity. The judges were then asked to list the qualities which determined their ratings. Having thus obtained definitive terms into which creativity could be categorized, Sprecher could label creativity with specific characteristics.

Taylor, Smith, and Ghiselin have reported a study of physical scientists at an Air Force research center, in which 56 criterion scores were obtained. The scores included not only multiple ratings by supervisors, monitors, and peers, but also official records, consideration of reports and publications, membership in professional societies, project research, control variables, and self-ratings. Correlations of scores from supervisors, peers, and monitors were often significant; correlations between subjectively and objectively obtained data were usually negligible; correlations between scores by supervisors, between scores by peers, and between scores on research reports and publications generally showed as zero. On the whole, for each criterion, only 20 per cent of the other criteria correlated with it significantly. This result points up the difficulties in this line of work.

Saunders set up three performance tests for factors related to creativity. His criteria for all these tests were supervisory evaluation on the basis of success as respects job requirements, and necessity for filling appropriately the role that the job demanded in terms of the supervisor's requirements. One of his tests was a measure of inductive reasoning, which involved number series, e.g., given three complete sets of number series, fill in the blanks in the fourth series. This test differentiated the research people distinctly from all others. Others of Saunder's tests were consequences of a novel situation, and controlled associations.

Saunders examined the engineers with whom he was working for a measure of interest in ideas, things, people, and economic matters, and he found that those individuals involved in research and development—the most creative group—came out with the highest scores on interest in ideas. The same group had higher scores than did any of the less creative individuals in a study of liking-to-think.

These methods have contributed less to the knowledge of creativity than the tests of performance or personality. One reason is that these methods are not really studying or attempting to identify creativity. Supervisors' high ratings go to the all-around men in the industrial hierarchy, who fit the "company pattern," and these are not necessarily the most creative men. Groups of high creatives should be identified, then studied for their performances and methods of achievement. The initially groping works of Patrick, Laycock, Duncker and Maier have been more illuminative of creativity than the modern peer and supervisor ratings procedures.

Tests of Improvement in Creativity

The AC Spark Plug Test, used in conjunction with a creativity course, has been reviewed on pages 149-150. This course, and the GE course also described in Chapter 10 appeared to improve the creative performance of participants.

Parnes and Meadow have studied students in a creative problem-solving class at the University of Buffalo. The class, organized to teach brainstorming, begins with a discussion of perceptual, emotional, and cultural blocks to creative thinking. Perceptual blocks include difficulty in isolating problems, rigidity produced from narrowing the problem too much, and failure to use all the senses in observing; cultural and emotional blocks include the effects of conformity, excessive faith in reason or logic, fear of mistakes and failure, self-satisfaction, perfectionism, reliance on authority, and negative outlooks. The students are taught the brainstorming principle of suspended judgment, and are given wide practice in the utilization of it. They are also given practice in examining a problem from a variety of viewpoints, and they are taught to analyze problems, considering such items as simplification, possible combinations of techniques and procedures for solution adaptation, etc. Forced relationship techniques, in which relationships within a list of possible solutions must be made, emphasize freedom in thought and the use of imagination. Students are taught to sense problems in their lives and to define these problems for creative attack.

In the first work by Parnes and Meadow, an experimental group of students who had been enrolled in the course was matched against a control group. The experimental group made significant gains over the control group on measures for both quantity and quality of ideas.

Further research was done to determine whether an increase in creative productivity in students who had taken the course was apparent a year or more after they had completed it. Again, the experimental group achieved significantly higher quality and quantity scores. These pieces of work indicate how increase in creativity has been tested for. Brainstorming itself can be a test, by counting the number and rating the quality of ideas produced.

Carrier Company Tests

Kubasta, at a meeting of the Special Libraries Association in Pittsburgh, in 1956, described the Carrier Corporation's test for a development engineer. The test includes both personality and performance facets:

(1) The Guilford-Zimmerman Temperament Survey, a multiple choice test comprising 300 questions, indicates a man's personality and disposition as they apply to his relations with other people, and covers such traits as energy, domination, sociability, emotional stability, objectivity, cooperativeness, and masculinity of emotions.

(2) Mechanical Comprehension includes some 60 problems dealing with such things as levers, gears, pulleys, and mechanical forces.

(3) Productive Thinking includes consequences of special hypotheses. An example is: "Chemical research has produced a new gas called 'Invane.' It has remarkable properties. It contracts when heated and condenses to a liquid at 90°C.

"Condensation results in the absorption of 300 calories per gram of 'Invane.' It is nonflammable and costs less than acetylene. What are the consequences of this discovery? What ideas occur?"

(4) Mathematical Formulation requires the individual to select mathematical expressions which are the correct solutions to problems stated in words.

(5) Spatial Visualization presents flat patterns and requires the subject to designate the particular three-dimensional objects into which they would fold.

Men who show a certain profile in these tests are said to make good Carrier development engineers. Creativity is only a part of the picture, in the work of the development engineer, as well as in the tests. Those tests which are especially related to creativity are Productive Thinking, and the tests for personality traits related to Cattell's creative characteristics, such as dominance.

New Methods of Testing

Modern knowledge makes it possible to select the more effective creative minds from a general population for creativity study. These subjects serve to evaluate new methods which will permit motivation and incubation to operate in ways largely denied by the preliminary screening tests. The selective tests are exemplified by the following:

> Bouthilet method used to identify prefocal rapport.
> Inverse use of factor analysis.

The first has already been discussed (p. 78). The "inverse use of factor analysis" is a phrase by which the present writer wishes to imply a new interpretation of suitable factor analysis data. As described above, the factor analysis method used the responses of subjects as source material to cluster tests related to certain analyzed partial aspects of creativity, such as originality of thought or idea fluency. The inverse or reverse of this is to use the responses in order to cluster the *subjects* who answer groups of tests well or poorly. This can be done for high or low levels of spatial or verbal abilities, as well as for creativity.

In most factor analysis tests, and many creativity tests of the past, emphasis has been on correlations, and the extraction of factors. So much has this been the case, that almost no study of subject-by-subject performance has been made to obtain, for example, the distribution of creative talent in a representative population of subjects. This could be done from the existing data of experiments referred to above. But the raw data are required, and partially because of printing costs, are rarely published. Therefore, unless the experimenter himself studies the creativity in his individual subjects, the chance is lost.

The following is a method, somewhat arbitrary, whereby the distribution of creativity in a sample population might be estimated, and the most creative subjects marked down for further intensive study. What is usually done is to correlate the tests of all subjects. What is now wanted is the reverse, that is, the correlation of subjects on all tests. But in order to isolate creativity, the tests must be ranked according to the amount of creative ability required to perform them. Criteria might be something like these:

If a simple judgment is required, and all the requisite material to make the judgment is supplied, place the test low on the scale.

If much must be supplied by the subject, rate high. For example, such verbal tests as writing a composition, or listing words beginning with s, or synonyms, or related words.

If little must be supplied by the subject, rate low.

If a method of solution must be created, even though all requisite material is given, rate high.

If the test is difficult, obviously requiring creative searching around in the mind, rate high.

Table 12–5 can then be set up:

TABLE 12–5

Tests, in Order of Creativity Required, 1 = Highest Creativity	Rank of Each Student in Each Test — Student —					
	A	B	C	D	E	F	G
1	1	24	2	5	16		
2	1	19	3	11	19		
3	1	12	15	21	8		
4	1	16	19	17	9		
5	2	10	4	23	13		
6	7	25	6	15	11		
.							
.							
.							
.							
.							
.							
n (say, 26)	23	17	19	3	9		

The correlation between each student's performance rank and the creativity rating can be obtained. The order of these correlations is the order of creativity of the subjects, as judged by the battery, and insofar as the assigned ranking of creativity of the tests is concerned. This ranking could be to a large extent validated by a panel. To the objection that the creativity ranking is arbitrary, the sufficient answer is that we know so little of creativeness, that this kind of work is useful anyway and should be followed up to see where it leads.

It would be interesting to validate the rankings of a group of subjects from an ordinary factor analysis, by giving a creativity battery. It would be helpful if the battery contained tests (a) deliberately oriented to creativity so that the ranking from high to low would be obvious and easily agreed to; (b) requiring students to supply as much material as possible; and (c) requiring the creative additions proposed below.

It would also be interesting to compare creativity rankings with those for general intelligence, or for particular factors. The first could be done if an intelligence test were part of the battery. For the second, a particular factor, it is realized that the best tests for the space factor, for example, have already been isolated by the factor analysis. These can be used to rank the students for spatial facility, and these ranks can be correlated with the creativity ranks. So also for other factors, or for other rankings that can be deduced from the data, including personality trait ratings if available. Rank correlations with age, health, sex, or general physical classification, also can be tested.

Other Methods

The present author's own ideas on methods for the study of creativity and general types of tests are based on the concept that the subject must add something or create something of his own in the tasks he undertakes. For verbal testing, he should write a "composition" on some subject. Puzzle solving and seeing an old item (a brick, a matchbox) in a new context are suitable. In some tests he may be asked to invent the *method* of solving. Requirements for selection of the key clue from a mass and for explication of needs should test aspects of creativeness. Finally, tests that are deliberately difficult are certain thereby to require creative solution.

The method of *addition to tests* is proposed as follows. Let it be assumed that a battery of psychological, mental tests has been given to a group. In each case, when a subject has finished a test, he is asked to write two further examples, first a better example, then an example with a new twist. These would have to be judged qualitatively. Such judgments can give satisfactory results, especially if made independently by members of a panel. The principle involved here is, again, creation to a model.

The following is suggested as a method of testing the subject's *ability and mechanism of attack*. A large and significant problem, such as the treatment of cancer, is posed, and the subject must provide: two significant analogies in the field; two searching questions which, if answered, might guide the research; two sidelines in related fields, the study of which might contribute to the problem; one wild guess of what might work, with a reason to support it, if available; and unusual facts of halo material which might stimulate another worker. For example, X-rays can be used against cancer, and cysteine gives a certain protection against some radiation effects of X-ray, so a more efficient compound might allow the use of considerably higher X-ray dosages than now.

Naturally, these replies would be subject to the experimenter's judgment for grading. The use of panels for rating would be helpful. Indeed, the use of good tests for creativity, even if difficult to score, is to be recommended over poor tests whose only merit is ease (and precision) of scoring. Precise scoring of worthless tests will not increase the knowledge of creativity.

Management

A study of creativity and success was made by Stein in an attempt to answer questions such as: What are the differences and similarities in skills and abilities necessary to achieve success, and necessary to achieve creativity? How do status levels differ between success and creativity? How do different members of society perceive the skills and abilities necessary to achieve creativity and necessary to achieve success? How do people at different levels of creativity compare with their top-level supervisors, who are successful but not necessarily creative, in their perception of skills and abilities necessary for success, and in their perception of what should be considered creative? How do more and less creative individuals differ from each other?

The study was carried out with individuals in the research divisions of several companies. Subjects were sorted into seven supervisory status levels: top administrator, a secondary level, and five lower-level groups. Individuals in the five lower groups were further classified into more and less creative groups on the basis of ratings by supervisors, peers, and subordinates. From analyses of the situations in which the researchers were employed, it was discovered that they played one of the following five roles: scientific, professional, employee, social, or administrative. Statements of eleven skills and abilities related to these roles were constructed, with the characteristic of autonomy related to a twelfth statement. Statements were presented to the subjects in two separate lists: One was introduced by asking subjects to rank the statements in terms of which abilities made for success in the company, and the other was introduced by asking the subjects to rank the statements in terms of abilities and activities that should be recognized and rewarded for the purpose of encouraging and promoting research activity in an organization.

There was good agreement among raters at each of the supervisory levels in the orderings they made for success and for creativity. In answer to the questions first set forth, apparently creativity and success seem much more similar to the top level administrators than they do to men lower in the hierarchy. The lower correlations between skills and abilities necessary for success and for creativity found among researchers suggest that these men perceive more value conflict than do top administrators. Different members of this society (i.e., research people and those successful in terms of having achieved high levels in management) seem to agree on at least several statements which relate to achieving both success and creativity: At all levels, a factor which seemed most relevant to success as well as to creativity was the ability to originate and develop ideas for useful products and processes, IGE (information gains, economic). The effective selling of ideas to management and customers, CE (communications, economic), was ranked for creativity lower than for success at all levels, but it was ranked particularly high by those in top level administration, which may reflect the importance attached by this group to communication with management and with customers.

The major discrepancies between what makes for success and what should be rewarded for creativity were in two of the scientific role items: IGT (information gain, theoretical), making original discoveries for theoretical gain in scientific knowledge; and CT (communication, theoretical), communicating ideas and findings effectively to other scientists. At all levels, IGT was ranked significantly higher for creativity than for success. CT, however, differed significantly in creativity over success only in the lowest level, and it became more important for success progressively through the three upper levels. This seems to show the importance of the scientific peer group to the administrators for evaluating each other's work. In addition, CT was rated as more important than IGT at the top levels, and at all other levels, IGT was rated as being significantly lower than IGE, suggesting that most individuals believe researchers must use their theoretical knowledge, but that it is more important to make contributions to economic gain than to theory.

That CT was rated as being more important than IGT suggests the importance of playing the role of scientific researcher, of being acknowledged and recognized as a scientist in the industrial environment. Autonomy was ranked as more important for creativity than for success, an explanation of which may be that carrying out a research problem with maximal effectiveness often depends on the work and ingenuity of a single individual working alone. For success, on the other hand, delegating and accepting responsibility and working with and convincing people is more important than working alone. It is also noteworthy that the lower supervisory groups ranked autonomy as being more important for creativity than did the upper echelons, which may be due to an increased feeling of pressure for group participation felt by those in the lower echelons.

In answer to the question of how more and less creative men compare with their top-level supervisors in their perceptions of what makes for success and what should be rewarded for creativity, no correlation was found between the more or the less creative men and their supervisors in regard to creativity. With respect to success, however, correlations of the more creative men with their supervisors increased with level, although the correlations between the less creative men and their supervisors did not vary over levels.

In comparing more and less creative men in each level, it was seen that in the lowest level, Level 1, the more creative men ranked CT and getting along well with colleagues (SI) as important to creativity; for success, however, the more creative group ranked working in close co-operation with salesmen and customers (SO) more important, and the less creative group ranked administration of research (AdR) and carrying out the scientific ideas of others (ES) as more important. At the next level up the scale, the less creative group ranked AdR lower and ES higher than did the more creative individuals; at Level 3, there were no significant differences between the groups.

Apparently, then, there is a subtle difference between creativity and other success irrelevant of drive or motivation. Perhaps it is a quality of the intellect or a facet of the personality, or some combination of the two, that can only be located by attempting to identify the characteristic qualities of creativity.

Summary

Early tests for originality or creativity had many elements of modern tests, but usually lacked criteria against which the tests could be evaluated. At least three criteria have gradually been developed:

1. The task is made so difficult that it is known to be creative or is obviously so. Then subjects are observed during the execution of the task (Patrick, Vinacke, Willman, Bahle).

2. The criteria against which to set performance in tests presumed to measure creativity are supervisor/peer ratings of creativity (Buel, Stein).

3. The criterion is the emergence of significant factors in mathematical analysis (Guilford).

These methods have been discussed and illustrated, along with creative personality tests (Cattell, Roe, Kubasta). Personality traits of creators have been given at length in Chapter 9. The studies of creative behavior have largely served to confirm these creative traits.

The most highly developed battery of performance tests for creativity is Guilford's; the most highly developed battery for personality evaluation is Cattell's.

The present writer has proposed certain new means of testing creativity. A group of CNB's could be profitably studied from this point of view. A needed direction of work is the intensive study of groups selected for high level of creativity.

PART III

FURTHER COMMENTS IN DEPTH

13. CREATIVITY FROM DIFFERENT VIEWPOINTS

Thus far we have reviewed the modern knowledge of creativity, and have discussed its applications to individual and group improvement and to industrial use. The ebb and flow of the creative process in stages and in relation to the creative personality have been explored, and aids and testing procedures have been described. We turn now to completion of the review of the literature, and presentation of certain new concepts developed by the author. Work done on problem solving, concept formation, and aging, in relation to creativity, must be covered. Applications of creativity in the field of education are due for discussion. This is the work that exists, and of which it is necessary to be aware, for a complete coverage of creativity. Finally, for a panoramic view of the subject, some special instances will be related, and an attempt will be made to dissect the inner nature of new combinations and the aids employed to evoke them.

Creation to Specific Stimuli

Bahle, and also Willman, asked authors to do creative work to specific stimuli. They studied the products. Their work had these special features: (1) many authors created to the same stimuli; (2) the creations were part of a psychological experiment; (3) a report—introspective, and secondary—was submitted by the author with his material.

Bahle asked composers to write music to one of eight poems, and keep a diary until the composition was begun. He got back twenty-seven compositions, eighteen to his own submitted poems. The distribution of these eighteen was 8-4-3-1-1-1-0-0. Two poems were judged unsuitable to stimulate musical composition and were not used.

Bahle divided his replies on the question of inspiration into those to whom the inspiration was a sudden idea, and those to whom it was a feeling preceding the idea. He "was concerned with the actual stimuli of the musical texts; equated creative urge to productive mood; and separated the 'artistic imperative' into a complex of psychic processes." In addition to the actual stimuli to inspiration and productive mood, Bahle detailed the more general attendant circumstances:

(1) The physical: health, season, weather, time.
(2) The mental: meditation, day-dreaming, thought, rest.
(3) The social: comments and criticisms aiding growth, challenging, etc.

Willman asked (by mail to each) a group of standard and a group of popular composers to prepare at least a few bars of music stimulated by each of the four diagrams, as shown in Figure 13-1. They

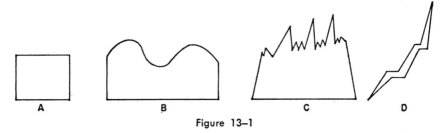

Figure 13-1

were asked for whatever comments they cared to make on the creation of the music.

Willman's thesis was the unity of the senses. "Appropriate stimulation of one will heighten the sensitivity of another." He states, for example, that with the left eye covered, the visual acuity of the right eye was enhanced:

By the sound of 2100 d.v.
By the smell of citronellol and xylenol.
By contact of a small weight on the back of the hand.
By the prick of a pin.

Willman found that the *form* of the notes of the musical compositions he received often followed the pattern of the diagram to which they were made. The trend of the notes *in the written music* tended to copy the diagrams. It might be continuously upward (D), or smoothly up and down (B), or sharply, even jaggedly, up and down (C). The composers were able to make a relation between the diagram and the music.

When the music was played back to listeners, and they were asked to match compositions heard to the four diagrams displayed on the wall, they—whether trained in music or not—were able to make the connection intended by the composer. The listeners to a significant degree chose the diagram to which the piece was composed, although the more complex figures, C and D, were harder to link up.

Again here is noted the profound effect of symbols on thinking. In this case, it influenced musical composition. Duncker showed how the flattened ellipse misled thought. He showed other cases where poor figures misled, good ones guided to the goal. Laycock points out the same thing in his spatial problem, to be discussed later in this chapter. In other work, a picture was stimulus for poems, and a poem for drawings.

Questionnaires

To continue the discussion of the ways used to study creativity, questionnaires were employed by Rossman, and by Platt and Baker, as already discussed. Hadamard lists the queries used in a questionnaire sent to mathematicians by *L'Enseignement Mathématique* (Vol. IV, 1902), but does not discuss the results in any specific detail. The methods of opinion study and market surveys have now so refined the questionnaire technique, both as to wording of questions and analysis of results, that information elicited should be far more precise today. Particularly, this is so because creativity is a subject of high current interest. A repeat of the Platt and Baker work is suggested.

Problem Solving

The method of studying creativity by having subjects comment aloud during a creative task has also been applied by many workers in the closely related fields of problem solving and concept attainment. This related psychological work is to be described in the present section.

First, however, it is desired to discuss the experiments of Laycock. He did not have his subjects talk aloud, but his studies show the rarity of creative talent and the difficulty of being creative. He forces us to the startling conclusion that just giving away the answer to a problem is not enough. When subjects are given the answer, and told that they have been given it, fifty per cent may achieve solution. This is supported by observations of Bulbrook and Duncker, and is known in a practical way to most teachers and educators.

Laycock presented to schoolboys problems of three types, and determined their ability to solve them with varying degrees of aid. The three types of problems were:

Pure psychological.
Pure spatial.
Mixed.

In each case, there were five degrees of aid:

(1) Non-pertinent.

(2) Pertinent help, but no comment, just presentation. The help took the form of parallel cases.

(3) The same pertinent help, plus (a) overt statement of the relation intended to be transferred to the problem, but (b) no statement that these parallel cases were related to the problem.

(4) The same pertinent help, plus (a) no statement of the relation to be transferred, but (b) the explicit declaration, these cases parallel your problem.

(5) The same pertinent help, plus *both* (a) statement of the relation to be transferred, and (b) the explicit declaration, "these parallel cases are given to help you."

The problems were as follows:

Pure psychological: A man sitting at his desk in his office alone after hours, suddenly looks up to be confronted by the gun of a burglar. What to do?

Pure spatial: Seeing the operation of a simple mechanical model from the front, with working parts concealed, the subject is to draw them.

Mixed: This was the Cyrus problem. Cyrus came to Babylon, found the wall too high to scale, and the inhabitants too well provisioned for siege. The Euphrates flowed through the city. Cyrus diverted the river, and marched in on the river bed to capture the objective.

There was very little success in solving the problems immediately after reading them. After the aids were given, the percentages of solution attainment were as shown in Table 13–1. The detailed data are tabulated in Appendix C.

TABLE 13–1

Aid	*% Subjects Solving Correctly, Averaged Over Three Tests*
None	2
Pertinent	8
Pertinent + Statement of Relation (a)	15
Pertinent + Advice—These Cases Are Hints (b)	17
Pertinent + Both (a) and (b)	34

In accordance with expectation, the combination of (a) and (b) with pertinent aids produced highest attainment of solution.

The level of successful solution was surprisingly low for the problems, apparently simple with the help given. For example, in the Cyrus problem the help was in the shape of appropriate stories. One related how a stream was diverted to solve a farm problem. Another related how a fleeing royal party came to a fork in the road, and the king took one path, while a henchman slowly fled along the other. He was not quick enough. The pursuers caught him, to learn he had been abandoned when his horse went lame, but was following as best he could. Thus, concluded the hint, (1) the stream of pursuers was diverted to a route other than that taken by the king for his successful escape; (2) this story should help you to determine what Cyrus did. There were three more such stories, which almost give the answer, and tell the subject that he is being given the answer—yet most failed.

The models problem revealed an important point. In one case, the help was to show the operation of training models, similar to but not identical with the problem model, saying, "These are similar to the problem." Solution frequency was 13 per cent. In another case, the help was to show the working parts of (similar but not identical) training models from the back, without a "these are hints" comment. Solution attainment was raised to 26 per cent. Let seeing the working models be equated to making a suitable drawing for some other problem. Then this observation shows how much progress may be expected in real problems when the right diagram has been visualized, or the most useful signs have been adopted, or a suitable model selected. This is Duncker's best model of search.

In an extension of this work, Laycock found the same inability to solve when he applied the method to students several years older. He noted that ability to solve difficult problems is rare. Subjects make absurd errors, and cannot draw analogies from parallel cases specifically pointed out. The danger is not reasoning by analogy, but *not* reasoning by analogy. People cannot spot the key point when, knowing the answer, the experimenter gives them the certainty: This is similar. But when no one knows the answer, the creator must first spot the similarity which is to lead him to it.

The work of Laycock shows the real difficulty of creative work, and the need to be alert to seize upon significant clues, and to learn to recognize and use them in new combinations.

Laycock's work has been confirmed by many other experimenters. Maier, in his pendulum problem, like Laycock, gave subjects different degrees of help. He supplied subjects with these materials: wooden strips, clamps, wires, chalk, and a heavy table (which was not to be moved) all placed in a large, otherwise empty room. The problem was to construct two pendulums to leave chalk marks on the floor at certain places. The solution was to jam a board, from the ends of which the pendulums were suspended, flush against the ceiling with another strip made long enough by C-clamping two shorter pieces together. The aids were demonstrations of making a plumb line, making a long strip by clamping two shorter ones, and wedging a double strip horizontally across the door frame. Direction was given to thinking by remarking that the problem would be easy if only there were nails in the ceiling. Without aid, one out of 62 solved the problem. With both demonstrations and particular direction, 8 of 22 (36 per cent) solved the problem. The degree of aid necessary to trigger a 50 per cent level of success in Duncker's thirteen problem will be recalled. These workers show that specific models plus proper set afford the best chance, which is none too good.

In exploring for a creative answer, a researcher must dig out his facts, sort the useful from the irrelevant, and by his scientific taste, developed from the study of creativity and the creative achievements of others, establish a correct "set" or "Einstellung."

Set

The effect of faulty set is murderous to creative success. Luchins did experiments in which three empty jars of 21, 127, and 3 quarts capacity were supplied, and it was required to measure out various exact volumes, such as 100 quarts of water. After several problems required the use of three jars, students continued to use them all even when volumes were asked for that were easier to obtain using two jars and omitting one. Then came the clincher: given jars of 3, 64, and 29 quarts, it was required to measure out 3 quarts. Then 52-85 per cent of the subjects solved the problem by filling the 64 quart jar, and removing from it, successively, 29, 29, and 3 quarts! Many a one has the answer, and knows it not. This is why Schiller said, "Open wide the gates, let the ideas flock, and only then survey the crowd."

All persons are creative, to various degrees. But the percentage who can solve *difficult* problems, requiring the use of the complete creative method, is indicated by Laycock's work to be, very likely, vanishingly small in the general population. It becomes small much faster than the decrement of general intelligence. A creator must be intelligent, but even a highly intelligent person is not necessarily creative.

Creativity demands intelligence, capacity for seeing problems, ability to sort out the wheat from the chaff in preparation, and courage to see insight through. It asks also personality traits permitting creation that occur in only a few in a high-conformity culture. Eras of highly creative achievements on a broad front have been times of relatively disorganized society, with the culture in a state of flux.

The follow-up by Terman on large numbers of gifted children with IQ of 140 did not reveal very many highly *creative* adults, though a large number were highly *successful*. The creative capacity is a special one. The creative person has *more* ideas, yet is able to suspend judgment about them. He has fewer blocks, does not fear to communicate new ideas, is able to communicate with the unconscious and to receive the material there selected to answer the problem. He easily breaks through set when it becomes a faulty adjustment to a group of specifications. He can even overcome a basic aspect of set in personality. A part of set is necessarily made up by the established rules one lives by, those things which are axiomatic, indisputable, not to be questioned. Therefore, a given set, or expectancy, may reject as an unfitting pattern a solution which is correct. The offered solution is rejected as not matching the temporary specifications, or as violating one's axiomatic truth.

Creativity requires the overthrow of set much of the time. That is why the creative person's personality is less well integrated. His lines of guidance for living are reined more loosely. The overthrow of set becomes more difficult with age. Set then includes all the "truth" one has allowed to become axiomatic in his chosen field of interest. Entering a new field may bring a resurgence of creativity.

A comment has been made to the effect that the great qualities for scientific work are memory, reasoning power, and imagination. Let these be separate abilities, and assume that one man in a hundred has gifts of memory, of reasoning power, or of imagination, which would qualify him as topnotch. They combine only $10^2 \times 10^2 \times 10^2$, or 1 in a million.

For a time in the development of psychology, the topic of set or *Einstellung* was in all the papers. Set determines whether one will solve *now*, or later when it has shifted. Unless one can shake a wrong set, it is questionable whether he will *ever* solve. Such sets are the established rules, and characterization of items as obvious or trivial or important, which have come to be regarded as axiomatic by a worker who is old in a field of work.

Several other things are similar to, or related to, set. One is direction. It has been seen, from Duncker and Laycock, that abstract aids are of little use. It will be shown later that even simple concepts are relatively hard to attain if abstract. But a general aid in the psychological field can be helpful by influencing problem set.

Maier obtained improved performance in the problem situation by a warning that "it is necessary to vary one's attack" and seek new combinations if old ones are not furthering progress. Luchins found improved performance of subjects who wrote at the top of the work-sheet the simple warning, "Don't be blind." The warning sets the relays on the trips at the dispersal points of the association paths.

Another trait related to set is functional fixedness, so harmful to creativity. To some people, a rose is a rose is a rose, and a hammer is a hammer is a hammer, and never anything else. How are such people to see a match-box as a candle support, or ink as a dye? One writes with ink—letters, and checks, and income tax forms. One dyes with ink only when it is spilled by accident, never intentionally. This *attitude* is often rooted in the deep layers of the unconscious, and may occur in a well-integrated personality, which maintains the integration by barring such shifts of basic tenets even from consideration. The creative person is necessarily less well-integrated. His concepts must be free, for every creative act is nonconformity. He exhibits these aspects of set in creativity:

(1) Changing set to meet new requirements and approach an answer—*adaptive flexibility*.
(2) Changing set in some new direction, and the oftener the better—*spontaneous flexibility*.
(3) Breaking an established set—*redefinition*.

The history of the mind and personality before a problem is presented affects the ability to solve it. This is broadly self-evident, but Prentice showed it can be carried down very fine indeed. His subjects were to discriminate between pairs of circles and squares, modified in size, color, and shape, and in the difficult cases scarcely distinguishable. Buttons were pushed to make choices—a correct choice actuated a light, a wrong choice, a buzzer. One group made a practice run of 20 trials in which the signals were reversed, then started the experiment as given above. This group was much slower than others to achieve success. Vinacke says: "Something is gained during periods of sheer exposure to the parts of a problem which is essential to ultimate success, even if it cannot be tangibly identified ... the gradual development of direction."

Bruner wrote: "A good idea in nebulous form appears several times before it is finally grasped. This is not a matter of an open mind, nor of incubation. It takes a tuned organism with a particular set to recognize the appropriateness of an idea."

Taton writes of Brucke that he had the requisite knowledge to invent the ophthalmoscope, just as Helmholtz had, but the orientation of his work did not let him ask the needed question.

Bulbrook observed the efforts of subjects toward the solution of a wide variety of problems. She gave each problem in printed form to the subject, with the instruction to "Proceed aloud" or "Comment aloud." For example, a nonuniform string of beads was to be made uniform by smashing the inappropriate ones. In another bead problem, the pattern was to be made uniform by using ink to *dye* a few beads to induce symmetry in the whole strand. In another problem, balls were thrown from central initial placement into peripheral pockets simultaneously by centrifuging. The problem was, to *think* of centrifuging. Other tests were, a complex tracing without lifting the pencil; a verbal puzzle; and two problems to learn and apply rules.

Bulbrook determined by the verbal reports and by interrogation the psychological functions brought into play: search, three forms of visualization—perceptive, memorial, and imaginational—inspection and comment, and finally, comprehension. She did not distinguish insight as sudden closure. Bulbrook observed that her subjects must be actively about solution—they would not wait for sudden appearance of the solution. According to her comments, there was always reason for what the subjects did.

Further Observations on Insight

The diffuse nature of insight begins to be evidenced in the several studies that have been reported in the previous chapters. Bulbrook does not find sudden insight. Patrick finds insight as a selection of a subject about which to write or draw following preliminary development. Duncker finds sudden grasp, but prefers the logical approach to solution. But Kohler clearly shows sudden closure even in experimental animals. Common experience—"it dawned on me" —verifies it, as do the reports of innumerable creative workers.

The explanation of this divergence is that the type of insight is partially dependent on the problem. Where information is totally lacking, there must be trial and error. A mathematical extension of a recognized theorem is best approached by logic, and insight is then of gradual onset. Discoveries which depend upon stepwise elimination flower slowly but surely. Problems to write or draw to a complex stimulus offer so many solutions that insight, as the one bright idea, is unnecessary—selection from a spectrum of possibilities is what is required. But in other problems, sudden illumination is a new combination not easily available to logic. In the many cases of insight caused by chance stimulus—a novelist meets or sees a potential strong characterization—logic is ruled out. Important insight is generally a new and *unusual* combination, and to that extent is less accessible to logic. Hence, a large percentage of major creations stem from a eureka experience.

Thus, creativity has been evaluated in problem-solving studies to demonstrate insight; the rarity of creative skill; the importance of models and set. The displacement of function has been most important—an analog of set, since the normal view of the subject must be broken, and a new look taken. The work of Laycock, Duncker, Maier, Luchins, and Bulbrook has been reported as representative.

Concept Formation

One of the mental processes important for creativity is concept formation—the organization of successive or related experiences in a conceptual fashion, or the classification of symbols into groups according to the well-known principles of likeness and contiguity.

Extensive work over many years has been done by Heidbreder in developing this field. In her work, stimuli were presented on cards to which the subject made a response, which in turn was communicated to him as correct or incorrect. The correct response was according to a preestablished arbitrary rule, and cards continued to be presented until the subject learned the rule. In Heidbreder's earliest work, subjects were allowed to comment aloud after making a response and before getting the information of correct or incorrect. In the more difficult problems in this early work, some fairly pointed hints were given.

The behavior of subjects in response was classified as participant or spectator. Participant behavior included trial and error, and gradual analysis, some hypothesis guiding each move. There were four classes of reaction: changes and repeats after success; changes and repeats after failure. Spectator behavior took such forms as responding without hypothesis, with the idea of gathering data. This is reminiscent of the advice, for creative aid, to open wide the gates, and let in as many ideas as possible. Heidbreder says that spectator behavior may facilitate processes of summation of material. Spectator behavior is often simply an appeal to the unconscious. Such appeal would be more likely in persons having exceptional rapport. In this sense, a tendency to spectator behavior may be a mark of creative facility.

With different problems, subjects achieved concepts of rule at rates having significance for creativity. There was a series of nine concepts, and such groups of nine, new examples each time, were run through until all could be correctly identified. Table 13–2 shows the mean number of times each concept of the nine was presented before it was learned:

TABLE 13–2

Concept	Name	Mean	t	Probability of Significance
Face	Relk	3.35		
Building	Leth	3.48	0.59	
Tree	Mulp	3.94	2.09	.05
O	Fard	4.46	2.00	.05
≠	Pran	5.05	1.31	
∝	Stod	5.19	0.31	
2	Ling	6.14	2.07	.05
6	Mank	8.76	4.68	.01
5	Dilt	10.22	2.86	.01

Thus, the subjects on the average connected Face with Relk at the 3.35th presentation, but did not connect (5) with Dilt until the 10.22th presentation. The t value is for the statistical comparison of each entry with the immediately preceding one. A value for t of at least 2.00 was required at the .05 level, and of at least 2.66 at the .01 level of statistical significance.

The diagrams which represent things were easiest to learn. Abstract diagrams were next, and most difficult were the number concepts. The familiar progress of the mind from concrete to abstract is evident. It was the concrete help, in the Laycock and Duncker experiments, that was effective. Obviously, in creative work, effort should be made to reduce the problem to concrete representation.

Leeper emphasizes these points about concept formation:

(1) Concepts may be formed and used without conscious awareness.

(2) In concept formation experiments, subjects report an exceedingly active mental process, with reasoning and hypotheses about the classifications.

(3) Different approaches to achieve the concept are available: analytical thinking; manipulation of the materials; spectator behavior; blends and alternations of these.

(4) "Concept formation is sometimes helped by starting with materials that reveal the principle in an extremely clear form"—the model effect.

Age and Achievement

H. C. Lehman has made intensive studies of the relation of age to creativity, or the production and publication of important insights. His method of investigation is to use reference works to obtain data as follows:

Creative Work	Author	Age at Time of Publication	Age at Death
x	x	x	x
x	x	x	x
	etc.		

From this table, he would (1) tabulate the number of creations by five-year intervals in the ages of the workers; (2) calculate the average number of creative contributions per *living* individual in each age bracket; (3) plot average number of creative contributions against age bracket.

Lehman found, with that monotonous regularity so desirable in scientific proof, an early maximum in creative production in practically all fields. The most commonly occurring age bracket for the maximum was 35-39 years, but it was less for a selection of the greatest creative works, and for works such as lyric poetry high in emotional content. A brief list is shown in Table 13-3.

TABLE 13–3

Field	Age Bracket for Maximum Av. No. of Contributions per Living Individual
Chemistry	26–30
Mathematics	30–34
Surgery	30–39
Astronomy	35–39
Physiology	35–39
Chamber Music	35–39
Grand Opera	35–39
Lyric Poetry	26–31
Tragedies	34–38
Novels	40–44
Oil Paintings	32–36

Lehman lists sixteen possible causes for these early maxima. The most important, in later life, are less drive, preoccupation with the large affairs of successful men, decline in health and vigor, and negative transfer, that is, interference to the acquisition and application of new learning. In general, creators are young, leaders are old. Yet many instances of high creative achievement are listed for both very young persons and aged ones, well below and well above the maximum brackets given above. It cannot be emphasized too strongly that these brackets are statistics, and have no meaning for any individual, but only for many individuals taken together.

Lehman's observation has been confirmed experimentally by Bromley. He tested 32 men and 32 women in each of four age groups,

Range:	17–35	35–51	51–66	66–82
Mean:	27	44	58	72

using a well-known test of ways of classification of blocks. Their ideas were graded as to quality, and the best ideas (A) were further divided into common A_c and unusual A_u. Results are shown in Table 13–4.

TABLE 13–4

Average Age	Total No. of Ideas	No. of Ideas of Type A	A_c	A_u	% of Total Represented by A_c	A_u
27	820	586	376	210	46	26
44	714	488	324	164	45	23
58	731	417	299	118	41	16
72	613	235	185	50	30	8

With increasing age, there is a fall in total ideas, and in per cent of good but common ideas, but most of all, in good and uncommon ideas.

In broad perspective, a man of creative bent with adequate training to create makes his important discoveries not long after he begins serious work in a field. He continues to make discoveries, or achieve creative successes, reaching his peak in the decade from 30 to 40 years of age. Thereafter, he has too many fixations to make contributions of equal quality.

He has fixed methods of attack that have worked for him in the past. He has grooved paths in his mind that take more and more for granted in developing any new project. He has large areas of territory to cover in the elaboration of the big achievements of his earlier years, and this is his line of least resistance, the easy path to maintenance of assured position. He has affairs to tend, the complacency of success, the lessened energy and drive of middle life. But there is one step that can give him a new start—a deliberate change of field. The chemist Ostwald achieved new creative success in this way. Another step is a clear understanding of the creative process, and deliberate efforts like Titchener's to visualize problems in different ways, with fresh, youthful viewpoints. It may be valuable to retain a capacity for the enjoyment of fanciful books, plays, and stories beloved of youth, and thus keep alive the youthful imagination. It is certainly fortunate if one can retain the eidetic abilities of childhood.

One of the characteristics of great age, of the order of seventy years or more, is known to be a tendency to turn back to sharp and clear recollections of childhood and youth. It may happen also that the viewpoints and ways of thought of youth strengthen again in aged creative workers. At any rate, this hypothesis can be used to explain an observation made by the present writer from analytical study of Lehman's data in his book, "Age and Achievement": There is a resurgence of creativity in advanced age, such that average creative achievement per living man is greater than in some considerably younger age brackets.

As evidence for this statement, the tabular data in "Age and Achievement" corresponding to graphs 1-99 were examined. Those graphs were selected for analysis where there was an entry for age

70 or more. The data taken note of were the number of times there were more creative achievements at the oldest age bracket given than at some previous age. The detailed analysis is given in Appendix D. The summarized results are:

No. of times last bracket is greater than a preceding entry	66
No. of times last bracket is less than a preceding entry	14
No. of times last bracket equals a preceding entry	3

This distribution is very highly significant in the statistical sense; that is, there is a resurgence of creativity at great age.

Six of the 14 negative cases occurred in the 85-89 age bracket. In five of these, production was greater at 80-84 than at 85-89. In all of these five, the 80-84 bracket value also surpassed at least one earlier value.

The above has been discussed at length because it appears to indicate a new aspect of creativity. Its meaning is of importance, by interpretation:

Resurgence of youthful recollection → Resurgence of creative achievement

Highlights

In brief summary, some of the highlights of the study of creativity have been:

Wallas: Four stages, theoretically.
Patrick: Four stages, experimentally; they interweave.
Vinacke: The four stages are a dynamic process.
Rossman:
Osborn: By subdividing, seven stages.
Hutchinson: Incubation = frustration.
Duncker: Form a model of search.
Bouthilet: Solution may forerun conscious explication.
Heidbreder: Find the rule.
Flesch: Thinking is the manipulation of memories.
Roe: Absorption in the task undertaken is the creative personality highlight.
Laycock: Creation is hard, and the ability rare.
Lehman: Creative ability reaches an early maximum.

Eidetic Ability

Eidetic ability—richly detailed recollection—is a very common phenomenon in childhood. Retained eidetic ability is one of the very common, though by no means universal, characteristics of genius. For example, Mozart, Weber, and Tschaikovsky were auditory eidetics in adulthood. Let the eidetic look at a picture with rich detail for a short time, then ask him about it a little later. He will visualize it before his eyes, and look at it, and read back the answer of something which he perhaps did not even observe consciously at the start. Painters have been able to project the picture they wished to draw on the canvas and then trace the requisite lines. A man did calculations by mentally moving the parts of a visualized slide rule. Another may simply in his mind turn the pages of an encyclopaedia to the required page and read off the required information.

It is easy to understand how such retained eidetic capacity would aid creative work. It may be hypothesized that this capacity is just another of those childhood traits that persist into the adulthood of many high creatives, others being gullibility, tolerance of ambiguity, analogic imagination, readiness to question even naively—but searchingly—and capacity to wonder. Sophistication is the opposite of these. Sophistication means critical judgment and it has overtones of flippancy, and all three are the enemies of creativity.

It is remarkable that the average person can produce eidetic recall under hypnosis. "A subject will be brought into a strange room for a few minutes. When asked subsequently to list every item that he has seen, he will reproduce twenty or thirty items. Thereupon, under hypnosis, he will go on to reproduce another two hundred items. All of this indicates how much intake, registering, recording, and recalling can occur without participation of conscious awareness at any step in the process. It follows that there must be an incessant bombardment with preconscious stimuli all day long in every life, and probably in reduced amounts at night as well." (Kubie)

Retained eidetic ability, then, *may* mean better rapport with the unconscious of the type considered important for creativity by Thurstone. In that case, the eidetic starts on a creative career with the definite advantage of better rapport. Since eidetic recall is possible, all this material is available to unconscious cerebration. The problem is activation through motivation, the stirring-up effect of intense preparative labor—and rapport.

The Eidetic Faculty and Education. The subject of eidetic imagery provides a place to digress for a moment and consider one phase of education. It would clearly be advantageous to retain the eidetic faculty. Methods to promote this might be found by psychological studies. One suggestion is to use the faculty constantly. Those children who are fortunate enough to possess it should be encouraged to exercise it every day. For example, let the normal procedure for detecting eidetic ability (experience, then reproduce, a detailed observation) be used in the special class for eidetics as daily practice. A picture is shown, or a page read, or a story told, or quick, complex play-action put on. The students must recall all they can. The aim is not 80 per cent recall but 99 per cent. Mozart and Weber did not recall only 80 per cent of the music they created or heard. They recalled it all. Where this ability exists, if it is retained, it is bound to be a firm pillar of the individual's later achievement.

This training is part of a three-point program for educating students to be more creative. First, a basic atmosphere is needed: permissive atmosphere with control, weakening of conformity pressures, reduction of anxiety of separation by willingness to lend an unprejudiced ear without a trace of flippant derogation. But these are general. The following aims are specific:

(1) Keep eidetic ability.
(2) Train in forced substitution and ultimate utilization.
(3) Practise creation to models.

Training in Substitution

Chapter 6 discussed the effect of a frugal upbringing on avoiding unnecessary purchase by substitution of function—a plastic bag in which food was purchased becomes a plastic bag for travel use; and to get maximum use of worn articles by transfer to another use— dress clothes become work clothes, or a newspaper becomes a table cloth at a picnic, and later a garbage-wrapper. Clearly, upbringing in a frugal home is not the only way, and not necessarily even the best way, to learn these lessons. But they *are* important, so that a hammer is no longer seen as a hammer, but as a T-shaped article made of wood and iron. Scouting in the woods, with its improvisations, teaches these things. But why not a deliberate classroom method? Here, the pendulum device of Maier, the ink-the-white-beads device of Bulbrook, and the match-box candle-holders of Duncker, themselves undergo transfer of purpose, and become not tests but teaching materials. In the Materials Substitution Class, some amounts of some materials are laid out, and the class works, individually and/or as a group, to:

(1) List and carry out all the things they can think of to do with the materials, with or without supplements they can readily procure.

(2) Devise ways to carry out specific projects set them by the teacher, and actualize these. It is not even necessary that the materials be able to do the job, since not all problems are soluble. Supplementary materials requested can be permitted or denied, as seems expedient.

After materials are used for one problem, they are saved, and the used pieces serve a more plebeian purpose the next day. Perhaps a colored garment was pulled apart to get from it a special, colored thread. The next day, it is a rag, or heat or sound insulation.

Students who do this every day, or every week, for years, will almost inevitably become creative. Perhaps admission to the class is allowed only to students who seem able to profit from it. The class will need, for textual aid, a well-designed kind of laboratory manual serving as a guide. The manual lists materials and articles and a wide variety of things that can be done with them. It shows ideas for combinations, like "20 things to do with bricks, string, a box, and a dozen tacks." It instances the many models one can build with a few standard pieces of a Tinkertoy or Erector set, or the many experiments done with a few chemicals by the toy chemistry sets.

This type of thing is practiced in a desultory way in scouting. It is prominent in the devices and adaptations of amateur theatricals; one of the reasons they are popular is that people enjoy improvisation. The much-from-little deductions of Sherlock Holmes that are so entertaining partake of this same quality of substitution and ultimate utilization. One also recalls in the Count of Monte Cristo the remarkable improvisations of the imprisoned Abbé.

Means must also be devised for practice in the more difficult area of forcing substitution in working with non-material things. One example may be writing a brief term-paper on a set subject with only the large Webster as source material. Let the subject be the Elizabethan Period. Then look up Elizabeth, Tudor, Shakespeare, Raleigh, Marlowe, Jonson, alchemist, England, Scotland, Armada. From these definitions get more suggestive words. With enough material in hand, select a narrow subject within the scope of the main one, and write.

There is no reason why there should not be a "substitutions" class for adults.

Creation to Models

The training discussed above is only superficial if not followed or supplemented by real and appreciated creation. In general, let the students have a chance to create. The continuous learning of facts, and relaying them back for grades, is not more important than this. In the class described above, models are provided for the creative teaching in the "lab manual" at the start, in the form of the variety of things that can be done with some common and basic materials. Later in the course the students provide their own ideas. In art, forms are established; in poetry, the sonnet; in music, the fugue and sonata. To the given form, one creates as best he can.

The present writer well remembers that one of the most pleasant assignments he ever had in high school English was to write an original Sir Roger de Coverley adventure. This was strictly creation to a model. The format and character were established. It was only necessary to invent incidents and bits of business to bring out the facets of the de Coverley character. Such assignments were far too rare, and they remained rare in college. Eighteen years in school exercised the learning faculty, the memory faculty, the reasoning faculty, the verbal reconstruction for the teacher faculty, the conformity faculty, the social adjustment faculty—everything but the creative faculty: There wasn't time for that.

Give the students models, then, and let them create. Let the models first be simple or specific; then more general and diffuse. Finally, let the model be so general that the product built on the framework is a genuine creation (of whatever quality) and some students begin to design the models themselves.

The value of the model appears even in the study of animals. Lashley "has demonstrated that rats may require more than 150 trials ... to learn a discrimination between a lighter and darker gray. But if trained first to discriminate black from white, which they learn in perhaps 10 trials, they are then able to transfer without further training to the difficult pair of grays. In other words, out of clearly different materials, the animals can learn something, in a few trials, that then can be applied to a more difficult problem on which more training would have been required."

Care should be taken to expose the means and mechanisms by which great creators have adapted the models to their purposes. This is for development of creative taste, and to give fullness of meaning to the model. Those with low creative skill will be unable to create to the models or will slavishly ape. Others will shoot wildly, as though to be merely different were to be creative. A few will use a free restraint. They are the ones to watch, to help.

In *Harper's* for October, 1960, Jacques Barzun emphasizes the distance between average creative efforts of ordinary people and creative masterpieces, and reserves the term "creative" to the masters. However, one must crawl before walking, and walk before running, and run before sprinting distances in record time. An important part of the definition of creativity in the present work is the ability to produce solutions of social value to difficult problems. The "creations" in school are not this; they are practice aimed at this that a few will achieve, in the hope that the number of the few will be larger; that one or two will shoot farther than they otherwise would; and that the large group will get more from their lives by profiting from the knowledge of creative approach and achievement. Such training will have this advantage also—a counterirritant to the creeping paralysis of conformity in modern American life.

Unusual Instances of Creativity

Let us consider some insights and creative results which occurred under rather unusual circumstances and conditions, and occasionally seem a little aside from the usual creative process.

There is first the contrast of the multiple invention and the un-accepted solo one. Creations that were before their time have been mentioned above—those by Mendel, Tswett, and Waterston. Ross-man, on the other hand, tabulates a large number of multiple inventions, showing the very common occurrence of the same insight to more than one person at about the same period of time. (See Table 13–5.)

TABLE 13–5. A LIST OF SOME INVENTIONS AND DISCOVERIES MADE INDEPENDENTLY BY TWO OR MORE PERSONS

Discovery of the planet Neptune	By Adams (1845) and Leverrier (1845)
Logarithms	By Burgi (1620) and Napier-Briggs (1614)
Calculus	By Newton (1671) and Leibnitz (1676)
Discovery of oxygen	By Scheele (1774) and Priestley (1774)
Liquefaction of oxygen	By Cailletet (1877) and Pictet (1877)
Method of liquefying gases	By Cailletet, Pictet, Wroblowski and Olzewski (all between 1877 and 1884)
Molecular theory	By Ampère (1814) and Avogadro (1811)
Process for reduction of aluminum	By Hall (1886), Heroult (1887) and Cowles (1885)
Photography	By Daguerre-Niepe (1829) and Talbot (1839)
Kinetic theory of gases	By Clausius (1850) and Rankine (1850)
Mechanical equivalent of heat	By Mayer (1842), Carnot (1830), Seguin (1839) and Joule (1840)
Pneumatic lever	By Hamilton (1835) and Barker (1832)
Telegraph	By Henry (1831), Morse (1837), Cooke-Wheatstone (1837) and Steinheil (1837)
Electric motors	By Dal Negro (1830), Henry (1831), Bourbonze and McGawley (1835)
Electric railroad	Claimed by Davidson, Jacobi, Lilly-Colton (1847), Davenport (1835), Page (1850) and Hall (1850-1)
Ring armature	By Pacinotti (1864) and Gramme (1860)
Microphone	By Hughes (1878), Edison (1877-8), Berliner (1877) and Blake (1878)
Telephone	By Bell (1876) and Gray (1876)
Theory of the infection of micro-organisms	By Fracastoro (1546) and Kircher
Relation of micro-organisms of fermentation and putrefaction	By Latour (1837) and Schwann (1837)

Laws of heredity	By Mendel (1865), De Vries (1900), Correns (1900) and Tschermarck (1900)
Balloon	By Montgolfier (1783), Rittenhouse-Hopkins (1783)
Flying machine	By Wright (1895-1901), Langley (1893-7) and others
Reapers	By Hussey (1833) and McCormick (1834)
Double-flanged rail	By Stevens and Vignolet
Cylinder printing press	By Koenig-Bensley (1812-13) and Napier (1830)
Typewriter	By Beach (1847-56), Sholes? (1872) and Wheatstone (1855-60)
Trolley car	By Van Doeple (1884-85), Sprague (1888), Siemens (1881) and Daft (1883)
Centrifugal pumps	By Appold (1850), Gwynne (1850), and Bessemer 1850)

From Rossman, "Psychology of the Inventor," Inventor's Press, Washington, D.C.

The importance of desire to the attainment of insight in major problems has been emphasized, and rightly. All the evidence attests this: the burning ambition of creators, their drive to achieve in the face of no matter what obstacles, their willingness to sacrifice, their courage to lay down a plan requiring years or a lifetime to bring to fruition. Milton, as a young man, visualized the "Paradise" which only as an old man, and blind, did he complete.

But there is also creation without desire oriented in that particular direction, deriving from:

(1) The role of chance.
(2) The principle of the incomplete pattern, and
(3) The effect of side thoughts.

Chance, and incomplete pattern, have been covered in Chapter 7.

Advantage must be taken of the presented chance. It is worth repeating J. F. Young's comment to the effect that a creative man possesses a host of incomplete patterns all awaiting some event to close the gap.

On the effect of side thoughts, Knowlson's comment on inspiration is applicable: "When the mind has a set to discovery, its energies may develop a conception aside from immediate purpose, or make a chance discovery of a different nature." Appleby, in reply to Rossman's questionnaire, said: "I have found no rest for weeks at a time, until I would finally seek seclusion and pencil in hand jot down certain things that would reveal themselves but which previously were in unrecognizable form in my mind. Sometimes I did not know what they were about, although I would be conscious of a constant urge in my mind to stop and interpret them into intelligent ideas. In most cases they were absolutely new ideas in the field to which they pertained . . . in some cases they were entirely foreign to anything that I desired to perfect."

The creative works mentioned in the preceding paragraphs often had no strongly motivated attack or intricate formal preparation, or any real frustration. There *was* insight—the true basic of creation. These works fit into creative theory in this way: a *generalized* motivation to create; a prepared mind; a match to factors; and a match to personality. Philosophers like to muse upon broad questions. Some inventors like to improve mechanical gadgets, and cannot bear to see one that is not in working order. Researchers may be at their best in utilizing by-products, or in the meticulous detailing of an analytical procedure, or in the general correlation of accumulated factual information.

There are further unusual instances of other kinds. For example, there is the result without labor—during sleep. Hadamard tells how, "being very abruptly awakened . . . a solution long searched for appeared . . . and in quite a different direction from any of those which I had previously tried to follow."

F. E. Ives replied to the Platt and Baker questionnaire: "I studied the problem of halftone process. I went to bed one night in a state of brain fag over this problem, and the instant I awoke in the morning saw, before me, apparently projected upon the ceiling, the completely worked out process and equipment in operation."

E. B. Spear replied to Platt and Baker: "The . . . of my invention were too costly. I discussed the entire matter . . . went to bed . . . slept for several hours. At 3 o'clock in the morning I awakened with an entirely new process clearly before my mind's eye."

"Otto Loewi, professor of pharmacology at the University of Graz, awoke one night with a brilliant idea. He reached for a pencil and paper and jotted down a few notes. On waking next morning, he was aware of having had an inspiration during the night, but to his consternation could not decipher his notes. All day at the laboratory in the presence of familiar apparatus he tried to remember the idea and to decipher the note, but in vain. By bedtime he had been unable to recall anything, but during the night to his great joy he again awoke with the same flash of insight. This time he carefully recorded it before going to sleep again." (Beveridge)

There is the result without explication. This was observed in the concept studies of several workers. The present writer once used a new result in planning work for two weeks without "knowing" he was using it.

There is the result without proof. Poincaré told how a mathematical notion came to him as a sudden insight with immediate certainty of truth. Gauss even said on one occasion, "I have the result, but I do not yet know how to get it."

Goldenstein replied to Rossman as follows: "An idea may come to me ... all of a sudden ... and at first all I may know is that I feel that certain results can be obtained without my knowing how to accomplish the desired results."

Insights in the form of prognostications have been reported quite commonly. Different types have been marked by greater and lesser degree of certainty, and greater or lesser degree of explication of premises.

Leonardo's flying machine and Jules Verne's submarine were proposed only as future possibilities, and too early in history for their authors to describe any close-to-the-mark means of making them work. Similarly, Swift had no real *reason* to predict, 150 years ahead of his time, that Mars had two moons, quite close to the planet. The chemist Prout declared the atomic weights would turn out to be integers even while the fractional values were being so carefully (and usefully) determined. Many decades later it required the concept of isotopes to confirm Prout.

On an entirely different level of certainty was the prediction by the Russian chemist Mendelejeff of the properties of then undiscovered elements on the basis of the Periodic Law. (See Table 13–6.)

To this may be compared, in astronomy, the prediction of the existence of the planet Neptune, and later Pluto, together with the precise specification of where to look for them. Comparable, too, is the supreme confidence of Michelson, whose "intuition gave him the equation for some complicated tidal phenomena, and when an expert mathematician reported a different result from his calculations, Michelson sent him away to find, as he did, an error."

TABLE 13–6

Property	Predicted for "Eka-aluminum"	Found for Gallium
Atomic Weight	69	69.9
Melting Point	Low	30.1°
Sp. Gravity	5.9	5.93
Action of Air	None	Slight at red heat
Action on H_2O	Decompose at high temp.	Decompose at high temp.*

* Adapted from "Elementary Principles of Chemistry," Brownlee *et al.,* page 519, Allyn and Bacon, 1921.

Hadamard quotes from mathematics several interesting cases in his chapter on "Paradoxical Cases of Intuition." His carefully selected instances show that exceptionally intuitive minds may develop theorems of which some links, or even the entire method, of orderly proof remain unknown to the thinker, and then for a time to all workers.

Fermat (1601-1661) announced that he possessed a certain proof by a statement in the margin of a book, which concluded that he lacked room to inscribe it. Three centuries later, that proof is still sought for. The partial proof of Fermat's last theorem utilizes algebraic theories unknown in Fermat's time, and of which no notion appears in his writings.

Rieman (1826-1866) obtained results from a mathematical expression which he did not publish. Some thirty years later, Hadamard was able to prove all of them but one. Hadamard's proofs utilized material completely unknown in Rieman's time.

Galois (1811-1831) announced conclusions for which the bases were not developed until long after his death. He spent the night before the duel in which he died in collating his notes. In a letter to a friend he enunciated "a theorem on the periods of a certain kind of integrals ... these periods had no meaning in the state of science of that day; they acquired one only by means of some principles ... found ... a quarter of a century after the death of Galois."

The simplicity of many results, when they come, is worthy of note. Watson was wont to remark, after Holmes had explained a deduction, that it was so simple that anyone could have seen it. So, when needs or new ideas are explicated, they often seem so simple as to be self-evident. Such is not the case. The expriments of Laycock, Bulbrook, Duncker, Bouthilet, and a host of others show how poor a rate of creative problem solution is attained. We have already remarked that a good idea is often something that everybody knows but nobody has yet thought of.

Good ideas from time to time will come to mind, only to be tossed aside by immediate judgment as of little worth. Later, in a more complete, or a different setting, they regain recognition, at their true value.

Thoughts for Management

Management should consider that discoveries on a smaller scale of values may follow the pattern of the big successes in their intuitive workers. The discoveries, for instance, may be aside from original purpose. Creativity is rare, and if wanted, the nonconformist character of the creative man must be accepted.

The creative men should be helped with encouragement and model shop and draftsman support to develop the powerful aid of models. The strength of this aid has been amply shown, and the models can be drawings, diagrams, or specifications, as well as physical objects.

The surest way management has to get a research request fulfilled is to furnish clear specifications of the thing desired.

Two rather daring ideas for management are:

(1) Take a man who was extra-creative in his thirties; give him a raise in salary and status; then start him to work in a field entirely new to him. While a specialist is lost, there may be a resurgence of creative skill.

(2) Contact a few 75-80 year old retirees who were great creators, and hire them to create for the company.

14. THE BASIC NATURE OF CREATIVE WORK

The immediate concern of a human being in society is to find a useful niche in which his service as a valuable instrument of social design earns social recognition and reward. Be he a laborer, a book-keeper, a baseball player, or an executive, he does something worth paying for. In general, society is interested in each individual's being a valuable instrument, and not much more. If the instrument is not one of the few *required* to be creative, then the road to creativity is hard. Battering against this social barrier is the psychic force in most individuals. They want to be more than instruments. As Rogers declares, "The mainspring of creativity appears to be the same tendency which we discover so deeply as the curative force in psychotherapy—man's tendency to actualize himself, to become his potentialities."

Thus, at the very start, there is a basic conflict between forced instrumentality and the urge to create. Creativity—the ability to produce a new and socially useful combination—has the aspects of:

The creative product itself—what and wherefore it is.

The way the insight developed.

The ability to create, and the growth of this ability.

The Creative Product Itself

The thing itself is art or science, including the esthetic, the philosophic, political, or objective, arising usually from a man's vocation or avocation. Its nature and scope depend upon the man—what he is able to do, and what he is attuned to grasp. Some see in little with a meticulous detail that gives greatness; some see grandly in large without a clear visualization of detail; the greatest—the great creators—see both in large and in detail. Such men were Darwin,

Beethoven, Mozart, Shakespeare, Newton, and Pasteur. As their visions went beyond those of ordinary men, so also did the fusion into unity of even the smallest pieces they put together to work out the visions.

A problem has foreground and background material, and a variety of facets only some of which are key ones. Different men look at a problem and tab different things as foreground, background, and key. Perhaps one makes the right mosaic out of all these things, and *he* makes the discovery. But others make different mosaics, and *they* make other discoveries.

A creation may arise from a vocation, avocation, conflict, or an observed need touching a sensitive spot in the personality. One person will respond to "It can't be done"; another to "What a terrible waste!"; still another to "How terribly inconvenient and slow!" A thorn in the flesh to one is not so to another.

The distinguishing thing in creativity is the moment of insight. Thinking thereafter is different than before. In the definition of this book the insight must be of such scope as to mean the creation of a new and socially valuable concept or object. This means time in "the deep well." The process for creative achievement will now be discussed.

The Basic Nature of A + B → C

The basic nature of A + B → C is two fundaments and a relation between them: both *moon* and *apple fell.*

This is closely related to an analysis of the nature of ideas by Spearman. He pointed out that if two items called fundaments are given, then a relation between them called the correlative may be perceived; or a given item and a relation may generate another item. Given dog and cat, one readily develops chase; or, given dog and chase, one readily develops—rabbit. Relations, or correlates, have the basic character of likeness, evidence, or conjunction. More specific examples are given in Table 14-1, to show different types of relations between fundaments.

It is most important in connection with creativity to note that the fundaments are nouns and the correlates verbs. In part, this has been discussed previously. The importance is, that in a majority of cases

(1) The invention is itself a verb.

(2) The relation is the root of mental set in regard to the problem—and changing the verb can modify the set.

TABLE 14–1

		EXAMPLE	
Relation	*Fundament*	*Relation*	*Fundament*
Attribution	Lemon	has	Yellow Color
Identity	A	=	B
Time	Thunder	follows	Lightning
Space	Gift	is smaller than	Box
Constitution	Bread	sandwiches	Meat
Cause	Sun	grows	Plants

This ability to shake free from fixation or set or established dicta is a fundamental characteristic of creators. Creation is often defined as a new combination, that is, essentially, a new relation—which is nothing else than a new correlate, the establishment of a verbal connection between two previously unrelated fundaments.

Regarding this, consider first the common creativity test, uses of a brick. This is a test of *monopolar* ideas fluency. It is also Spearman's case where one fundament (brick) and a relation (is useful for) are given, and it is required to generate other fundaments. And that is the way the mind works. It turns up other nouns, one by one, and asks, how is a brick useful in relation to that? Soon a list grows:

> Brick is door-stop
>   "   " missile to throw
>   "   " weight for paper, or ballast
>   "   " unit in wall.

Now each of these can have the idea put in verbal form also:

> Brick stops door
>   " is thrown at something
>   " weights paper
>   " fills place in wall.

The more interesting case in the present discussion is the creative method of forced relationship described by Whiting and others. In this method, two items are selected as poles, and the mind is allowed to free-associate between them. This is *bipolar* idea fluency. An example of the present writer's already described was to seek relations between *clock* and *lamp* such as

(1) Lamp has clock built into its support.
(2) Clock turns on lamp at preset time as antiburglar measure.
(3) Clock turns on lamp at preset time and it shines or blinks in a man's face to wake him up, providing a soundless alarm.

It will be seen that:

(1) These are nothing more than Spearman's fundaments and a correlate-relation between them.
(2) The inventions (if any) are verbs: clock (a) *turns on* lamp and (b) *wakes up* man. The clock to turn on a lamp is certainly an old idea; the twist of using this as a soundless alarm is somewhat newer; both the old idea and the twist derive from verbs.

There has been much discussion about verbs in the field of writing. Forceful writing needs relatively short sentences, and the preponderant use of active rather than passive verb forms. In the highest form of writing, namely poetry, quality and economy and extra suggestion of imagery are attained by selecting meaningful and unusual verbs to replace excess words otherwise needed to supply the meaning. So true is this, that, in assessing the quality of the poetic work of even the good poets, it has been said, "by their *verbs* ye shall know them."

Since verbs are the heart of creation, an obvious way to improve creativity is to study and understand and use more, and unusual, verbs. This may be useful as a test in the following way.

The 100 words of the Kent-Rosanoff work association test as given in Appendix E include no verbs—that is, there are no obvious verbs, though a few words are capable of verbal interpretation as their more remote connotation, e.g., needle, trouble, sleep. Since in giving the test most of the stimulus words are unequivocally nouns, a strong *set* is established to interpret even the amphoteric ones as nouns too.

If one further examines the distribution of responses to the Kent-Rosanoff test, it is found that *responses* which are *verbs* have very low incidence. Now, let it be assumed that the number of verb responses to such a word association test may be an index of creativity. This can be justified as an hypothesis by the following line of reasoning: Creation is to perceive unusual relations; these perceptions take the form of verbs; most people do not readily perceive unusual relations; so they give few verbs in the Kent-Rosanoff test; creative people perceive more relations, and produce more verbs in such a test.

Now the minds of children are actively creative in the sense that they readily entertain fantasy, and they are less subject to fixation. Their reactions to word association are less superficial, less stereotyped, and more likely to dig into the meanings of the stimulus. Children tend to produce verb responses more than adults. An example from tests is given in Table 14–2.

TABLE 14–2

		Per Cent	
Stimulus	*Response*	*Children*	*Adults*
Table	Eat	36	5
	Chair	2	30
Man	Work	17	1
	Woman	1	48

Children do not have ironed-in responses, or highly developed clusters, and they give verbs as readily as nouns for responses. In adults, the response to a verb is significantly slower than to a noun, as six separate investigators showed. In an adult, a verb response is less usual, and to that extent less fixed and more creative than the entrenched noun response. When a noun is given as stimulus, another noun in the cluster, or concept, is readily responded. But to give a verb response to the noun requires going outside the superficial noun and adjective complements, and mentally developing a relation.

The present writer examined the results of the Kent-Rosanoff test administered to a subject engaged in a creative livelihood, on two occasions two years apart. The results showed:

Verb responses, like *"thief*-steal"	26%, 35%
Phrase completions, like "thief in the night"	30%, 31%
Other responses, like "thief-robber"	41%, 34%

Since the Kent-Rosanoff test comprises 100 words, there were, from the first number in the first line above, 26 words that elicited a verb response. These words would normally elicit verb responses only 7 per cent of the time. Indeed, for a group of 21 of the 26 words there would be verb responses only 2 per cent of the time. But the subject under discussion gave 26 verb responses to the 26 words. The *average* verb responses to the 74 other words in the Kent-Rosanoff

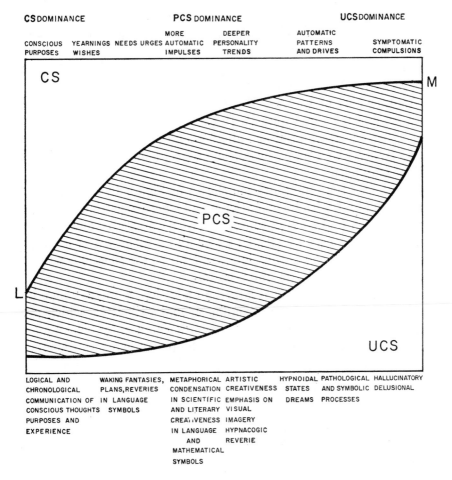

CS DOMINANCE　　　　　　　　　**PCS** DOMINANCE　　　　　　　　　**UCS** DOMINANCE

		MORE	DEEPER	AUTOMATIC	
CONSCIOUS	YEARNINGS NEEDS URGES	AUTOMATIC	PERSONALITY	PATTERNS	SYMPTOMATIC
PURPOSES	WISHES	IMPULSES	TRENDS	AND DRIVES	COMPULSIONS

CS

M

PCS

L

UCS

LOGICAL AND	WAKING FANTASIES,	METAPHORICAL	ARTISTIC	HYPNOIDAL	PATHOLOGICAL	HALLUCINATORY
CHRONOLOGICAL	PLANS, REVERIES	CONDENSATION	CREATIVENESS	STATES	AND SYMBOLIC	DELUSIONAL
COMMUNICATION OF	IN LANGUAGE	IN SCIENTIFIC	EMPHASIS ON	DREAMS	PROCESSES	
CONSCIOUS THOUGHTS	SYMBOLS	AND LITERARY	VISUAL			
PURPOSES AND		CREATIVENESS	IMAGERY			
EXPERIENCE		IN LANGUAGE	HYPNACOGIC			
		AND	REVERIE			
		MATHEMATICAL				
		SYMBOLS				

Figure 14–1

(From Kube, "Neurotic Distortion of the Creative Process," p. 40, University of Kansas Press)

list are correspondingly as low as the 2-7 per cent figures given. The fewness of verb responses to the standard list by the general population is surprising.

Taking the number of verb-replies as an index of creativity is subject to check by computing the median frequency value of all the individual's responses and comparing with standard values. If this median value is high, the individual runs to common responses; if low, he runs to unusual responses, which may be extra-high grade, eccentric, or incoherent, and this is subject to judgment by the test-giver. Naturally, the use of this method for creativity evaluation would need validation against other criteria. If applied to a homogeneous group of working scientists, its diagnostic value to estimate creativity would be interesting.

Another part of the $A + B \rightarrow C$ equation is the $\rightarrow$. This stands as a symbol for these questions: How does the new combination occur, become recognized as valuable, and presented to consciousness? In order to discuss these, some concepts modified from Kubie will be employed.

Kubie uses the representation shown in Figure 14-1 to represent the whole mind, with its operational and affective gradations. There are conscious (CS) and unconscious (UCS) divisions, and between them, the preconscious (PCS), which the present writer considers as that section of the unconscious available to the conscious without external, i.e., psychiatric, intervention.

In a creative man, PCS is larger. In addition, a creative man has a gained or intuitive understanding of and with UCS, which provides the larger PCS, and allows less interference, by blocking and fixation, with the creative function. The preconscious contains:

> The never-conscious.
> The forgotten.
> The problem.
> The worked-over preparative material.
> The motivation.

The line LM in Kubie's figure is a kind of *interface,* through which material enters the conscious, and through which falls the material displaced. If several ideas suddenly crowd the mind, and one starts to record them, it sometimes happens that one idea may plunge deep into the PCS again, and be irrevocable. One only knows that something was thought of but cannot be written down.

A new, valuable combination may slip through the interface LM into the shaded zone in Figure 14-2 which is fringe consciousness,

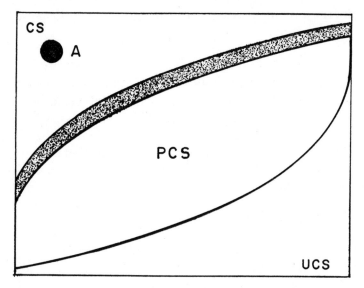

Figure 14–2. Showing zone of fringe consciousness and attention center A.

or Galton's antechamber, and if not noted, fall back again. Or it may rush out sharply and seize the center of attention, A.

The imparting to consciousness comes: as an image; a verbalization; pictures of A and B; a kinesthetic feel of putting A and B together. The new idea is often like a meteor: fleeting, bright enough to be easily seen, but gone unless immediately noted.

The ⟶ depends on the personality of the person, especially,

(1) Did he state the problem clearly?
(2) Did he send good, adequate, well-worked-over preparative material to the preconscious?
(3) What is the nature and size of the person's preconscious?
(4) What is his rapport with the preconscious and unconscious?
(5) Is he a verbal, auditory, or kinesthetic thinker?
(6) Is he an intuitive or deliberative thinker?

(7) Is he eidetic, a clear visualizer, dim, weak, or imageless?
(8) Will he notice, and record, and use?

The slow and complex development of creative ability takes place from adequate inheritance of intelligence and developable factors, and from the growth of creative personality from childhood to adulthood.

Factors

As stated on page 197, factors are basic human abilities that have been identified by mathematical analysis of extensive batteries of tests. Now, if an individual should take a group of tests which represent a factor of human ability, and do well in them, he clearly is strong in that ability; if he should do poorly in them, he would be weak in the ability. This is reverse factor analysis, to identify abilities in people. The thesis here is:

(1) These factors are part of heredity.
(2) Strong factors in a person's intellectual makeup develop easily to relatively high levels; but weak factors do not, there being less tendency to use them, and absolute inability to raise them to levels that the strong factors reach easily.

Duncker gave subjects six matches with which to construct four equilateral triangles. Some after a while thought of three dimensions and constructed a tetrahedron, but others, said Duncker, had "fixation to the plane too strong." To this the present writer adds, *or* had too weak a space factor.

It is necessary to know a man's favorable development of factors. A research director should not give an assignment in stereochemistry to a man with a weak spatial factor, nor a primarily writing job to a man with a weak verbal factor. This kind of thinking is just as sensible as choosing for managers men who can handle people skillfully. It is just as sensible as giving a problem on how to use a by-product to a man who can't stand waste; or a problem needing Gordian knot cutting to enhance speed to a man from an openhanded background. A reference relates how an overly critical man did poorly in several departments, until given a job where intensely careful inspection was needed, when he did very well.

Welch's work, already described, showed how artists surpassed students on two tests requiring a well-developed space factor. But the students did as well as the artists in two tests requiring verbal skill. As a matter of interest, Roe showed that, even in eminent men, an above-average space factor may be accompanied by below-average verbal skill. Social scientists tended to have verbal skill. Biologists rated poorer than physicists in the spatial test. In the class of physicists, the theorists rated considerably higher than the experimentalists in verbal facility.

The reverse of factor analysis to identify creative people has been described in Chapter 12.

A relation between factor analysis and concept formation seems to the present writer very probable, though he has not found it in the psychological literature. This relation is that if a subject has more difficulty in learning to identify one concept than another, then he will be found to have low loading of the factors needed for closure on that concept. The individual's + and − factors (his assets and liabilities) will be reflected in the types of concepts he finds easy to form or hard to form. The clusters of concepts involving factors of high loading will be rich; of concepts involving weak factors, poor. The man will create only with difficulty, if at all, when the accomplishment of the task rests heavily on the small abilities of his intellect. "Small abilities" means that he does poorly on tests in the groups representing those abilities in factor analyses.

Growth

For creation of the scope under consideration, it is first needful that the man inherit intelligence and developable factors to a degree at least somewhat above the average. Next, it is needful to foster growth of the ability to create, and a liking for it. The home life especially serves to develop the creative personality. The home and school combine in education to accouter the intelligence with information, and to cultivate the factors needed for subsequent creation to their above-average levels. In the course of education, the individual learns to use his "good" factors and almost instinctively shies away from tasks that utilize his "weak" ones. There are not many mistakes here. A person soon learns what he can do more easily, and what he can do less easily, and what he cannot do at all. Misfits arise from laziness to develop existing talent (i.e., high-loaded factors), from parents who force children into wrong occupations, and from occasional tragic errors like the talentless artist Fanny Price in "Of Human Bondage."

The home environment nurtures the prepared mind for creation. The prepared mind is ready, from childhood, to be able to, and dare to, make the creative leap. It derives from the physical conditions and the psychological atmosphere of the home. The resolution of basic conflicts must be favorable, and must somehow instil in the child an extra drive to excel and willingness to pay the price it may demand. Economic influences operate. A frugal atmosphere directs effort against waste and damage, and toward substitution. In a more opulent atmosphere, one may learn to think big, and ignore the costs of getting things done faster, or more conveniently. The attitude in the home must be favorable to things of the mind, since nearly all creations of value are things of the mind. This automatically provides acquaintance with the great creations of the past. There must be permission to diverge, that is, to create. In the home this permissiveness means willingness, in love, to let the child try a new thing and fail, and then encourage him to try again. This fosters the daring to be different, which creation—by definition, nonconformity—demands. For a creator is a nonconformist who must learn to conform enough to get by without excessive social friction in his life situation.

In such home atmosphere the desire to create blossoms. Necessary stern discipline of practice is undertaken willingly on one's own, and is broadly encouraged. It is possible to fail without recrimination, and bask in the sunshine of praise for success—that furthers more success and more daring.

Then from childhood a kind of set to create is established, and fostered by training. It burgeons in all directions where factors are freely manipulable by the individual. Learning the effective direction of one's work is set, too. There develops a liking for certain areas, and an individual style in handling them. Mozart, for instance, liked best to write opera. In orchestral composition, he liked certain instruments more than others. He avoided certain keys.

From the home background of firm support, the child goes forth to school. There he is met with the insidious, creativity-throttling tentacles of formal education which takes away his time for dissociated thought and instead gives him "activities"; which is a factory for the reproduction of facts; which makes him forget that a problem may have more than one, unique answer; which teaches him in solving to use all the given, no more and no less; which teaches him to judge and judge and criticize and analyze, with never a *chance* to create.

Of course, the obverse side of this is that there is so much to learn and so much to do. Weisskopf writes, "The constant activity enforced by many educators does not give young people the leisure which is an essential prerequisite for intellectual or artistic creation. ... We keep the secret of biological creation from small children, and the secret of intellectual creation from youth." And so the creative spirit is weakened—a significant falling off appearing in the fourth grade. Meanwhile, the stern conformity pressures of our culture begin to operate: from peer groups; from the need to conform to win acceptance of the opposite sex; from the over-riding educational philosophy of adjustment, to teach not subjects but girls and boys. The easy way to obtain adjustment is to teach conformity.

The leader does his work within the pattern of group conformity by *surpassing*. The creator must go outside the conformity pattern and do his work by *surprising*. He must then win group concurrence, or suffer rejection.

The formal education is necessary. Man must build on the past; he does not create in a vacuum. He needs stimulative contacts with teachers, peers, ideas, and broadening experiences. What would help is a shift of attitude, granting *laissez faire* to the creative as well as the conforming student. The home training may save the situation, and while the formal training shapes his factors and sharpens his use of these tools, the man may find the stimulus of contact with a creative environment suited to his abilities.

There remains to find a life situation which shall propound a series of problems matched to his factors; and to achieve conditions where solutions bring the desired rewards. The reward is matched back to basic personality pattern. The problems must match, besides factors, the man's unconscious wishes, experience, motivation, and drives. They should not run seriously counter to material buried in the self-inaccessible unconscious. This is to say, a man's work should match his factors and his personality, according to the development of creative personality described in Chapter 9. The man becomes his own creative instrument, self-charged by skilled polypreparation, and tuned to see and understand his unique answer when in some quiet time it shall appear.

What, then, favors the great creator? These particulars:

(1) Big factors with average or big intelligence (p. 256).
(2) High childhood furtherance and desire to excel (p. 183).
(3) Retention of full, or more than average, eidetic ability (p. 237).
(4) Confidence.
(5) Readiness to sacrifice time, and energy, and other desires, in order to attain the creative goal.

Of Coleridge, Lowes wrote that at the time of his association with Wordsworth, Coleridge had come upon themes good for him, and was working out techniques for their expression. The effort and care expended were tremendous. Techniques acquired through such strong, conscious effort become in time unconscious in their exercise, when one is free to create. He has forged the tool and can use it.

Prescott says, "Poetic creation is seeing the thing sufficiently . . . the word that will describe the thing follows of itself from such clear, intense sight of the thing."

What kinds of characteristics appear in the course of the birth, education, growth, and fruition of creativity?

(1) *Many are childlike.* Lehman's data say, when age begins to hark back to childhood, there comes a resurgence of creativity. Students have noted these creative traits:
   Spirit of wonder.
   Capacity for rapture.
   Eidetic elements.
   Gullibility.
   Retained capacity for enjoyment of amusements similar to children's; for example fantasy.
(2) *Home environment fixes these:*
   Sexual attitudes.

Drives and energy.

Self-dependency.

Frugality, open-handedness, etc.

Willingness to be alone.

(3) *Growth into adulthood brings these:*

Deferment of judgment, and its other face, ability to see others' viewpoints; may lead to apparent vacillation or indecision. This is partly true, but partly comes from insistence on keeping as many avenues of choice open as long as possible.

Confidence.

Learning to apply tension to produce insight (for example by obtaining oblique thoughts when working at moderate tension along an unrelated line).

Learning to establish creative set, to break unfruitful set.

Learning to choose puissant signals.

An eternal vying, so that it is waving a red flag to say, *it can't be done, has never been done, is impossible.*

15. SOME IMPORTANT
ISSUES IN CREATIVITY

The startling growth of the research and development industry since the war, as evidenced by the Chart on page 179, has caught American management by surprise. This is suddenly big business, but without a tangible product, and basically geared to operate at a loss on the account books. It must be tolerated, and even stimulated, because half the company products a decade from now will flow from it. The basic scientific work it produces will by far outlive the company itself in the published journals of science. No one knows quite what to do about all this. The articles pour forth. For the present, the conservative approach has won, and the method has been to try to run R&D like any other department of the business, making grudging concessions to its special nature and importance as those concessions become inevitable, because without them the engine ceases to run.

The other aspect of this has been that the manpower to implement this vast expenditure has not been available except by lowering standards. The management system has been revised to keep a large influx of men of average competence busy doing fairly useful things. The means to this end has been to break up the job into parts, and let each man do his bit of piecework, and relay it to a minor research executive for coordination.

There are organized groups of these research teams in a large laboratory, and breakthroughs are brought in from the outside for them to work on. This combination puts the situation into familiar management territory—a labor force to till a boundaried field. This over-all position says to the men: Limit your creativity to cultivation of this demarcated territory, and change your scientific aspirations to the goal of middle management.

Unfortunately, this system is reaching out through control of funds to hamper the men capable of big discovery, and attempt to establish the objectives for all scientific endeavor. Even the universities are coming under control. They seek and receive allocations of funds for work in certain areas. The allocation is dependent on a more or less detailed project write-up. Then professors are advertised for, not with the time-honored privilege of working on whatever they are curious about, but to work in the particular area of the allocation. The researcher may turn up something interesting outside the Great Plan and find there is neither authorization nor funds for it. These controls are bad. History shows:

It is the following of unrestricted curiosity that brings the big discovery. This policy cannot be followed in industry. Its traditional place has been the university. If control is exerted there also, there is no chance for major new departures.

Research to obtain breakthroughs—the function of the university —cannot be planned. Only the thread can be followed. The discovery will be a chance observation a good share of the time. The proper objective of the true scientist is to satisfy his curiosity; his only proper directive is: Discover the new.

Even when projects *are* carefully planned, the percentage of successful completions according to plan is not very good. The proper thing to plan carefully is the upcoming experiment. It will tell you what to do next. Big discoveries are beyond logic. They come from the emotional fire and the creative methods that this book is about. Attempts to control discovery in the way industrial verification teams are controlled will simply end discovery.

The administration of American science has the responsibility to foster breakthroughs as well as direct the efforts of verification teams to use them. It is well-geared for the latter; it is failing in the former, the area of basic research, because different methods are required. The attitude is too pragmatic.

When, in order to get allocations for their work, the detailed projects are submitted by scientists as required, the kinds of reasons given for rejection (*Science,* **132**, 1532, 1960) are scarcely to be believed.

A reason for many rejections was, "The investigator does not have adequate experience or training for this research." What do you think of that, Pasteur, a mere chemist studying disease?

Another reason was, "The problem is of insufficient importance to produce any new or useful information." Well, Mendel, those garden peas! Why waste your time?

Another reason was, "The problem is more complex than the investigator appears to realize." What do you think of that, Perkin, attempting the hopeless synthesis of quinine, and discovering only mauve?

Another reason was, "The equipment contemplated is outmoded and otherwise unsuitable." Well, Faraday, do you *really* expect to get anything from that old magnet and soft iron core?

Another reason was, "The institutional setting is unfavorable." Well, Fleming, how do you expect to accomplish anything in that mouldy old building? Why, sometimes your plates even get contaminated!

Another reason was, "The proposed research is based on a hypothesis that is unsound." What about that, Francis Bacon? Didn't you write that a hypothesis can be very fruitful without being correct? Haven't a hundred discoveries come directly out of erroneous hypotheses?

All these objections have ignored that if a man will work, discovery will come, and no man can predict where or whence. It doesn't *matter* what the discovery is, it will find its place. Should it be a girl when a boy is wanted, rest content—she may be a Marilyn Monroe, or even a Marie Curie.

One of the curious aspects of modern American life is a willingness to give all kinds of extra "breaks" to those who can accomplish little even with them; but to deny "breaks" to those who, with them, would help themselves to big things—and in so doing help us all to better things. Our basic and fundamental research suffers because it goes so much against the American grain to support a man in style while he simply explores some aspect of nature that happens to interest him. We will spend much more to educate a child with an IQ of 60 than one of 160. We will spend far more to educate a child who cannot hear than one who possesses absolute pitch. We can, and should, help the unfortunate. But why can we not see that aiding big talent will help *them* best—and help us too?

We must find ways to favor talented individuals within the framework of democracy—or despite it.

We need more creativity. We need to study and know more about it. And we need to enlarge it in our education.

Education

Previous discussions (pp. 258-259) on education have pointed out some of the hampering effects of formal education on creativity; have mentioned the general aspects of scholastic atmosphere favorable to creativity; and have given three specific ways in which creativity might be fostered:

(1) Preserve eidetic ability.
(2) Train in substitution.
(3) Provide opportunity for creation to models.

The subject of creativity in relation to education has recently been in active discussion (Weisskopf, Andersen, Patrick). The chief comments have been:

First, that the emphasis on social adjustment over subject information not only decreases the acquired information but pressures conformity as the easy way to "adjustment."

Second, that the time needed to develop creative skill is expended, along with energy, in feverish extra-curricular activities.

Third, that there is too much insistence on unique-answer problems. The student needs experience in open-end problems, even some where the answer is unknown, and his grade depends upon his *attack*. This would prevent the industrious gatherer/reproducer of facts from achieving a higher place than he deserves.

Fourth, that organization for the average holds back the superior creative student. This retardation comes from the curriculum, diluted to the average level; and from the rules that lay down the curriculum by age and by requirements for the diploma. Joel Hildebrand daringly proposed that students be allowed to concentrate on their majors in the first years of college, while interest burns high. Then later, and more relaxed, they should take supporting courses to broaden education. This would favor creativity in a special way, because the earlier a student gets the training he can then take, the better for his success. Many indeed are the instances of significant youthful creation in all fields.

In the United States there is a foolish overinsistence on democracy in education. The bright student shall receive no break over the norm. Yet it can only be to the advantage of our culture to give bright students all they can take, and disadvantageous to force on others what they cannot take.

Integrated with the desire for children is the desire for them to do well, and for the culture to do well. The *maintenance* of the culture is entrusted to leaders who thereby earn rich rewards. For the *progress* of the culture we are dependent in each generation on a few thousand nonconformist creators. They also deserve reward, and the aid of education designed to foster their achievements.

Attempts need to be made, continuously and at every stage of learning, to relate what is taught to its creative significance, or how it may be used creatively. In studying poetry, one is taught to recognize the simile, the metaphor, onomatopoeia, and the other figures of speech. Mostly, these are pointed out as merely different from the general run of thought. Occasionally their purpose—to expound the writer's thought on something less familiar in terms of something more familiar to the reader—is made clear. But why not add the most important thing: in analogy lies the secret of all creative activity? The simile and the metaphor are analogies. The onomatopoeia is a sound analogy, and its words were probably supercharged for the author. A new combination is the sum of two old fundaments transferred by analogical imagination to new settings. Aristotle remarked, "Metaphor is the special mark of genius, for the power of making a good metaphor is the power of recognizing likeness."

When this has been explained, the figure of speech will acquire significance for the student. He will detect it with the enhanced pleasure of increased understanding. He may strive to go farther, to analyze what was in the author's mind as he developed the analogy and perceived point by point the similarities worked out in such marvelous detail in, for example, the long similes of Homer, or "Sohrab and Rustum."

The teacher can then complete the job on this segment of education—the figures of speech—by asking the student to develop analogies on his own, to watch for them in his thinking, to write down all the analogies that occur to him in a week, finally, to use them habitually. He can thus become a more creative person.

The nature of the creative process should be explained each year in more advanced terms as the child grows. Usually, it is never explained at all. The inspiring stories and anecdotes of the literature on this subject should be drawn upon freely. It is possible to demonstrate the process and let the students use it for themselves.

For example, let an essay on a choice from a list of subjects be an English assignment on Friday. The teacher asks the student to select his subject, and spend the last fifteen minutes of class time making notes of his material. He is then instructed to put away this material until Sunday, when the theme is to be written. Can he observe how the material has added to itself, and organized and jelled, in the intervening time? Did additional suggestions of material flash into his mind before Sunday? Did he write them down? Did he forget some useful items because he failed to record them? Did he find the conscious mind reverting to the theme-subject, if only momentarily, in the intervening time?

A few themes written in this way, with the students asked to notice and reply to such questions as those posed, should have value far beyond being exercises in English composition. The teacher may be able to show the class that this is not just for English; it can be used for algebra too, and is, indeed, a general problem-solving method which each must develop for himself, as far as applying it to his own problems is concerned. Cannon's description of how he prepared an address (p. 67) may be worth quoting—without, however, recommending that the high-schoolers rise at night to make records—and there is considerable similar material by other writers.

Why not tell the student overtly that it is most worthwhile to cultivate in yourself a facility with this method? Worthwhile, because it is the way at least some will in the future *create:* new designs, new ideas, new literature.

Students of all ages will respond favorably when the teacher points out convincingly the potential broad usefulness of his material. Work with language can aid in building creative technique by explaining one simple thing—that a foreign language is a crystallization of a foreign culture. It is then worthwhile to activate the mind to grasp the whole meaning of the foreign words. This in turn entails restructuring, and the words represent new symbolizations, and full appreciation of them enforces off-trail viewpoints.

In all courses, the values of diverse symbolization should be pointed out. There will be more interest in drawing and in geometry if the pupil knows that a by-product of his work will be a most useful versatility in symbolization. Especially in the art course, as Cantor said, one can learn how to distort symbols to gain help in problem solving. If you draw it conventionally, and then later distort the symbol, even though some departures lead you away, others will move toward the optimum model of search.

The mechanism of new ideas should be explained. They are combinations of things already known, in new patterns. The student is told: "You have to learn the things; and you have to learn how to evoke the combinations; and you do it the same way you wrote the theme!" Give a model: Then create to it.

Let the student, then, in his mathematics class, devise some original problems, perhaps with a new twist, perhaps a trifle more difficult, than the ones in his current lesson. In his science class, let him devise other experiments to illustrate a law, and other ways of stating the law. Can he think of any off-the-beaten-track implications?

In English class, let him take a poem, and replace some of the lines with his own. Let him try to make them better than the original. Perhaps he can add six lines to a lyric and expand the thought. Perhaps he can remove a speech from a play and replace it with one of his own. Let him try to invent entirely new poetical forms, new meters, new lengths of line, new rhythms, new rhyming schemes. In such exercises his primary purpose is not to create literature, but to develop in himself the means and method to create anything he wants.

The student needs the thrill of creating the novel, of making new combinations, of seeing that the frontier beyond which lies the unknown is not so far away as he had thought. And with youth so educated, and drilled from childhood in the technique of creation, and experienced in application of that technique to all fields and aspects of life—may we not confidently anticipate the future, confidently anticipate, too, the solution of social and psychological problems at a tempo to match the currently out-of-step march of physical science?

The burden so far has been, while the student is learning things, let him practice making new combinations of them. Let him practice creating. This can be done in moderately advanced studies, with examples like the following drawn from the field of science, although parallels should readily occur to readers experienced in other disciplines.

One proposal, designed for seniors majoring in chemistry, may be called the 100-compound problem. The student will select about a hundred chemical compounds of his own choosing, tabulate their properties from the literature, and then derive what relationships he can from the data. If he desires, he can verify a derived relationship on still other compounds.

Now, the compounds might be selected pretty much at random, or according to some plan. For example, he might take a hundred ketones, aliphatic, alicyclic, aromatic, substituted and unsubstituted. Or he might select a hundred C_5 compounds. Or he might choose the different metal acetates, hydroxyacetates, chloroacetates, dichloracetates, trichloroacetates, mercaptoacetates, and the like. Or he might elect to compare the sodium, potassium, and ammonium salts of a list of organic acids comprising acetate, propionate, citrate, tartrate, malonate, hydroxyacetate, maleate, fumarate, etc. Or he might select fifteen compounds existing in the C_1 to C_7 form (105 altogether). There will be a measure of both taste and industry in the physical properties the student decides to record. Finally, what analogies or relationships can he deduce or imaginatively project from the material he assembles?

This problem would provide an excellent final term paper for chemistry seniors. Their selection of compounds and properties would reveal the beginnings of scientific taste as discussed by Hadamard and by Beveridge. Their ability to see possibilities in the data would be a clue to research potentialities. Occasionally, some new correlation or principle would be unearthed. The student will not be blind to his chance of turning up something valuable in this, actually his first formally assigned research problem.

The best students will try by luck and taste to feel their way toward placing such limitations on their selection of compounds and properties as will be optimal for the occurrence of new combinations.

This method lets the student try his wings without reference to his professor. He must depend on himself. He must learn to use the library. For the first time in his life he will handle masses of data that he himself first decided to accumulate, then located and tabulated, and must now define as to meaning. Like any other research, he may get something important, he may discover the already known, or he may get nothing for his pains.

The Creativity Interview

The present writer in no way wishes to imply that there is any considerable innovation for the field of personnel-interviewing claimed in the following. All that is intended is to propose an unusual slant, an unusual method, and a way to get a potential extra for the recruiting money.

In nearly every hiring situation, the personal interview is decisive in selecting a person for an assignment. This is as true for scientific personnel as for other employees, and large sums of money are spent in recruiting them. The employment offer, if made, follows upon a considerable number of personal interviews. These are calculated to evaluate a man's poise, judgment, energy, personality, interests and hobbies, and knowledge of his profession. Each interviewer will often fill out a rating sheet concerned with these. Now in employing scientists, creativity is a prime consideration. Yet this factor does not appear overtly on the rating sheet, nor does it usually enter into the discussion of an applicant among interviewers: They say, he's a "nice guy," he "knows his stuff," he's a "live wire," he "talks well about his work"—all fine qualities. But does he have ideational fluency or exceptional creative ability? No answer.

One person should talk to an applicant to evaluate creativeness. The type of creativity interview suggested would last 30-45 minutes and would consist in the actual consideration of a problem by interviewer and interviewee.

In this visualization, the man is frankly told that the Company would like to see how many ideas and fruitful associations he can produce to a problem. There is no expectation to solve it, but only to see what avenues he can open up and how he follows them. He is on his mettle. The problem is then stated: for example, how might aqueous solutions be produced having lower surface tension than any now known, and what would their special properties and advantages, for washing and otherwise, be? Some information helpful to thinking is presented, oriented to the applicant's training. It might include, for example, a graph of surface tension vs. concentration for sodium laurate; a small table of surface tension minima:

Water, 0°C	76 dynes
Water, 100°C	59 "
Soap	30 "
Perfluoro Soap	10 "

Some stimulative questions would be given:

(1) How can surface tension of a *soap solution* be decreased? Can an addition be imagined that would decrease surface tension? What would it have to do? How might it work?

(2) What are forces which produce surface tension? How can they be weakened? How does rise in temperature weaken them? How does soap affect them?

The applicant should be able to produce some ideas to these stimuli. They should be used sparingly, because even while they stimulate they also condition to certain avenues and render others, in the applicant's experience, less probable of receiving consideration. If an applicant makes a good start without them, the aids may perhaps be used late in the discussion, or not at all. The interviewer must be ready and alert to follow any avenue the applicant may open. Suppose, for instance, that he skips the question of how to *produce* the low surface tension, and begins to imagine its effect on washing soiled fabrics, and goes from there to some theory of a relation between most recalcitrant soil and the size of the contact angle to loosen it, and from there to his pet method of removing carbon black that becomes firmly embedded in the skin. It is the duty of the interviewer to contribute his ideas to help the creative discussion along, to show interest, and to help build new associations springing from the ones the applicant has produced.

The interview will provide a good evaluation. Notes will have been made on the ideas developed and approaches opened up by the candidate. The quality and quantity of these can be compared against the results of previous interviews, which will have (1) given a concept of average production, as well as (2) built up for the interviewer a firm knowledge of needed facts, avenues often taken, and means of stimulation. If the creativity on the job of some of these interviewees is known, the judgment on the present applicant will be even more useful.

Now for the bonus. A record has been kept of the previous interviews, to provide a standard of what kind, what quality, and how many associations are usually produced. These ideas have been produced in each case by cooperative thinking with young minds, well-informed, well-grounded in fundamentals, of many different environments and scholastic backgrounds, each with a new viewpoint, and each of optimum age for the production of new ideas that may be startlingly new, even revolutionary. Some of these ideas will be valuable, particularly if after fifty or a hundred interviews, the coordinator is capable of a creative synthesis, to produce a really significant new combination.

Summary

Creativity—the ability to form new combinations to solve difficult problems—has been discussed as occurring in four dynamic stages:

> Preparation.
> Incubation.
> Insight.
> Verification.

These may so interweave or telescope that they have been regarded chiefly as convenient divisions for discussion. Together they constitute the creative process. But for this process to occur, two other things are necessary: a perceived problem, and motivation to attack it.

When these two are present, and solution fails, the principles of creativity to be used are the recognized knowledge in detail about each of the creative stages. This knowledge about the stages suggests the ways in which solution may be promoted and attained. These ways include a basic understanding of the mechanism of creation, and a realization that it is compounded of the interaction of preparative material and personality traits. The problem must match the inherited factors of skill and the environmentally determined attitudes in a creatively fostered outlook. There must be in the offing the chance of recognition and reward.

The view is held that the distinctive feature of creation is insight. The insights obtained as solutions to difficult problems occur as the result of unconscious work.

Aids to achievement are summarized on page 177; blocks and killer phrases on pages 157 and 166. These may affect favorably/unfavorably the progression of one or more of the stages. Broad study *helps* suggest directions in which to prepare. Worry *blocks* creative detachment. An atmosphere on the job which is negative to creativity is a major *hindrance* and spawns frequent use of the killer phrases.

Aids may be major or minor, individual or group. The easiest one to use is to record the ideas that arrive. Individual aids are check lists and deliberately polypreparational effort. Group aids range from the fast procedure of brainstorming to the slow evolution of the Gordon procedure, and include the casual and free-associational creative discussions with colleagues. The Collective Notebook Method (page 151) is powerful for groups, individuals, and suggestion systems.

The attempt has been made to analyze particular aids to promote new combinations and factor them in several closely related ways:

As two fundaments and a relation.
As two nouns and a verb.
As the symbolic equation, $A + B \longrightarrow C$.

Here A is an item plus a question, B is a second item, and C is the solution to the question in terms of a new view of the combination AB.

Good industrial climate for creativity accepts the need to limit creativity to the requirements of the organization, while asking the organization for especially loosened structural bonds. For favorable climate the most basic grants are freedom to work and recognition of achievement. Plant and services are secondary. Management's best steps are: efforts to find and pay the kind of reward the creative man is seeking; and efforts expended to apply his work creatively and keep its direction to a minimum. It is necessary to understand the creative process and give it a chance to occur, and this is a patience-trying task for management in attempting to get things done on schedule.

Regarding creativity, many moves are to be recommended, among them:

(1) A generally tolerant and favorable attitude toward the non-conformity the creator must exhibit.

(2) Revamping of education to steer all students toward a more creative outlook; careful, special training for the talented, in specifically mentioned ways.

(3) Study of creativity, by selecting creatively talented groups and testing and training them.

REFERENCES

1. Anderson, H. H., "Creativity as Personality Development," in H. H. Anderson (Ed.)," "Creativity and Its Cultivation," New York, Harper & Brothers, 1959.
2. Anderson, H. H., "Creativity in Perspective." *Ibid.*, Ref 1.
3. Armstrong, E. A., "Shakespeare's Imagination," London, Lindsay Drummond, 1946.
4. Arnold, J. E., "Creativity in Engineering," *S. of A. E. Trans.*, **64,** 17-23 (1956).
5. Bahle, J., "Eindfall und Inspiration in Musikalischen Chaffen," *Arch f. d. ges. Psychol.*, **90,** 495-503 (1934).
6. Barron, F., "The Disposition towards Originality," *J. Abn. Soc. Psychol.*, **3,** 478-485 (1955).
7. Barron, F., "The Psychology of Imagination," *Sci. Amer.*, p. 150 (Sept. 1958).
8. Barron, F., "The Needs for Order and for Disorder as Motives in Creative Activity," in Second Research Conference on the Identification of Creative Scientific Talent, Salt Lake City, University of Utah Press, 1958.
9. Barzum, J., "The Cults of Research and Creativity", *Harper's Magazine*, p. 69 (Oct. 1960).
10. Benger, *Ind. Eng. Chem*, **22,** 572.
11. Berlioz, Hector, in Ref. 40.
12. Beveridge, W. I. B., "The Art of Scientific Investigation," New York, W. W. Norton & Company, Inc., 1950.
13. Bittel, L. R., "How to Make Ideas Come Eeasy; Creative Thinking," *Factory Management*, pp. 84-90 (Mar. 1956).
14. Bittel, L. R., "Brainstorming: Better Way to Solve Plant Problems; Group Attack; Factory Special Report," *Factory Management*, pp. 98-107 (May 1956).
15. Blanshard, B., "Workshop of the Unconscious," *Am. Mercury*, p. 693 (Dec. 1945).
16. Bloede, V. G., in Ref. 123.
17. Bloom, B. S., "Report on Creativity Research at the University of Chicago," in First University of Utah Research Conference on the Identification of Creative Scientific Talent, Salt Lake City, University of Utah Press, 1956.
18. Bloom, B. S., "Some Effects of Cultural, Social, and Educational Conditions on Creativity," Second University of Utah Research Conference on the Identification of Creative Scientific Talent, Salt Lake City, University of Utah Press, 1958.

19. Bouthilet, L., "Measurement of Intuitive Thinking," University of Chicago Thesis, 1948.
20. Bromley, "Experimental Tests of Age and Creativity," *J. Gerontology,* 11, 74 (1956).
21. Bronowski, J., "The Creative Process," *Sci. Amer.,* p. 58 (Sept. 1958).
22. Brown, H. C., "What Is Wrong with Industrial Research?" *Res. and Dev.,* p. 101 (Nov. 1960).
23. Bruner, J. S., "What Social Scientists Say about Having an Idea," *Printer's Ink* (July 12, 1957).
24. Buel, W. D., "Rating Scales for Industrial Creativity," *J. Appl. Psychol.,* 44, 407-412 (1960).
25. Bulbrook, M. E., "An Experimental Inquiry into the Existence and Nature of Insight," *Am. J. Psychol.,* 44, 409-453 (1932).
26. Cannon, W. B., "The Way of an Investigator," New York, W. W. Norton and Company, Inc., 1945.
27. Cantor, S. M., "Education in Art: a Lesson for Chemistry," *Chem. Eng. News,* pp. 5406-10 (Nov. 5, 1956).
28. Cattell, R. B., Committee report on predictors of creativity, in C. W. Taylor (Principal Investigator), Third University of Utah Research Conference on the Identification of Creative Scientific Talent, Salt Lake City, University of Utah Press, 1960.
29. Cattell, R. B., The Personality and Motivation of the Researcher from Measurements of Contemporaries and From Biography, in C. W. Taylor (Principal Investigator), Third University of Utah Research Conference on the Identification of Creative Scientific Talent, Salt Lake City, University of Utah Press, 1960, b.
30. Cattell, R. B., and Drevdahl, J. E., "A Comparison of the Personality Profile (16 P. F.) of Eminent Researchers with that of Eminent Teachers and Administrators and of the General Population. *Brit. J. Psychol.,* 44, 248-261 (1955).
31. Cattell, R. B., and Stice, G. F., "The Sixteen Personality Factor Questionnaire," I.P.A.T., Champaign, Illinois, 1955.
32. Chassell, "Tests for Originality," *J. Ed. Psychol.,* 7, 317-328 (1916).
33. Claparede, E., "La Genese de l'Hypothese," *Arch. de. Psychol.,* 24, 1-154 (1934).
34. Clark, C. H., "Brainstorming," New York, Doubleday & Company, Inc., 1958.
35. Cowell, H., *Am. J. Psychol.,* 235 (1926).
36. Cranbach, Lee, "Essentials of Psychological Testing," p. 261, New York, Harper & Brothers, 1960.
37. Danielson, L., "Characteristics of Engineers and Scientists," p. 24, University of Michigan, 1960.
38. Dashiell, J. F., "Fundamentals of General Psychology," Boston, Houghton Mifflin Company, 1937.

39. Dimnet, E., "The Art of Thinking," New York, Simon & Schuster, Inc., 1928.

40. Dorian, Frederick, "The Musical Workshop," Harper & Brothers, 1947.

41. Dow, A. B., "The Creativeness of Life," in H. H. Anderson (Ed.), "Creativity and Its Cultivation," New York, Harper & Brothers, 1959.

42. Drevdahl, J. E., "Factors of Importance for Creativity," *J. Clin. Psychol.*, 12, 23-26, 1956.

43. Drevdahl, J. E., and Catell, R. B., "Personality and Creativity in Artists and Writers," *J. Clin. Psychol.*, 14, 107-111, 1958.

44. Duncker, K., "On Problem Solving," *Psychol. Monograph*, No. 270 (1945).

45. Easton, W. H., "Creative Thinking and How to Develop It," *Mech. Eng.*, pp. 694-704 (Aug. 1946).

46. Eindhoven, J., and Vinacke, W. E., "Creative Processes in Painting," *J. Gen. Psychol.*, p. 47 (1952).

47. Elder, A. L., "What Management Expects of the Young Professional," *Chem. Eng. News*, pp. 78-81 (Dec. 7, 1959).

48. Eyring, H., "Scientific Creativity," in H. H. Anderson (Ed.), "Creativity and Its Cultivation," New York, Harper & Brothers, 1959.

49. Ferren, Skytop Symposium, *cf.* Ref. 163.

50. Flesch, R., "The Art of Clear Thinking," New York, Harper & Brothers, 1952.

51. Flory, C. D., "Developing and Using Our Creative Abilities," *Chem. Eng. Progr.*, pp. 676-678 (Dec. 1953).

52. *Fortune*, "New Approach to Research and Development," p. 212 (May 1958).

53. Friedman, P., "The Principles of Scientific Research," New York, Pergamon, 1960.

54. Frokel, in Ref. 40.

55. Ghiselin, B., "The Creative Process," New York, New American Library, 1952.

56. Ghiselin, B., "The Nature of Imaginative Action," Third Research Conference on the Identification of Creative Scientific Talent, Salt Lake City, University of Utah Press, 1960.

57. Girard, R. W., "The Biological Basis of Imagination," *Sci. Monthly*, pp. 477-499 (June, 1946).

58. Gordon, W. J., "An Operational Approach to Creativity," *Harvard Business Review*, pp. 41-51 (Dec.-Jan. 1957).

59. Guilford, J. P., "Creativity," *Am. Psychologist*, 5, 444-454 (1950).

60. Guilford, J. P., "Factors in Problem Solving," *ARTC Inst. J.*, 4, 197-204 (1954).

61. Guilford, J. P., "The Structure of Intellect," *Psychol. Bull.*, 53, 267-293 (1956), a.

62. Guilford, J. P., "The Relation of Intellectual Factors to Creative Thinking in Science, in C. W. Taylor (Principal Investigator), First University of

Utah Research Conference on the Identification of Creative Scientific Talent, Salt Lake City, University of Utah Press, 1956, b.

63. Guilford, J. P., "A Revised Structure of Intellect," *Rep. Psychol. Lab.*, No. 19, Los Angeles, University of Southern California, 1957.

64. Guilford, J. P., "Basic Traits in Intellectual Performances, in C. W. Taylor (Principal Investigator), Second University of Utah Research Conference on the Identification of Creative Scientific Talent. Salt Lake City, Utah, University of Utah Press, 1958.

65. Guilford, J. P., "Intellectual Resources and Their Value as Seen by Creative Scientists, in C. W. Taylor (Principal Investigator), Second University of Utah Research Conference on the Identification of Creative Scientific Talent, Salt Lake City, University of Utah Press, 1960.

66. Guilford, J. P., Wilson, R. C. and Christensen, P. R., "A Factor-Analytic Study of Creative Thinking," II. Administration of Tests and Analysis of Results., *Rep. Psychol. Lab.*, No. 8, Los Angeles, University of Southern California, 1952.

66a. Guilford, J. P., Wilson, R. C., Christensen, P. R., and Lewis, D. J., "A Factor-Analytic Study of Creative Thinking, I. Hypotheses and Description of Tests." *Rep. Psychol. Lab.* No. 4., Los Angeles, University of Southern California, 1951.

67. Guth, L. W., Discovering and Developing Creative Engineers," *Machine Design*, pp. 89-94 (Mar. 1949).

68. Hadamard, J., "The Psychology of Invention in the Mathematical Field," Princeton University Press, 1945.

69. Haefele, J. W., and Broge, R. W., "The Synthesis and Properties of Mercaptans Having Different Degrees of Acidity of the Sulfhydryl Group," Proceedings of the Scientific Section of the Toilet Goods Association, Dec. 1959.

70. Hagen, D., "Careers and Family Atmospheres: An empirical test of Roe's Theory." Harvard Studies in Career Development, No. 10A. Cambridge, Mass., Graduate School of Education, Harvard University, 1959.

71. Harmon, L. R., "Social and Technological Determiners of Creativity," in C. W. Taylor (Principal Investigator), First University of Utah Research Conference on the Identification of Creative Scientific Talent, Salt Lake City, University of Utah Press, 1956.

72. Harmon, L. R., "The Development of a Criterion of Scientific Competence, in C. W. Taylor (Principal Investigator), Second University of Utah Research Conference on the Identification of Creative Scientific Talent, Salt Lake City, University of Utah Press, 1958.

73. Harris, R. H., and Simberg, A. L., "AC Test of Creative Ability," Examiner's Manual, Flint, Michigan, AC Spark Plug Division, General Motors Corp., 1953.

74. Hart, Hornell, "Technique of Social Progress."

75. Hart, Hornell, "Science of Social Relations," New York, Henry Holt and Company, Inc., 1927.

76. Heidbreder, Edna, "An Experimental Study of Thinking," *Arch. Psychol.*, No. 73 (1924).
77. Helmholtz, in Wallas' "Art of Thought," Ch. 4, New York, Harcourt, Brace & Company, Inc., 1926.
78. Heyel, Carl, "Handbook of Industrial Research Management," New York, Reinhold Publishing Corp., 1959.
79. Hills, J. R., "The Relationship between Certain Factor-Analyzed Abilities and Success in College Mathematics," *Rep. Psychol. Lab.*, No. 15, Los Angeles, University of Southern California, 1955.
80. Housman, A. E., in Ghiselin, "Creative Process," *cf* Ref. 55.
81. Hull, C. L., "Quantitative Aspects of the Evolution of Concepts," *Psychol. Monograph*, No. 123, (1920).
82. Humphrey, G., "Thinking," New York, John Wiley & Sons, Inc., 1951.
83. Hutchinson, E. D., "How to Think Creatively," Nashville, Abingdon-Cokesbury, 1949.
84. James, William, "Principles of Psychology," Vol. 1, p. 582; Vol. 2, p. 360.
85. Kekulé, F., in Kekulé Memorial Lecture by Japp, *J. Chem. Soc.* (London) p. 100 (1898).
86. Kelton, "Evaluation of Scientific Personnel," *Research Management*, **2**, 185-198 (Autumn 1959).
87. Kent, G. H., and Rosanoff, A. J., "A Study of Association in Insanity," *Am. J. Insanity*, **67**, 37-96 (1910).
88. Kleitman, N., in Flesch, "Art of Clear Thinking," *cf*. Ref. 87.
89. Knapp, R. H., Personality Committee Report, First Research Conference on the Identification of Creative Scientific Talent, Salt Lake City, University of Utah Press, 1956.
90. Knowlson, T. S., "Originality," New York, J. B. Lippincott Company, 1918.
91. Kohler, W., "Gestalt Psychology," New York, Liveright, 1947.
92. Kubie, L. S., "Neurotic Distortion of the Creative Process," Lawrence, University of Kansas Press, 1958.
93. Lashley, K. S., "Preliminary Studies of the Rat's Capacity for Detail Vision," *J. Gen. Psychol.*, **18**, 123-193 (1938).
94. Laycock, S., "Adaptability to New Situations," Baltimore, Warwick and York, 1926.
95. Leeper, R., in "Handbook of Experimental Psychology," S. Stevens, (Ed.), p. 743, New York, John Wiley & Sons, Inc., 1951.
96. Lehman, H. C., "Age and Achievement," Princeton University Press, 1953.
97. Lowell, Amy, in Ghiselin, "The Creative Process," see Ref. 55.
98. Lowes, J. L., "The Road to Xanadu," New York, Houghton Mifflin Company, 1940.
99. Luchins, A. S., "Mechanization in Problem Solving: the Effect of Einstellung," *Psychol. Monograph*, No. 248 (1942).
100. Maier, N., *Brit. J. Psychol.*, **24**, 144-155 (1933).
101. Maier, N., "Reasoning in Humans, I. On Direction," *J. Comparative Psychol.*, **10**, 115-143 (1930).

102. Maslow, A. H., "Creativity in Self-actualizing people," in H. H. Anderson (Ed.), "Creativity and Its Cultivation," New York, Harper & Brothers, 1959.
103. May, R., "The Nature of Creativity," in H. H. Anderson (Ed.), "Creativity and Its Cultivation," New York, Harper & Brothers, 1959.
104. McClelland, D. C., "The Calculated Risk: an Aspect of Scientific Performance," in C. W. Taylor (Principal Investigator), First University of Utah Research Conference on the Identification of Creative Scientific Talent. Salt Lake City, University of Utah Press, 1956.
105. McKellar, Peter, "Imagination and Thinking," New York, Basic Books.
106. McPherson, J. H., "What is Creativity," Am. Management Bull. 4, 9-14 (1960).
107. Meadow, A., and Parnes, S. J., "Evaluation of Training in Creative Problem Solving," J. Appl. Psychol. 43, 189-194 (1959).
108. Mortimer, Charles G., "The Clarkson Letter," (n.f.i.).
109. Mozart, W. A., in Ghiselin, "The Creative Process," see Ref. 55.
110. Murphy, G., "The Freeing of Intelligence," Psychol. Bull., 42, 1-19 (1945).
111. Nelles, Maurice, "Deliberate Creativeness in Science and Engineering," Chem. Eng. News, 31, 1520 (1953).
112. Omwake, Louise, "Visual Responses to Auditory Stimuli," J. Appl. Psychol., 24, 468.
113. Osborn, Alex, "Applied Imagination," New York, Charles Scribner's Sons, 1957.
114. Pacifico, C., "For Creativity—Ignorance Helps," Chem. Eng. News, pp. 52-55 (May 12, 1958).
115. Parnes, S. J., and Meadow, A., "University of Buffalo Research Regarding Development of Creative Talent, in C. W. Taylor (Principal Investigator), Third University of Utah Research Conference on the Identification of Creative Scientific Talent, Salt Lake City, University of Utah Press, 1960.
116. Parnes, S. J., "Description of the University of Buffalo Creative Problems Solving Course," Buffalo, N. Y., Creative Education Office, University of Buffalo, 1958.
117. Parnes, S. J., "Effects of "Brainstorming Instructions on Creative Problem Solving by Trained and Untrained Subjects, J. Educ. Psychol., 50, 171-176 (1959).
118. Patrick, C., "Creative Thought in Poets," Arch. Psychol., No. 178 (1935).
119. Patrick, C., "Creative Thought in Artists," J. Psychol., 4, 35-73 (1937).
120. Patrick, C., "Scientific Thought," J. Psychol., 5, 55-83 (1938).
121. Patrick, C., Psychology, 8, 253.
122. Patrick, C., "What Is Creative Thinking?" New York, Philosophical Library, 1955.
123. Platt, W., and Baker, R. A., "The Relation of the Scientific Hunch to Research," J. Chem. Educ., 8, 1969 (1931).
124. Poincaré, H., "Mathematical Creation," in Ghiselin, "Creative Process," See Ref. 55.

125. Polya, Gyorgy, "How to Solve it," Princeton University Press, 1945.
126. Porterfield, A. L., "Creative Factors in Scientific Research," Duke University Press, 1941.
127. Prentice, W. C. H., "The Interruption of Tasks," *Psychol. Rev.*, 51, 329-340 (1944).
128. Prescott, Frederick, "The Poetic Mind," Cornell University Press.
129. Pressey, S. L., "Nature and Nurture of Genius," *Sci. Monthly* (Sept. 1955).
130. *Printer's Ink*, p. 28 (Feb. 17, 1956).
131. Quinn, J. B., *Harvard Business Review* (Mar.-Apr. 1960).
132. Rees, H. J., and Israel, H. E., *Psychol. Monograph*, No. 210 (1935).
133. Reiss, Otto, "How to Develop Profitable Ideas," New Jersey, Prentice-Hall, 1945.
134. Rhodes, J. M., University of Arizona Thesis, 1957.
135. Ribot, T., "Essay on the Creative Imagination," Chicago, Open Court, 1906.
136. Roe, Anne, "A Psychological Study of Physical Scientists," *Genet. Psychol. Monograph*, 43, 123-255 (1951).
137. Roe, Anne, "A Psychological Study of Biological Scientists," *Psychol. Monograph*, No. 331 (1951).
138. Roe, Anne, *Sci. Amer.*, p. 25 (Nov. 1952).
139. Roe, Anne, "A Psychological Study of Eminent Psychologists and Anthropologists, and a Comparison with Biological and Physical Scientists. *Psychol. Monograph*, 67, (1953). (Whole No. 352.)
140. Roe, Anne, Early Differentiation of Interests, in C. W. Taylor (Principal Investigator), Second University of Utah Research Conference on the Identification of Creative Scientific Talent. Salt Lake City, University of Utah Press, 1958.
141. Roe, Anne, Personal Problems and Science, in C. W. Taylor (Principal Investigator), Third University of Utah Research Conference on the Identification of Creative Scientific Talent, Salt Lake City, University of Utah Press, 1960.
142. Rogers, Carl, "Toward a Theory of Creativity," *ETC—Review of General Semantics*, 11, 249-260 (1954).
143. Rossman, J., "The Psychology of the Inventor," Washington, Inventor's Publishing Co., 1931.
144. Royce, J., "Psychology of Invention," *Psychol. Rev.*, 5, 113-144 (1898).
145. Saunders, D. R., "Some Measures Related to Success and Placement in Basic Engineering Research and Development," First Research Conference on the Identification of Creative Scientific Talent, Salt Lake City, University of Utah Press, 1956.
146. Shapero, Harold, in Ghiselin, "Creative Process," *cf*. Ref. 55.
147. Sharp, E., "Individual Psychology," *Am. J. Psychol.*, 10, 329-391 (1899).
148. Sprecher, T. B., "A Proposal for Identifying the Meaning of Creativity," Third Research Conference on the Identification of Creative Scientific Talent, Salt Lake City, University of Utah Press, 1960.
149. Smith, W. R., "Favorable and Unfavorable Working Conditions Reported

by Scientists at Two Research Centers," Third Research Conference on the Identification of Creative Scientific Talent, Salt Lake City, University of Utah Press, 1960.

150. Smoke, K., "Objective Study of Concept Formation," *Psychol. Monograph*, No. 191 (1932).

151. Spearman, C., "The Creative Mind," New York, Appleton-Century-Crofts, Inc., 1931.

152. Stein, M., "Creativity and the Scientist," in "The Direction of Research Establishments," London, H. M. Stationery Office, 1957. 3pl.

153. Stein, M., Heinze, S. J., and Rodgers, R. R., "Creativity and/or Success," Second Research Conference on the Identification of Creative Scientific Talent, Salt Lake City, University of Utah Press, 1958.

154. Tappi, "Symposium on the Management of Research," (Dec. 1953).

155. Taton, R., "Reason and Chance in Scientific Discovery," New York, Philosophical Library, 1957.

156. Taylor, D., and Jordan, R. C., "Developing Creativity in Engineering," *Mech. Eng.* (Feb., 1958).

157. Taylor, C. W., "Some Variables Functioning in Productivity and Creativity, in C. W. Taylor (Principal Investigator), Second University of Utah Research Conference on the Identification of Creative Scientific Talent. Salt Lake City, University of Utah Press, 1958.

158. Taylor, D. W., Smith, W. R., and Ghiselin, B., "Analyses of Multiple Criteria of Creativity and Productivity of Scientists, in C. W. Taylor (Principal Investigator), Third University of Utah Research Conference on the Identification of Creative Scientific Talent. Salt Lake City, University of Utah Press, 1960.

159. Taylor, D. W., "Variables Related to Creativity and Productivity among Men in Two Research Laboratories, in C. W. Taylor (Principal Investigator), Second University of Utah Research Conference on the Identification of Creative Scientific Talent. Salt Lake City, University of Utah Press, 1958.

160. Taylor, D. W., Berry, P. C., and Block, C. H., "Does Group Participation When Using Brainstorming Facilitate or Inhibit Creative Thinking?" Tech. Rep. No. 1, Contract Nonr. 609 (20) NR 150-166. New Haven, Conn., Dept. of Psychology, Yale University, 1957.

161. Teeple, J. E., in Ref. 10.

162. Thomas, H. M., "Establishing the Proper Climate for Creative Effort," *Am. Management Bull.*, 4, 15-21 (1960).

163. Thurstone, L. L., in "The Nature of Creative Thinking," Skytop Symposium Monograph sponsored by the Industrial Research Institute, pp. 35, 38, and 40, 1952.

164. Thurstone, L. L., "Primary Mental Abilities," Rep. No. 50, the Psychometric Laboratory, University of Chicago, Sept., 1948.

165. True, G. H., "How to Be Creative," *Printer's Ink*, p. 19 (Jan. 4, 1957).

166. Tumin, Melvin, "Obstacles to Creativity," *ETC*, p. 261 (Summer 1954).

167. Tuska, C. K., "Increasing Inventive Creativeness," *J. Franklin Inst.* **260,** 93-98 (Aug., 1955).

168. Vinacke, W. E., "The Psychology of Thinking," New York, McGraw-Hill Book Co., Inc., 1952.

169. Von Fange, E. K., "Understanding the Creative Process," *Gen. Elec. Rev.,* (July and Sept. 1955).

170. Wallace, A. R., "My Life," London, Chapman Hall, Ltd., 1908.

171. Wallas, Graham, "Art of Thought," New York, Harcourt-Brace, 1926.

172. Weber, C., in Squires, P. C., "The Creative Psychology of Carl Maria von Weber," *Character and Personality,* **6,** 203-217 (1938).

173. Weinland, C. E., "Creative Thought in Scientific Research," *Sci. Monthly,* **75,** 350-354 (Dec. 1952).

174. Weisskopf, E., "Intellectual Malfunction and Personality," *J. Abn. Soc. Psychol.,* **46,** 410 (1951); *J. Ed. Psychol.,* **42,** 185 (1951).

175. Welch, L., *J. Appl. Psychol.,* **30,** 638; **31,** 280.

176. Wertheimer, M., "Productive Thinking," New York, Harper & Brothers, 1945.

177. Whipple, G. M., "Manual of Mental and Physical Tests," Vol II, Baltimore, Warwick and York, 1921.

178. Whiting, C. S., "Creative Thinking," New York, Reinhold Publishing Corp., 1958.

179. Wiegand, W. B., "Motivation in Research," *Chem. Eng. News,* **24,** 2772-2773 (1946).

180. Wilbur, in Skytop Symposium, *cf.* Ref. 163.

181. Willman, R. R., "An Experimental Investigation of the Creative Process in Music," Psychol. Monograph, No. 261 (1944).

182. Wilson, R. C., Guilford, J. P., and Christensen, P. R., "The Measure of Individual Differences in Originality," *Psychol. Bull.* **50,** 362-370 (1953).

183. Wood, H., in Ref. 123.

184. Woodworth, R. S., and Schlossberg, H., "Experimental Psychology," Rev. Ed., p. 51, New York, Henry Holt & Co., 1954.

185. Yerkes, R. M., "The Mind of a Gorilla," *Genet. Psychol. Monograph,* No. **2,** 1-193 (1927).

186. Young, J. F., "Developing Creative Engineers," *Mech. Eng.,* pp. 305-314 (Dec. 1945).

187. Young, J. W., "Technique for Producing Ideas," Chicago, Advertising Publications, Inc., 1940.

Notes to References

The author has the following comments on what he considers the more important references in the above list. The items in each category are listed in order of importance for the general reader, the first item being rated most important, the second next in importance, etc. Numbers refer to the list.

Books

Beveridge, 12: excellent material, technical orientation, well-written.

Hadamard, 68: thoughtful, inspirational, thought-provoking, especially the unusual instances of creativity, which must be fitted to any comprehensive theory.

Patrick, 122: good material.

Knowlson, 90: thoughtful material on the creative process; makes point, the worker can know too much to succeed.

Hutchinson, 83: good on theory, overemphasis on frustration.

Rossman, 143: good summary of good work.

Flesch, 50: popular style, well-written, some new viewpoints.

Wallas, 171: chapters three and four good for themselves and for historical perspective.

Collected Papers

Ghiselin, 55: broad spectrum of papers culled from the literature.

Anderson, 1: from a University of Michigan symposium.

Utah Series: these are the collected papers from three symposia, and they are mentioned in references 17, 8, and 28. Since the sessions were related to the identification of creative scientific talent, emphasis is heavily on personality and ratings by judges.

NYAS Series: ten papers on thinking, with three included on creative thinking, in *"The Psychology of Thinking,"* Annals of the New York Academy of Sciences, **91,** 1-158, Dec. 23, 1960. Contains Guilford summary of the dimensions of mind. An excellent group for the serious student.

Textbook

Osborn, 113: very fine work, and a manual for teachers is available to supplement it. Heavily slanted to brainstorming, of which Osborn is prime advocate. Especially good for practical exercises, and the only place the author has found these in organized form.

Articles and Papers

Duncker, 44: every scientist should be familiar with this work; hard to follow, but worth it.

Easton, 45: for its clarity, conviction, and inspiration.

Platt and Baker, 123: interesting, and the wealth of material is convincing. (Their original protocols should be analyzed by someone experienced in market research interview methods.)

Arnold, 4: for its analysis of blocks to creativity.

Bittel, 13: for its summary of helps to creativity.

Gordon, 58: for its exposition of the take it slow, and from way back, method.

Gerard, 57: good presentation, by a biologist.

Murphy, 110: importance of reflective thought, and time for it.

Bulbrook, 25: interesting.

APPENDICES

APPENDIX A

PATRICK'S WORK ON CREATIVE THOUGHT IN ARTISTS AND POETS

(*Referred to on p. 16*)

Not only creativity, but also concept formation and problem-solving in general have been studied by observing subjects at work and soliciting their comments aloud in the course of their activity. These methods were used for the study of creativity by Catharine Patrick, one of the foremost modern authorities on the subject, later commissioned to write the article on Creative Thinking for the "Encyclopedia of Psychology."

For her first study, Patrick presented to 55 poets and 58 non-poets a picture— a mountain scene—carefully selected for potentiality to stimulate poetic thought. Subjects were asked to compose a lyric suggested to them by the picture, and to think aloud during composition. Thoughts were recorded in shorthand and later analyzed. The chief points discussed in the resultant paper were: (1) the occurrence of the stages of creative thought as specified by Wallas; and (2) the differences between poets and non-poets.

Patrick recorded the total time of the work of each subject. The method of analysis of her data was to count out for each quarter of the total time the number of new thoughts and the number of recurrences and modifications. Usage of figures of speech and other verbal elements was also noted. "If a thought had been modified sufficiently that a new sentence was necessary, it was considered a thought change." Poets also replied to a questionnaire on their methods of work.

The experiment with poets was followed by a parallel study of professional artists and a non-artist control group. Partly, this was to furnish the additional factor, that the progress of a drawing could be followed objectively as well as by listening to the creator as work progressed. In this case the stimulus was a poem which might be fruitful in suggesting material to paint: a passage from Milton's "L'Allegro." Timing began with presentation of the poem. The progress of the work of drawing was noted and analyzed. The actual writing or drawing required an average of about twenty-five minutes. The compositions may be regarded as genuine creative acts, since some of the poets' compositions were later judged worthy of publication.

The significant data from this pair of experiments appear in Table A-1. Analysis reveals the stages of the creative process:

Both poets and non-poets got ideas from the picture, and did some preliminary elaboration (preparative stage) of them. These ideas were then temporarily submerged (incubation) but reappeared occasionally until decision was made on the subject and basic content of the poem (insight). Then followed composition and revision (verification stage). Patrick was the first to show interweaving of the stages: Revision work started early; insights to embellish occurred even when the lyric was nearly completed.

Patrick found that the poets and the non-poets, those with and without technical training, both showed the four stages of creative thought. They showed no difference in time to write, or in average speed of composing per line, or in per cent use of adjectives, strong verbs, or weak words. Poets more often referred to the supernatural and more often employed allegory, simile, metaphor, and personification. Poets more often let the picture start ideas about other things. Non-poets stayed closer to the presented stimulus.

In the replies on methods of work, some poets said they incubated a mood. All but one said the essential structure of a lyric came at one sitting. As many as 90 per cent said part came automatically; 74 per cent said content came first, then form; 81 per cent wrote in a warm emotional state. If interrupted in composition, many felt they might as well throw the manuscript away.

Patrick interpreted the results to mean that the lyric insight emerged by fading of unimportant material, rather than unconscious rearrangement of the preparative work during the stage of incubation.

The paper on artists confirmed the earlier results for poets on the stages of the creative process. The professional artists, like the poets, went far afield from the presented stimulus to the final creation, if so moved. Most thought changes occurred in the first and second periods, three-fourths of the revisions in the third and fourth periods. Revisions were of the nature of shadings, additions of detail, stopping to survey the whole structure, etc.

Patrick, then, differentiated the four creative stages experimentally; showed that they interwove; and made clear the importance of early ideas, and how often they appear in the final product.

TABLE A–1. TYPES OF WORK BY POETS (P) AND ARTISTS (A) IN THE SUCCESSIVE INTERVALS OF A CREATIVE TASK, DIVIDED BY QUARTERS.

Material	Group	1st		2nd		3rd		4th	
		P	A	P	A	P	A	P	A
% of Thought Changes	Experts	54	80	33	15	10	3	3	2
	Controls	70	76	26	16	3	4	1	4
% Lines as 1st Drafted or General Shapes 1st Drawn	Experts	9	20	36	42	33	29	22	9
	Controls	10	18	32	44	41	32	17	12
% Revisions	Experts	1	3	12	17	26	34	61	46
	Controls	2	2	13	21	26	35	59	42

The first number, 54, means that, of all the thought changes noted for the poets, on the average 54% occurred in the first quarter of the working period. In row three, the poets drafted 36% of their lines in the second quarter of the working period. In row five, the poets did 61% of their revisions in the last quarter of the working period. The other numbers in the Table are to be interpreted in the same way as indicated.

WORK OF EINDHOVEN AND VINACKE
ON CREATIVE THOUGHT IN ARTISTS

(Referred to on p. 17)

Eindhoven and Vinacke also observed painters in action, and added these features to their experiment: The workers did not report aloud; the drawing was done in several sessions, giving more time for the creative process to occur; a variety of drawing materials was allowed. The creative task was a drawing suitable for a publishable illustration for the poem "Night" by Charles Peguy. Artists and non-artists were compared. The data obtained are given in Table B–1.

The stages of creative thought were again identified. The interplay of the stages was further clarified: The stages are continuing, the process is dynamic. The stages of creativity are not stages at all, but processes which occur during creation. "They blend together and go along concurrently."

Artists spent less time on preliminary drawing, more on final product. Non-artists spent about the same time on both.

Artists made more early sketches, with less elaboration, and they made fewer sketches in the periods after the first.

Artists' early sketches were smaller than non-artists'. Larger preliminary sketches would partially account for non-artists taking more time with preliminary work. The ability to blow up a small sketch may be a part of professional experience.

TABLE B–1. DATA FOR ARTISTS AND NON-ARTISTS FROM A LABORATORY
PROJECT TO ILLUSTRATE PEGUY'S "NIGHT."

| | Workers | *Laboratory Period* | | | |
		I	*II*	*III*	*IV*
% Time Spent in	A	67	87	91	
Sketching	N	70	82	76	
Mean No. of	A	3.6	1.1	1.4	0.5
Sketches	N	1.7	2.1	1.8	1.3
Number of Sub-	A	13	12	8	2
jects Attend-	N	14	12	10	4
ing Session					

The first number, 67, means that the trained artists (A) spent 67% of the first laboratory period in sketching. During this time, from row three, they averaged 3.6 sketches. These values are averaged, from row five, over 13 artists who attended. The other numbers in the Table are to be interpreted in the same way.

TABLE B–2. AVERAGE SUCCESS OF THREE CLASSES OF SUBJECTS IN
CERTAIN RUNS IN BOUTHILET'S "MEASUREMENT OF
INTUITIVE THINKING."

(*Summary Table of Bouthilet's work on preconscious rapport in concept formation, as described on page 78.*) Three classes of subjects were demarcated:

(1) Those who discovered the rule, and proved it by correctly marking all 20 of the new words in their final series, *and* who showed a significantly high level of correctness in the last run preceding their 20 correct.

(2) Those, again, who succeeded, but who did *not* show a significantly high level of correctneses in their last run preceding the 20 correct.

(3) Those who failed to discover the rule.

Class	No. of Subjects	Av. No. of Series	Av. No. of Correct Choices in Series Preceding Final Run by		
			One	Two	Three
1	7	10	15	9	5
2	6	8	5	3	6
3	7	20	4	5	3

In Class 1, there were 7 subjects; they needed 10 series to "get" the rule. In the 9th series, they got 15 of 20 right, in the 8th series they got 9 of 20 right, in the 7th series, they got 5 of 20 right. The expectation of correct choice by chance alone is 4. Getting 15 right would happen by chance only one time in a hundred.

APPENDIX C

TABLE C–1. INCIDENCE OF SOLUTIONS TO THREE PROBLEMS (AFTER LAYCOCK).
(*Summary Table of Laycock's work on the low incidence of problem-solving ability, as described on page 225.*)

		% of Subjects with Correct Solution to Problem of		
	Aid Type	Burglar	Model	Cyrus
1	None	–3	4	4
2	Pertinent	7	9	7
3	Pertinent + a	9	26	9
4	Pertinent + b	21	13	17
5	Pertinent + a + b	39	32	29

(a) statement of relation
(b) statement: "this is a hint"

–3 means 3% fewer subjects solved the problem after study without aid, than were successful in another group after initial reading. (This is a non-significant variation between groups.) When a pertinent story related to Cyrus was told, 7% of subjects got the answer. If told the story, and given the relation of diversion, 9% solved. If told the story, and apprised that it was a hint, 17% solved. If told the story, given the relation of diversion, and apprised that the story was a hint, 29% solved.

APPENDIX D

AGE AND ACHIEVEMENT

(The method of tabulation employed to derive the results on page 236.)

The Tables in Lehman's "Age and Achievement" were studied, and a special table was derived according to the following rules:

(1) Use 5 year intervals, exclude tables with other intervals.
(2) An entry preceding the oldest bracket must be finite; .000 is not counted.
(3) Table 85b was excluded because many workers are still living.
(4) If two Tables appear for the same data, only the one for "number of works" is counted.

For example, in Lehman's Table I, the oldest age bracket shown is 80–84. There were .004 notable contributions per living individual 80–84 years old. But in the same Lehman Table I, at another age bracket greater than age 40 but less than 80, there were only .002 notable contributions per living individual in that bracket. (This is not surprising until it is found to happen 66 out of 80 times.)

The partial tabulation, Table D–1, shows how the data were developed further:

TABLE D–1. PARTIAL TABULATION OF INCIDENCE OF CREATIVE WORK IN CERTAIN AGE BRACKETS (after Lehman).

Lehman Graph	Av. No. of Contributions in Oldest Bracket Shown	Lowest Av. No. of Contributions in Another Bracket at Age > 40
1	.004 (80–84)	.002
3a	.031 (80–84)	.014
3b	.021 (80–84)	.013
4	.006 (70–75)	.005
5	.048 (85–89)	.016
6	.003 (80–84)	.003
13	.010 (70–75)	.005
14	.003 (70–75)	.006
15	.014 (80–84)	.007
	Etc.	

APPENDIX E

KENT-ROSANOFF WORD LIST

1. Table	26. Wish	51. Stem	76. Bitter
2. Dark	27. River	52. Lamp	77. Hammer
3. Music	28. White	53. Dream	78. Thirsty
4. Sickness	29. Beautiful	54. Yellow	79. City
5. Man	30. Window	55. Bread	80. Square
6. Deep	31. Rough	56. Justice	81. Butter
7. Soft	32. Citizen	57. Boy	82. Doctor
8. Eating	33. Foot	58. Light	83. Loud
9. Mountain	34. Spider	59. Health	84. Thief
10. House	35. Needle	60. Bible	85. Lion
11. Black	36. Red	61. Memory	86. Joy
12. Mutton	37. Sleep	62. Sheep	87. Bed
13. Comfort	38. Anger	63. Bath	88. Heavy
14. Hand	39. Carpet	64. Cottage	89. Tobacco
15. Short	40. Girl	65. Swift	90. Baby
16. Fruit	41. High	66. Blue	91. Moon
17. Butterfly	42. Working	67. Hungry	92. Scissors
18. Smooth	43. Sour	68. Priest	93. Quiet
19. Command	44. Earth	69. Ocean	94. Green
20. Chair	45. Trouble	70. Head	95. Salt
21. Sweet	46. Soldier	71. Stove	96. Street
22. Whistle	47. Cabbage	72. Long	97. King
23. Woman	48. Hard	73. Religion	98. Cheese
24. Cold	49. Eagle	74. Whiskey	99. Blossom
25. Slow	50. Stomach	75. Child	100. Afraid

CATTELL PROFILE OF THE CREATIVE PERSONALITY

Mean 16 P.F. Profile of Eminent Researchers (N=140)
in Physics, Biology, and Psychology

Personality Dimension Label at Lower Pole	Mean Stens	Plotted Mean Sten Scores 1 2 3 4 5 6 7 8 9 10	Personality Dimension Label at Upper Pole	
A—Schizothymia	3.36	. . . .	Cyclothymia	A
A—Low Intelligence	7.64	. . . .	High Intelligence	B
C—Low Ego Strength	5.44	. . . .	High Ego Strength	C
E—Low Dominance	6.62	. . . .	High Dominance	E
F—Desurgency	3.15	. . . .	Surgency	F
G—Low Group Super Ego	4.10	. . . .	High Group Super Ego	G
H—Threctia	6.01	. . . .	Parmia	H
I—Harria	7.05	. . . .	Premsia	I
L—Low Protension	5.36	. . . .	High Protension	L
M—Praxernia	5.36	. . . .	Autia	M
N—Simplicity	5.50	. . . .	Shrewdness	N
O—Low Guilt Proneness	4.38	. . . .	High Guilt Proneness	O
Q₁—Conservatism	7.00	. . . .	Radicalism	Q
Q₂—Low Self Sufficiency	7.52	. . . .	High Self Sufficiency	Q
Q₃—Low Self Sentiment	6.44	. . . .	High Self Sentiment	Q
Q₄—Low Ergic Tension	4.91	. . . .	High Ergic Tension	Q

From "The Third (1959) Research Conference on the Identification of Scientific Talent," Page 82. University of Utah Press.

APPENDIX G

MUSICAL CREATION AS A SPECIAL INSTANCE

The present writer feels that musical creation has been better described in the literature than any other kind. It has been done so well that knowledge of music is not needed to follow the line of thought. The discussions emphasize the importance of models, and how creation arises spontaneously from them.

In "The Musical Workshop," Dorian describes three stages of composition:

Inspiration—end result is tones.
Elaboration—use of technical equipment of the musician.
Synthesis of the parts—bridging, coda, unifying.

Three composers developed their skill in remarkably similar ways.

Berlioz embarked on a methodical study of the opera. He would take the score of the announced work with him and follow it attentively during the performance from a seat where he had sufficient light. In this practical way, Berlioz grew to understand the handling of an orchestra, and recognized the function and timbre of most of the instruments, even if he could not grasp their mechanism. By a careful comparison of the means used by an admired master with their end results, Berlioz perceived the subtle connection which exists between musical expression and the special art of instrumentation.

Vivaldi's concertos for the violin were published and Frokel took them and "conceived the happy idea of arranging them all for the clavier. He studied the chain of the ideas, their relation to each other, the variations of the modulations, and many other particulars. The change necessary in the ideas and passages composed for the violin, but not suitable to the clavier, taught him to think musically. So that after his labor was completed he no longer needed to expect his ideas from his fingers, but could derive them from his own fancy. Thus prepared, he wanted only perseverance and unremitting practice to reach a point where he could not only create himself an ideal of his art, but might also hope, in time, to attain it."

Cowell wrote:

"As a child, I was compelled to make my mind into a musical instrument because I had no other, but desired to hear music frequently. I formed the habit at concerts of deliberately rehearsing the compositions I heard and liked, in order that I might play them over mentally whenever I chose. At first the rehearsal was very imperfect. I could only hear the melody and a mere snatch of the harmony, and had to make great effort to hear the right tone quality.... No sooner did I begin this self-training than I had at times curious experiences of having glorious sounds leap unexpectedly into my mind—original melodies and complete harmonies such as I could not conjure forth at will, and exalted qualities of tone such as I had never heard nor before imagined. I had at first not the slightest control over what was being played in my mind at these times; I could not bring the music about at will, nor could I capture the material sufficiently to write it down.... I was intensely curious concerning the experiences and strove constantly to gain some sort of control over them and finally found ... I could bring one of them about. I practised doing this until I became able to produce them with ease." *

[Eventually], "I was able by virtue of studying notation to write down the thought, after going over it until it was thoroughly memorized. I have never tried to put down an idea until I have rehearsed it mentally so many times that it is impossible to forget the second part while writing down the first."

This has been summarized as a method by Shapero:

If a composer finds himself sympathetic to the classical quality of expression, he can derive immense benefit from a detailed examination of the melodic procedures of the three great Viennese masters. He will find it logical to begin his studies with the trio forms, such as the minuet and scherzo, for these do not demand the complexities of episodic treatment, and present the clearest examples of the simple musical sentence. As a technical exercise he may copy down the soprano line of one of these sentences and attempt to supply the accompanying parts, comparing his result with that of the master. He will find that with practice he is able to duplicate the original accompaniments or supply alternatives which are equally proficient technically. As a further step he may begin writing accompanying parts to soprano lines which he has himself composed in imitation of his models. Gradually his mind will acquire the ability to direct a phrase which starts in the tonic to the dominant, mediant, submediant, or other destinations, as well as to extend it to any desired length. It is then that he will understand that if he focuses his attention on a definite key and beats mentally in a chosen meter, musical images will be set in motion in his mind, and the entire musical texture generated in this way. It is extremely important to practice these exercises in all keys and all rhythms so that the greatest degree of fluency may be attained. The importance of daily practice also cannot be overemphasized, for without it the bridge established between the conscious and the creative unconscious by technical exercise is soon blocked by non-musical associations. Just as the function of daily ritual and prayer, as related to the intuitive realization of deity, is that of preserving the

---

* Cowell, American Journal of Psychology, 1926, Vol. 37, p. 235.

thread of connected thoughts which lead to the intuition itself, so the function of daily technical practice, as related to musical composition, is that of maintaining free the inroad to that corner of the mind from which the music comes.

In science, such blueprints are rare, because scientific papers substitute order of proof for order and method of discovery. But the careful study of series of papers, in which a discovery is reported, expanded, proved, modified, and refined, may serve the same purpose, i.e., to get inside the mind of the creative scientist and see what made him tick, creatively speaking. How was the discovery prepared for, seen, and elaborated? What guided the selection of directions in which year-by-year development was carried out? What was missed, and why? Such models should be searched out by the teacher and given to the students. They should be taught how to explore such literature to learn the creative ways of the masters. In the same way that a manual is written for the lab, another manual should be written called "The Creative Development of a Chemist," comprising the analysis of a man's extensive series of papers elaborating a particular field, with such notes as the author can devise as pointers for the students' creative development. A paper somewhat of this nature has recently been written, by H. C. Brown, *Research and Development,* November 1960, page 101.

A PANEL METHOD FOR THE STUDY OF CREATIVITY

The market research methods employed in consumer usage testing of new products can be used to afford a new approach to the study of creativity.

A number of neatly boxed kits with carefully worded instructions are prepared for distribution to a panel. The purpose of these kits is to offer recipients the opportunity to create in one of several selected fields of their choice. For example:

(1) A kit is fitted with materials for drawing and painting: charcoal, oil, and water colors; one or two outlines to paint; a résumé of painting and drawing basics: balance, composition, how to use oil, etc.; also, some suggestions and idea-starters for artistic productions.

(2) A kit is fitted with materials for writing: some suggestions and idea-starters for an article, essay, or short story; references for a short article; one or two complete reprints as models; a picture or outline as basis for a story.

(3) A kit is fitted with materials to make something in wood or plastic, perhaps adapted from construction toys; or wood, a knife, and models for whittling.

(4) A kit is fitted with materials to do something in the field of science: perhaps adapted from "Things of Science," Chemcraft sets, etc.

These kits are shown to each panel member, who chooses one. He takes it home, uses it a week, and is then interviewed and/or fills out a questionnaire. Each kit carries a notebook for daily entries of what the subject thought about in connection with using the kit. The notebook and item created are studied. The interview/questionnaire asks:

How did you plan to do the things you did?
What suggested this specific thing? Give details of the where and when
  of the suggestive spark.
How did you go about enriching the original idea?
What are your thoughts about the purpose of this kit?
What did you like about working with the kit?
What did you dislike about working with the kit?
Do you like your product?
What would you do the next time?
Etc.

These questionnaires can be analyzed by the methods used in market research, and some analysis of the creative thinking can be made. The procedure has the good aspect of mental play, but motivation is weak and significance of the immediate objective is low. However, good subjects may try hard because the real objective—knowledge of creativity—*is* significant.

The panel should be interested in the experiment; they should understand its purpose. They should if possible be creatively inclined, or have a high C. Q. (creativity quotient), and it would be best of all if they were selected for creative skill, for example, by reverse factor analysis. In that case, the subject's high-level factors should be checked against the kit chosen.

Also, special methods from market research might be used to get at what subjects think about creativity, and their own abilities and methods to create. Included here are the depth and projective tests simplified from the TAT and Rorschach; filling in cartoon blanks; quoting Mr. Jones; and discussing aspects of creativity in groups with planted members to enlarge the permissivity of discussion at intervals.

APPENDIX I

EXPERIMENTAL STUDY OF THE ROLE OF THE UNCONSCIOUS

It is now possible, in modern psychology, to do experimental studies of one of the most important aspects of creativity—the role of the unconscious. The vast majority of all writers on creativity, including the most modern thinkers, have held this theory of "unconscious work." Indirect experimental evidence has been obtained by Bouthilet, Hull, and Smoke, and also derives from anecdotes of sudden insight, and from the popular advice to "sleep on it." But direct experimental evidence does not seem to have been sought. Such evidence would be: solution is imparted to the unconscious; is not known to the conscious; and is attained. The present writer proposes experiments along the following lines:

Devise a problem and solution and set it up in the A + B → C manner. Select a group of subjects to whom all three items are unknown. To half the group, under hypnosis, reveal a series of items (1) through (6) of which one is B. Then set the problem in the form A to the conscious of all the subjects. Is the incidence of solution higher when B was deliberately inserted into the unconscious?

INDEX

DATE DUE

MAY 4 '68			
APR 9 '68			
APR 1 4 '69			
APR 2 4 '69			
GAYLORD			PRINTED IN U.S.A.